ART GALLERY THEOREMS AND ALGORITHMS

THE INTERNATIONAL SERIES OF MONOGRAPHS ON COMPUTER SCIENCE

EDITORS

John E. Hopcroft, Gordon D. Plotkin, Jacob T. Schwartz
Dana S. Scott, Jean Vuillemin

Art Gallery Theorems and Algorithms

JOSEPH O'ROURKE

Department of Computer Science
Johns Hopkins University

New York   Oxford
OXFORD UNIVERSITY PRESS
1987

Oxford University Press

Oxford New York Toronto
Delhi Bombay Calcutta Madras Karachi
Petaling Jaya Singapore Hong Kong Tokyo
Nairobi Dar es Salaam Cape Town
Melbourne Auckland

and associated companies in
Beirut Berlin Ibadan Nicosia

Library of Congress Cataloging-in-Publication Data
O'Rourke, Joseph.
Art gallery theorems and algorithms.
(International series of monographs on computer science)
Bibliography: p. Includes index.
1. Geometry—Data processing.   2. Combinatorial geometry.
I. Title.   II. Series.
QA447.076 1987   516'.0028'5   86-19262
ISBN 0-19-503965-3

1 3 5 7 9 8 6 4 2
Printed in the United States of America on acid-free paper

To My Students

PREFACE

This book is a research monograph on a topic that falls under both combinatorial geometry, a branch of mathematics, and computational geometry, a branch of computer science. The research described is recent: the earliest dates from the mid 1970s, and the majority is from the 1980s. Many of the results discussed have not yet been published. Advances continue to be made, especially on the algorithms side of the topic, and I have suffered the frustration of seeing each draft grow out of date before it was completed. Although the area of art gallery theorems has not stabilized, I believe the time is ripe for a survey, for two reasons.

First, the material is fascinating and accessible, and should be made available to a wider audience. Although this monograph is not a traditional textbook (there are no exercises, for example), I have used some of the material to great effect in a graduate/undergraduate course on computational geometry. The only prerequisites for understanding the material are basic graph theory, data structures, and algorithms. Thus it is easily accessible to upper-level undergraduates, or indeed to the "amateur." I have found that students can become very excited at finding themselves so quickly at the frontier of knowledge, with a chance of extending the frontier themselves (and several of mine have).

Second, I hope that this monograph will accelerate the maturing of the field by drawing attention to the many open problems. These consist of two types: finding more succinct proofs of the theorems, and proving or disproving the conjectures. There is a history in this field of proofs being drastically shortened after a few years, and I expect some of the more ungainly proofs in this book also will be similarly upstaged. The conjectures are certainly not all equally difficult. Some may be open only because no one has tried hard enough to settle them (edge guards?), some are open because they appear to be genuinely difficult (polygons with holes?), and some seem to await the new idea that will solve them in a single stroke (prison yard problem?). I will be disappointed if many of the unsolved problems posed in this book are not solved in the next decade.

The plan of the book is partly chronological, and partly determined by the logical progression of the topics. The first chapter covers the original art gallery theorem ($\lfloor n/3 \rfloor$ guards are necessary and sufficient), and basic polygon partitioning algorithms. I have found this material to form a suitable introduction to computational geometry. Chapter 2 focusses on the important subclass of orthogonal polygons, and offers several proofs of the orthogonal art gallery theorem ($\lfloor n/4 \rfloor$ guards are necessary and sufficient).

Chapter 3 extends the two main theorems of the previous chapters to "mobile" guards. Several miscellaneous results are gathered together in Chapter 4. These first four chapters cover the best-developed aspects of the topic, and contain few open problems.

Chapter 5 discusses polygons with holes, containing proofs of one-hole theorems for general and orthogonal polygons. No general theorems for multiple-hole polygons have been obtained to date. Chapter 6 investigates exterior visibility, and establishes a pleasing counterpart to the original art gallery theorem ($\lceil n/3 \rceil$ guards are necessary and sufficient for the exterior). This chapter also discusses the "prison yard" problem, another tantalizing unsolved problem. Chapter 7 presents several results and questions from recent investigations into the properties of visibility graphs. The central problem of characterizing such graphs remains far from solution. The topic of Chapter 8, visibility algorithms, is in considerable flux at this writing, but the critical problem of computing visibility graphs in subquadratic time remains unsolved. Chapter 9 establishes the intractability of most questions of optimal guard placement. The challenge here is to find tractable restrictions. Chapter 10 closes with several related miscellaneous results and unsolved problems.

Baltimore   J.O'R.
August 1986

ACKNOWLEDGMENTS

I am indebted to three people for their assistance at different stages of the preparation of this book. Godfried Toussaint introduced me to art gallery theorems, and essentially "gave" me the topic by sharing with me his generalizations and conjectures. His encouragement convinced me to switch my research to computational geometry, which I have found a congenial home. Alok Aggarwal wrote his Ph.D. thesis on art gallery theorems under my direction, and the many beautiful results he obtained first made it clear to me that a monograph should be written. Collaboration with Alok was a pleasure, and his interest and assistance have been invaluable throughout the development of this book. Thomas Shermer became fascinated by art gallery theorems as a sophomore and has made several original contributions since then. He read the entire manuscript under time pressure and still managed to solve several of the open problems posed in the initial draft.

In addition, I thank Dean Pendleton for the care with which she drew the figures, and Daniel Barrett for a close reading of Chapter 5. I am grateful for the generous financial support of my research that I received from the National Science Foundation, General Motors, Martin-Marietta, and IBM.

Finally, I thank Marylynn Salmon for her patience, understanding, and support.

CONTENTS

ART GALLERY THEOREMS AND ALGORITHMS

1

POLYGON PARTITIONS

1.1. INTRODUCTION

In 1973, Victor Klee posed the problem of determining the minimum number of guards sufficient to cover the interior of an n-wall art gallery room (Honsberger 1976). He posed this question extemporaneously in response to a request from Vasek Chvátal (at a conference at Stanford in August) for an interesting geometric problem, and Chvátal soon established what has become known as "Chvátal's Art Gallery Theorem" (or sometimes, "watchman theorem"): $\lfloor n/3 \rfloor$ guards are occasionally necessary and always sufficient to cover a polygon of n vertices (Chvátal 1975). This simple and beautiful theorem has since been extended by mathematicians in several directions, and has been further developed by computer scientists studying partitioning algorithms. Now, a little more than a decade after Klee posed his question, there are enough related results to fill a book. By no means do all these results flow directly from Klee's problem, but there is a cohesion in the material presented here that is consistent with the spirit of his question.

This chapter examines the original art gallery theorem and its associated algorithm. The algorithm leads to a discussion of triangulation, and a reexamination of the problem brings us to convex partitioning. The common theme throughout the chapter is polygon partitioning. Subsequent chapters branch off into specializations and generalizations of the original art gallery theorem and related algorithmic issues.

1.2. THE ORIGINAL ART GALLERY THEOREM AND ALGORITHM

1.2.1. The Theorem

Problem Definition

A *polygon P* is usually defined as a collection of n vertices $v_1, v_2, \ldots, v_n$ and n edges $v_1v_2, v_2v_3, \ldots, v_{n-1}v_n, v_nv_1$ such that no pair of non-consecutive edges share a point. We deviate from the usual practice by

1

defining a polygon as the closed finite connected region of the plane bounded by these vertices and edges. The collection of vertices and edges will be referred to as the boundary of P, denoted by ∂P; note that $\partial P \subseteq P$. The term "polygon" is often modified by "simple" to distinguish it from polygons that cross themselves, but in this book all polygons are simple, so we will drop the redundant modifier. The boundary of a polygon is a "Jordan curve": it separates the plane into two disjoint regions, the interior and the exterior of the polygon. A polygon of n vertices will sometimes be called an n-gon.

Let us say that a point $x \in P$ *sees* or *covers* a point $y \in P$ if the line segment xy is a subset of P: $xy \subseteq P$. Note that xy may touch ∂P at one or more points; that is, line-of-sight is not blocked by grazing contact with the boundary. For any polygon P, define $G(P)$ to be the minimum number of points of P that cover all of P: the minimum k such that there is a set of k points in P, $\{x_1, \ldots, x_k\}$, so that, for any $y \in P$, some x_i, $1 \le i \le k$, covers y. Finally, define $g(n)$ to be the maximum value of $G(P)$ over all polygons of n vertices.

Klee's original art gallery problem was to determine $g(n)$: the covering points are guards who can survey 360° about their fixed position, and the art gallery room is a polygon. The function $g(n)$ represents the maximum number of guards that are ever needed for an n-gon: $g(n)$ guards always suffice, and $g(n)$ guards are necessary for at least one polygon of n vertices. We will phrase this as: $g(n)$ guards are occasionally necessary and always sufficient, or just necessary and sufficient.

Necessity

A little experimentation with small n quickly establishes a lower bound on $g(n)$. Clearly a triangle needs exactly one guard, so $g(3) = 1$. Even a non-convex quadrilateral can be covered by a single guard, so $g(4) = 1$. It is slightly less obvious that $g(5) = 1$, but there are only three distinct "shapes" of pentagons possible: those with 0, 1, or 2 *reflex* vertices (those with interior angle larger than 180°), and all three can be covered with one guard; see Fig. 1.1. For $n = 6$, there are two shapes (also shown in Fig. 1.1) that need two guards, so $g(6) = 2$. The second shape easily generalizes to a "comb" of k prongs and $n = 3k$ edges that requires k guards (Fig. 1.2) (Chvátal 1975). This establishes that $g(n) \ge \lfloor n/3 \rfloor$.

This situation is typical of the art gallery theorems that we will examine later: it is often easy to establish a lower bound through a generic example that settles the "necessity" of a particular formula. The difficult part is establishing sufficiency, as this needs an argument that holds for *all* polygons. Before showing our first sufficiency proof, we will briefly explore a few approaches that do not work.

False Starts

The formula $g(n) \ge \lfloor n/3 \rfloor$ could be interpreted as: one guard is needed for every three vertices. Phrased in this simple form, it is natural to wonder if

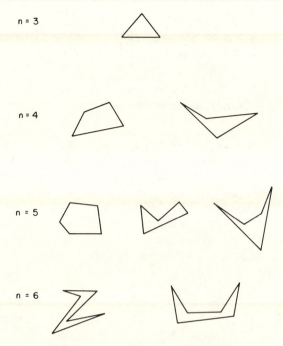

Fig. 1.1. Polygons with 5 or fewer vertices can be covered by a single guard, but some 6-vertex polygons require two guards.

perhaps a guard on every third vertex is sufficient. Figure 1.3 shows that such a simple strategy will not suffice: x_m in the figure will not be covered if guards are placed on all vertices i with $i \equiv m \pmod 3$.

A second natural approach is to reduce visibility of the interior to visibility of the boundary: if guards are placed such that they can see all the paintings on the walls, does that imply that they can see the interior? Not necessarily, as Fig. 1.4 shows: guards at vertices $a, b,$ and c cover the entire boundary but miss the internal triangle Q.

A third natural reduction is to restrict the guards to be stationed only at vertices. Define a *vertex guard* to be a guard located at a vertex; in contrast, guards who have no restriction on their location will be called *point guards*. Define $g_v(n)$ to be the number of vertex guards necessary and sufficient to cover an n-gon. Is $g_v(n) = g(n)$? Certainly there are particular polygons where the restriction to vertices weakens the guards' power: Fig. 1.5 shows one that needs two vertex guards but a single point guard placed at x suffices

Fig. 1.2. Each prong of the comb requires its own guard. Here $n = 15$ and 5 guards are needed.

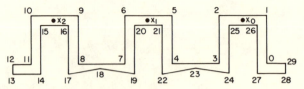

Fig. 1.3. Guards on every third vertex will not cover one of the points x_0, x_1, or x_2.

to cover the entire polygon. But $g(n)$ summarizes information about *all* polygons, so this particular case has no more impact on our question than does the existence of n-gons needing only one guard have on the value of $g(n)$. It turns out that in fact $g_v(n) = g(n)$ and that the reduction is appropriate. Its validity will fall out of the sufficiency proofs presented below, so we will not establish it independently. The reader is forewarned, however, that we will encounter many problems later for which the reduction to vertex guards is a true restriction and changes the problem in a fundamental way.

Fisk's Proof

We will step out of chronological order to sketch Fisk's sufficiency proof, which came three years after Chvátal's original proof (Fisk 1978; Honsberger 1981). Fisk's proof is remarkably simple, occupying just a single journal page. Its explication will introduce several concepts to which we will return later.

The first step in Fisk's proof is to "triangulate" the polygon P by adding internal diagonals between vertices until no more can be added. It is not obvious that a polygon can always be partitioned into triangles without adding new vertices this way; it is even less obvious how to perform the partition with an efficient algorithm. Triangulation is an important topic,

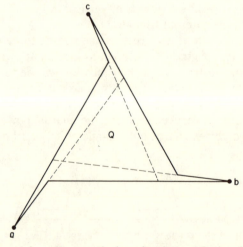

Fig. 1.4. Guards at a, b, and c cover the boundary but not the interior of the polygon.

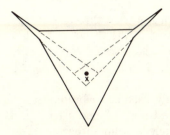

Fig. 1.5. Point guards are more powerful than vertex guards.

and will be covered in depth in Section 1.3. For now we will just assume that a triangulation always exists.

The second step is to "recall" that the graph of a triangulated polygon can be 3-colored. A *k-coloring* of a graph is an assignment of colors to the nodes, one color per node, using no more than *k* colors, such that no two adjacent nodes are assigned the same color. The nodes of the triangulation graph correspond to the vertices of the polygon, and the arcs correspond to the original polygon's edges plus the diagonals added during triangulation. Because a triangulation graph is planar, it is 4-colorable by the celebrated Four Color Theorem (Appel and Haken 1977). We will have to wait for the discussion of triangulation to formally prove that triangulation graphs of polygons are 3-colorable. Let us here just make the claim at least plausible via an example.

Consider the triangulation shown in Fig. 1.6a. Pick an arbitrary triangle, say *acg,* and 3-color it as shown with the colors 1, 2, and 3. The three diagonals *ac, cg,* and *ga* force the nodes *b, e,* and *i* to be colored 3, 1, and 2, respectively. Now diagonals involving the just-colored nodes force other colorings, and so on. The result is the coloring shown in Fig. 1.6b, which is unique given the initial arbitrary coloring of the first triangle: every "move" is forced after that, and since the polygon has no holes, the coloring never wraps around and causes a conflict. This argument will be formalized in Section 1.3.1.

Let us assume that the triangulation graph of a simple polygon can be 3-colored, and finish Fisk's proof.

The third step is to note that one of the three colors must be used no more than 1/3 of the time. Although this is obvious, let me be explicit since

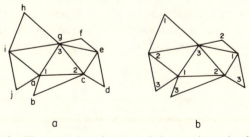

a   b

Fig. 1.6. Three-coloring of a triangulation graph starting from *acg.*

variants of this argument are used throughout the book. Let a, b, and c be the number of occurrences of the three colors in a coloring, with $a \leq b \leq c$. The total number of nodes is n, so $a + b + c = n$. If $a > n/3$, then the sum of all three would be larger than n. Therefore, $a \leq \lfloor n/3 \rfloor$ (since a must be an integer).

Let the least frequently used color be red. The fourth and final step is to place guards at every red node. Since a triangle is the complete graph on three nodes, each triangle has all three colors at its vertices. Thus every triangle has a red node and thus a guard in one of its corners. Moreover, since the triangles form a partition of P, every point in the polygon is inside some triangle, and since triangles are convex, every point is covered by a red guard. Thus the guards cover the entire polygon, and there are at most $\lfloor n/3 \rfloor$ of them.

This establishes that $\lfloor n/3 \rfloor$ guards are sufficient to cover the interior of an arbitrary polygon. Together with the necessity proved earlier, we have that $g(n) = \lfloor n/3 \rfloor$.

Chvátal's Proof

The first proof of Chvátal's Art Gallery Theorem was of course given by Chvátal, in 1975 (Chvátal 1975). His proof starts with a triangulation of the polygon, as does Fisk's, but does not use graph coloring. Rather the theorem is proven directly by induction. Although Chvátal's proof is not as concise as Fisk's, it reveals aspects of the problem that are not brought to light by the coloring argument, and we will see in Chapter 3 that Chvátal's argument generalizes in cases where Fisk's does not.

Define a *fan* as a triangulation with one vertex (the fan *center*) shared by all triangles. Chvátal took as his induction hypothesis this statement:

Induction Hypothesis: Every triangulation of an n-gon can be partitioned into $g \leq \lfloor n/3 \rfloor$ fans.

For the basis, note that $n \geq 3$ since we start with an n-gon, and that there is just a single triangulation possible when $n = 3$, 4, and 5, each of which is a fan; see Fig. 1.7. Thus the induction hypothesis holds for $n < 6$.

Given a triangulation with $n \geq 6$, our approach will be to remove part of the triangulation, apply the induction hypothesis, and then put back the deleted piece. We will see in the next section that there is always a diagonal (in fact, there are always at least two) that partitions off a single triangle. But note that this only reduces n by 1, and if we were unlucky enough to start with $n \equiv 1$ or $2 \pmod 3$, then the induction hypothesis partitions into $g = \lfloor (n-1)/3 \rfloor = \lfloor n/3 \rfloor$ fans, and we will in general end up with $g + 1$ fans

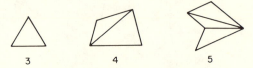

        3   4   5

Fig. 1.7. Triangulations of up to five vertices are necessarily fans.

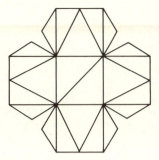

Fig. 1.8. No diagonal of this triangulation cuts off exactly three vertices.

when we put back the removed triangle. The moral is that, in order to make induction work with the formula $\lfloor n/3 \rfloor$, we have to reduce n by at least 3 so the induction hypothesis will yield less than g fans, allowing the grouping of the removed triangles into a fan.

So the question naturally arises: does there always exist a diagonal that partitions off 4 edges of the polygon, and therefore reduces n by 3? The answer is *no*, as established by Fig. 1.8 (this is not the smallest counterexample). Chvátal's brilliant stroke was to realize that there is always a diagonal that cuts off 4 *or* 5 *or* 6 edges:

LEMMA 1.1 [Chvátal 1975].   For any triangulation of an n-gon with $n \geq 6$, there always exists a diagonal d that cuts off exactly 4, 5 or 6 edges.

Proof.   Choose d to be a diagonal that separates off a minimum number of polygon edges that is at least 4. Let $k \geq 4$ be the minimum number, and label the vertices of the polygon $0, 1, \ldots, n-1$ such that d is $(0, k)$; see Fig. 1.9. d must support a triangle T whose apex is at some vertex t with $0 \leq t \leq k$. Since $(0, t)$ and (k, t) each cut off fewer than k edges, by the minimality of k we have $t \leq 3$ and $k - t \leq 3$. Adding these two inequalities yields $k \leq 6$.   □

Now the plan is to apply the induction hypothesis to the portion on the other side of the special diagonal d. Let G_1 be the triangulation partitioned off by d; it has $k+1$ boundary edges and hence is a $(k+1)$-gon (see Fig.

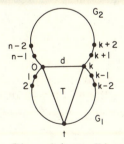

Fig. 1.9. Diagonal d cuts off k vertices in G_1.

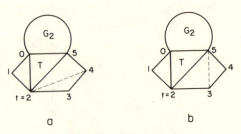

Fig. 1.10. G_1 is a hexagon.

1.9). Let G_2 be the remainder of the original triangulation, sharing d; it has $n - k + 1$ vertices. The induction hypothesis says that G_2 may be partitioned into $g' = \lfloor(n - k + 1)/3\rfloor$ fans. Since $k \geq 4$, $g' \leq \lfloor(n - 3)/3\rfloor = \lfloor n/3 \rfloor - 1$. Thus, in order to establish the theorem, we have to show that G_1 need only add one more fan to the partition. We will consider each possible value of k in turn.

Case 1 ($k = 4$). G_1 is a 5-gon. We already observed (Fig. 1.7) that every pentagon is a fan. Therefore, G has been partitioned into $\lfloor n/3 \rfloor - 1 + 1 = \lfloor n/3 \rfloor$ fans.

Case 2 ($k = 5$). G_1 is an 6-gon. Consider the triangle T of G_1 supported by d, with its apex at t. We cannot have $t = 1$ or $t = 4$, as then the diagonals $(0, t)$ or $(5, t)$ [respectively] would cut off just 4 edges, violating the assumed minimality of $k = 5$. The cases $t = 2$ and $t = 3$ are clearly symmetrical, so assume without loss of generality that $t = 2$; see Fig. 1.10. Now the quadrilateral $(2, 3, 4, 5)$ can be triangulated in two ways:

Case 2a.   The diagonal $(2, 4)$ is present (Fig. 1.10a). Then G_1 is a fan, and we are finished.

Case 2b.   The diagonal $(3, 5)$ is present (Fig. 1.10b). Form the graph G_0 as the union of G_2 and T. G_0 has $n - 5 + 1 + 1 = n - 3$ edges. Apply the induction hypothesis to it, partitioning it into $g' = \lfloor(n - 3)/3\rfloor = \lfloor n/3 \rfloor - 1$ fans. Now T must be part of a fan F in the partition of G_0, and the center of F must be at one of T's vertices:

Case 2b.1. F is centered at 0 or 2. Then merge $(0, 1, 2)$ into F, and make $(2, 3, 4, 5)$ its own fan. Now all of G is covered with $g' + 1 = \lfloor n/3 \rfloor$ fans.

Case 2b.2. F is centered at 5. Merge both $(2, 3, 5)$ and $(3, 4, 5)$ into F, and make $(0, 1, 2)$ a separate fan. The result is $g' + 1$ fans.

Case 3 ($k = 6$). G_1 is a 7-gon. The tip t of the triangle T supported by d cannot be at 1, 2, 4, or 5, as then a diagonal would exist that cuts off $4 \leq k < 6$ edges, contradicting the minimality of k. Thus $t = 3$. Each of the two quadrilaterals $(0, 1, 2, 3)$ and $(3, 4, 5, 6)$ has two possible triangulations, leading to four subcases.

Case 3a.   The diagonals $(3, 1)$ and $(3, 5)$ are present (Fig. 1.11a). Then G_1 is a fan centered at 3, and we are finished.

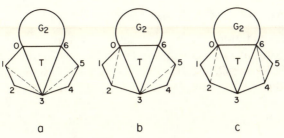

Fig. 1.11. G_1 is a heptagon.

Case 3b. The diagonals $(0, 2)$ and $(3, 5)$ are present (Fig. 1.11b). Join the quadrilateral $(0, 2, 3, 6)$ to G_2 to form a polygon G_0 with $n - 6 + 1 + 2 = n - 3$ vertices, which by the induction hypothesis can be partitioned into $g' = \lfloor n/3 \rfloor - 1$ fans. Let F be the fan of this partition to which the triangle $(0, 2, 3)$ belongs. The center of F must be at one of its vertices:

Case 3b.1. F is centered at 0 or 2. Merge $(0, 1, 2)$ into F and make $(3, 4, 5, 6)$ a separate fan.

Case 3b.2. F is centered at 3. Merge $(3, 4, 5, 6)$ into F, and make $(0, 1, 2)$ a separate fan.

In all cases, G is partitioned into $g' + 1 = \lfloor n/3 \rfloor$ fans.

Case 3c. The diagonals $(1, 3)$ and $(4, 6)$ are present. This is the mirror image of Case 3b.

Case 3d. The diagonals $(0, 2)$ and $(4, 6)$ are present (Fig. 1.11c). Merge T with G_2 to form a polygon G_0 of $n - 6 + 1 + 1 = n - 4$ vertices. Applying the induction hypothesis partitions G_0 into $g' = \lfloor (n - 4)/3 \rfloor \le \lfloor n/3 \rfloor - 1$ fans. Let F be the fan of the partition containing T.

Case 3d.1. F is centered at 0. Merge the quadrilateral $(0, 1, 2, 3)$ into F, and make $(3, 4, 5, 6)$ a separate fan.

Case 3d.2. F is centered at 3. Since all of G_2 is behind the $d = (0, 6)$ diagonal, it is clear that we can just as well consider F to be centered at 0, falling into Case 3d.1.

Case 3d.3. F is centered at 6. This is the mirror image of Case 3d.1.

In all cases, G is partitioned into $g' + 1 = \lfloor n/3 \rfloor$ fans.
This completes the proof. Placing guards at the fan centers establishes the theorem:

THEOREM 1.1 [Chvátal's Art Gallery Theorem 1975]. $\lfloor n/3 \rfloor$ guards are occasionally necessary and always sufficient to see the entire interior of a polygon of n edges.

Note that both Chvátal's and Fisk's proofs incidentally establish by construction that the guards can be chosen to be vertex guards. We now turn to designing an algorithm to perform the stationing of the guards.

1.2.2. The Algorithm of Avis and Toussaint

A naive implementation of the construction used in Chvátal's proof would
lead to an algorithm that is quadratic at best: $O(n)$ searches for the special
diagonal d would cost $O(n^2)$. However, Avis and Toussaint mimicked Fisk's
proof rather directly to obtain an $O(n \log n)$ algorithm (Avis and Toussaint
1981a).

Their algorithm follows the main steps of the proof:

Algorithm 1.1.
   (1) Triangulate P, obtaining a graph G.
   (2) Three-color the nodes of G.
   (3) Place guards at the nodes assigned the least-frequently used color.

Step (1) is a very difficult problem, the topic of the next section. We will see
that it can be accomplished in $O(n \log \log n)$ time. Step (2) is easy if you
assume that complete triangle adjacency information is contained in the
data structure for G output from Step (1). As the triangulation algorithm
papers were unconcerned with this issue, Avis and Toussaint assume only
that a list of the diagonals of the triangulation is available. Under these
minimal assumptions, 3-coloring is not so trivial.

They propose to 3-color by a divide-and-conquer strategy. Their divide
step partitions the polygon into two pieces, each of at least $\lfloor n/4 \rfloor$ vertices.
Recursively assuming that each piece is 3-colored, the merge step makes a
3-coloring of the whole by relabeling if necessary. Both the divide and the
merge steps require only $O(n)$ time, leading to the familiar recurrence
equation $T(n) = 2T(n/2) + O(n)$, whose solution is $T(n) = O(n \log n)$.

We now describe the division step.

LEMMA 1.2 [Avis and Toussaint 1981].   Any triangulation of a polygon P
of n vertices contains a diagonal d that partitions it into two pieces each
containing at least $\lfloor n/4 \rfloor$ vertices.

Proof.   Label the vertices of P $1, \ldots, n$. Partition the vertices into four
chains C_1, C_2, C_3, C_4, each of length at least $\lfloor n/4 \rfloor$: chain C_i consists of
vertices $(i-1)\lfloor n/4 \rfloor + 1$ through $i\lfloor n/4 \rfloor$ for $i = 1, 2, 3$, and C_4 consists of
$3\lfloor n/4 \rfloor + 1$ through n.

First note that there must exist an i and j, $i \neq j$, such that a vertex in C_i is
connected by a diagonal to a vertex in C_j. Otherwise an interior region
would be bound by at least four diagonals, contradicting the assumption
that the diagonals form a triangulation.

If there exists such an i and j with $|i - j| = 2$, the lemma is established by
the following argument. Let $i = 1$ and $j = 3$ without loss of generality, and
let d be a diagonal from C_1 to C_3. Then C_2 is on one side of d and C_4 on the
other; thus each piece is of size at least $\lfloor n/4 \rfloor$.

Finally, suppose there do not exist such an i and j with $|i - j| = 2$. Let $i = 1$
and $j = 2$ without loss of generality. Let v_1 be the lowest numbered vertex in
C_1 that connects to a vertex in C_2, and let v_2 be the highest numbered

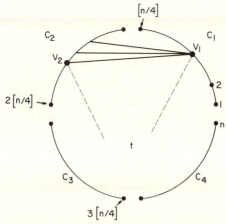

Fig. 1.12. The apex t of the triangle $v_1 v_2 t$ must lie in either C_3 or C_4.

vertex in C_2 that connects to a vertex in C_1. Clearly $v_1 v_2$ is a diagonal of the triangulation; see Fig. 1.12. Let t be the apex of the triangle supported by $v_1 v_2$ outside of the indices in the range $[v_1, v_2]$. t cannot be in either C_1 or C_2, as that would contradict the extremality of either v_1 or v_2 in their chains. If t is in C_3, then $v_1 t$ connects C_1 to C_3; if t is in C_4, then $v_2 t$ connects C_2 to C_4. Both cases contradict our assumptions, showing that this last case cannot occur. □

We will encounter a significant extension of this lemma in the next section.

Now that we have established the existence of an appropriate dividing diagonal, it is easy to see how to find one in linear time. Simply check each of the $n - 3$ diagonals (see Theorem 1.2 following) and see if its endpoints lie in either C_1 and C_3 or C_2 and C_4.

Finally, we consider the merge step. After recursively applying the algorithm, we have a 3-coloring of G_1 and G_2, the two graphs whose union is G. If the shared diagonal d is colored the same in each part, then no action is necessary. If the diagonal endpoints are assigned different colors in G_1 and G_2, simply relabel the colors in G_2 to accord with G_1's assignment to d. This relabeling will take $O(n)$ time, the size of G_2.

Step (3) of the algorithm clearly takes just linear time, resulting in an $O(n \log n)$ algorithm overall.

1.3. TRIANGULATION

We have encountered triangulations several times, and the concept will be used throughout the book: as the most basic polygon partition possible, its role in the field is analogous to the role of prime factorization in number theory. In this section we will first prove that triangulations exist, and then examine a series of algorithms for constructing a triangulation.

1.3.1. Theorems

When first confronted with the question, "Must all polygons admit a triangulation?," a natural reaction is, "How could they not?" Indeed, they cannot not, but this is still a fact in need of proof; a simple inductive proof follows.

THEOREM 1.2 (Triangulation Theorem).   A polygon of n vertices may be partitioned into $n-2$ triangles by the addition of $n-3$ internal diagonals.

Proof.   The proof is by induction on n. The theorem is trivially true for $n = 3$. Let P be a polygon of $n \geq 4$ vertices. Let v_2 be a convex vertex of P, and consider the three consecutive vertices v_1, v_2, v_3. (We take it as obvious that there must be at least one convex vertex.) We seek an internal diagonal d.

If the segment $v_1 v_3$ is completely interior to P (i.e., does not intersect ∂P), then let $d = v_1 v_3$. Otherwise the closed triangle $v_1 v_2 v_3$ must contain at least one vertex of P. Let x be the vertex of P closest to v_2, where distance is measured perpendicular to $v_1 v_3$ (see Fig. 1.13), and let $d = v_2 x$.

In either case, d divides P into two smaller polygons P_1 and P_2. If P_i has n_i vertices, $i = 1, 2$, then $n_1 + n_2 = n + 2$ since both endpoints of d are shared between P_1 and P_2. Clearly $n_i \geq 3$, $i = 1, 2$, which implies that $n_i < n$, $i = 1, 2$. Applying the induction hypothesis to each polygon results in a triangulation for P of $(n_1 - 2) + (n_2 - 2) = n - 2$ triangles, and $(n_1 - 3) + (n_2 - 3) + 1 = n - 3$ diagonals, including d. $\square$

COROLLARY.   The sum of the interior angles of a polygon is $(n - 2)\pi$.

Proof.   Each of the $n - 2$ triangles consumes π of the total interior angle. $\square$

Next, we make an important observation about the way the triangles in a triangulation fit together.

LEMMA 1.3.   The dual graph of a triangulation of a polygon, with a node for each triangle and an arc connecting two nodes whose triangles share a diagonal, is a tree with each node of degree at most 3.

Proof.   That each node has degree no greater than 3 is immediate from the

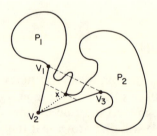

Fig. 1.13.   The line segment xv_2 is an internal diagonal.

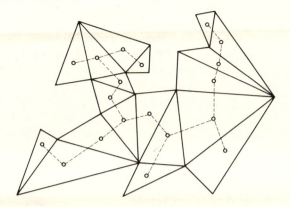

Fig. 1.14. The dual of a polygon triangulation is a tree.

fact that a triangle has 3 sides. Suppose the graph is not a tree. Then it must have a cycle. This cycle encloses some vertices of the polygon, and therefore it encloses points exterior to the polygon. This contradicts the definition of a polygon. ☐

Nodes of degree 1 are the leaves of the tree, nodes of degree 2 are parts of a path, and nodes of degree 3 are the binary branch points of a tree; see Fig. 1.14. We will see in Chapter 5 that Theorem 1.2 extends to polygons with holes (Lemma 5.1), but Lemma 1.3 does not.

The technical term for the dual used in the above lemma is "weak dual," weak because no node is assigned to the exterior face—that is, the exterior of the polygon. Throughout this book we will use weak duals but call them duals.

Lemma 1.3 yields an easy proof of the "two ears theorem" of Meister (1975). Three consecutive vertices v_1, v_2, v_3 form an *ear* of a polygon P at v_2 if the segment $v_1 v_3$ is completely interior to P. Two ears are *non-overlapping* if the triangle interiors are disjoint.

THEOREM 1.3 [Meister's Two Ears Theorem 1975].   Every polygon of $n \geq 4$ vertices has at least two non-overlapping ears.

Proof.   Leaves in the dual of a triangulation correspond to ears, and every tree of two or more nodes must have at least two leaves. ☐

This theorem in turn leads to a straightforward proof of the 3-colorability of a polygon triangulation graph by induction: cut off an ear triangle from the graph, 3-color the remainder by induction, and put back the removed triangle, coloring its degree 2 tip vertex the color not used on the cut diagonal.

Finally, we should note that in general a polygon has several distinct triangulations; only in special cases is the triangulation unique.

1.3.2. Algorithms

As is often the case, the proof of the existence theorem for triangulations leads directly to an algorithm for constructing one; and, as is again often the case, the algorithm is rather slow. Consider a naive implementation of the proof of Theorem 1.2. Determining whether a given diagonal is interior to the polygon requires $O(n)$ time. The chosen diagonal may partition the polygon into a small and a large piece; in the worst case the smaller piece could be a single triangle. Assuming the worst case at each step, complete triangulation requires

$$\sum_{k=n}^{1} O(k) = O(n^2).$$

Obtaining an optimal algorithm for triangulation is perhaps the outstanding open problem in computational geometry. To 1986, the best algorithms required $O(n \log n)$ time. The number and variety of these algorithms attest to the effort researchers expended on the problem. As this book was being revised, Tarjan and Van Wyk announced a breakthrough: an $O(n \log \log n)$ algorithm. Whether a linear-time algorithm is possible still remains open at this writing. In this section we will present several $O(n \log n)$ triangulation algorithms before sketching the latest algorithm.

The first $O(n \log n)$ algorithm developed proceeds in two stages: it first partitions the polygon into monotone pieces, and then triangulates each monotone piece individually. Thus we must first discuss monotone polygons and partitions, important topics in their own right.

Monotone Polygons

The concept of a *monotone* polygon was introduced in Lee and Preparata (1977) and has since proved to be a very fertile idea; it will be used at several critical junctures throughout this book. Let $p_1, \ldots, p_k$ be a polygonal path or a *chain*. A chain is called *monotone with respect to a line* L if the projections of $p_1, \ldots, p_k$ onto L are ordered the same as in the chain; that is, there is no "doubling back" in the projection as the chain is traversed. Two adjacent vertices p_i and p_{i+1} may project to the same point on L without destroying monotonicity. A chain is called *monotone* if it is monotone with respect to at least one line. We will use the convention that the line of monotonicity is the y-axis. A polygon is *monotone* if it can be partitioned into two chains monotone with respect to the same line. We will call them the *left* and *right* chains; see Fig. 1.15.

Lee and Preparata's monotone partitioning algorithm depends on an "obvious" characterization of monotone polygons, which, like so many such obvious statements, requires a careful proof. Define an *interior cusp* of a polygon as a reflex vertex v whose adjacent vertices either do not both have larger or do not both have smaller y-coordinates than v; picturesquely, interior cusps are stalactites or stalagmites. The following is proved in (Garey *et al.* 1978).

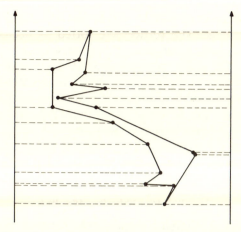

Fig. 1.15. The vertices of a monotone polygon project onto a line in a monotonically increasing sequence.

LEMMA 1.4 [Garey *et al.* 1978].   If a polygon P has no interior cusp, then it is monotone with respect to the y-axis.

Proof.   We will prove the contrapositive. Assume therefore that P is not monotone with respect to the y-axis. Then at least one of its two chains, say the right one, is not monotone. Let the vertices of the right chain be $p_1, \ldots, p_k$ from top to bottom, and let p_i be the first vertex of this chain such that the y-coordinate of p_{i+1} is greater than that of p_i; p_i must exist since the chain is not monotone. If p_{i+1} is to the right of the line $p_i p_{i-1}$, then p_i is an interior cusp and we are finished. So assume that p_{i+1} is to the left of $p_i p_{i-1}$. Now connect p_i to p_k with line L as shown in Fig. 1.16. Let p_j be a vertex of largest y-coordinate in the chain from p_i to p_k before it crosses L. Then p_j is an interior cusp: it is reflex since it is a local maximum in the y direction with the polygon interior above it, and neither of its adjacent vertices can have larger y-coordinate.   □

Lee and Preparata's algorithm removes all interior cusps by the addition of internal diagonals. It uses a general technique called "plane sweep"

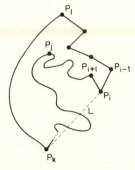

Fig. 1.16.   If p_i is not an interior cusp, then p_j is.

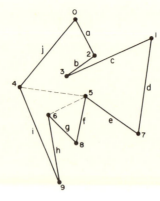

Fig. 1.19. Monotone partitioning example: diagonals (5, 4) and (6, 5) partition the polygon into monotone pieces.

are labeled with letters. Table 1.1 shows the values of the critical variables and the data structure S throughout the execution of the algorithm.

One can easily see that the algorithm is prepared to remove external cusps also, and it is only by checking whether v_i is reflex that we ensure that internal cusps are removed. Their algorithm was originally designed for planar point location, an application for which all cusps need to be removed.

We now turn to an analysis of the time complexity of the algorithm. The initial sorting step takes $O(n \log n)$ time. If the list S is implemented as a *dictionary*, say by a height-balanced tree (Knuth, 1973), then insertions and deletions can be performed in $O(\log n)$ time. As each vertex is processed only when it is passed by the sweeping line L, there are $O(n)$ such insertions and deletions, leading to an $O(n \log n)$ algorithm. The "trapezoidization"

Table 1.1

i	j	I	S	Output
0			$[-\infty, 0][j, 0][a, 0]$	
1	a	0	$[-\infty, 0][j, 0][a, 0][c, 1][d, 1]$	
2	j	1	$[-\infty, 0][j, 2][b, 2][c, 1][d, 1]$	
3	j	2	$[-\infty, 0][j, 3][d, 1]$	
4	$-\infty$	1	$[-\infty, 4][i, 4][d, 1]$	
5	i	0	$[-\infty, 4][i, 5][f, 5][e, 5][d, 1]$	$5 \rightarrow 4$
6	i	0	$[-\infty, 4][i, 6][h, 6][g, 6][f, 5][e, 5][d, 1]$	$6 \rightarrow 5$
7	e	2	$[-\infty, 4][i, 6][h, 6][g, 6][f, 7]$	
8	h	2	$[-\infty, 4][i, 6][h, 8]$	
9	$-\infty$	2	$[-\infty, 9]$	

algorithm in Tarjan and Van Wyk (1986), to be described shortly, improves this time complexity to $O(n \log \log n)$.

Finally we note that Preparata and Supowit have designed an algorithm to decide in linear time whether or not a given polygon is monotone with respect to any direction (Preparata and Supowit 1981).

Triangulation Algorithm of Garey, Johnson, Preparata, and Tarjan

The reason that monotone polygons have proven so useful is not due to their natural shape (they can be rather unnatural), but rather that often algorithms are much simpler if they are designed to work specifically on this restricted class. Triangulation is the best illustration of this: Garey *et al.* demonstrated that monotone polygons may be triangulated in *linear* time. Together with the $O(n \log n)$ algorithm for monotone partitioning just presented, this gives an $O(n \log n)$ algorithm for triangulating a polygon.

One might at first think that the dual of a triangulation of a monotone polygon must just be a simple path rather than the tree guaranteed by Lemma 1.3, but Fig. 1.20 shows that the structure can be quite complicated. Nevertheless, the situation is sufficiently constrained that Garey *et al.* were able to triangulate with a single stack algorithm.

Assume that the polygon P is monotone with respect to the y-axis. The first step of their algorithm is to sort the vertices in descending order by y-coordinate. Normally this would require $O(n \log n)$ time, but as the vertices on both the left and right chains of P are already sorted by y, the total sort can be obtained in linear time by a simple merge of the two sequences. Let $p_0, \ldots, p_n$ be the vertices in sorted order, with p_0 at the top. We will assume that no two vertices have the same y-coordinate to simplify the presentation.

The algorithm successively reduces P by chopping triangles off the top. At all times it maintains a stack of all the vertices examined so far but not yet completely processed. Let $v_0, \ldots, v_t$ be the vertices on the stack, with v_0 on the bottom and v_t on the top of the stack, and let P_i be the polygon remaining as step i commences. Then the following stack properties are

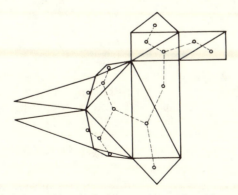

Fig. 1.20. The triangulation dual of a monotone polygon is not necessarily a path.

maintained throughout the processing:

(1) $v_0, \ldots, v_t$ decrease by height, v_t lowest.
(2) $v_0, \ldots, v_t$ form a chain of consecutive vertices on the boundary of P_i.
(3) $v_1, \ldots, v_{t-1}$ are reflex vertices.
(4)   The next vertex p_i to be processed is adjacent via a polygon edge of P_i to either v_0 or v_t (or to both).

The algorithm connects diagonals from the next vertex to the vertices on the top of the stack, pops these off the stack, and pushes the just processed vertex onto the stack.

Algorithm 1.3.   Triangulation of a Monotone Polygon
Sort vertices by decreasing y-coordinate, resulting in $p_0, \ldots, p_n$.
Push p_0.
Push p_1.
for $i = 2$ **to** $n - 1$ **do**
    if p_i is adjacent to v_0 **then** {Fig. 1.21a}
        begin
            while $t > 0$ **do**
            begin
                Draw diagonal $p_i \to v_t$.
                Pop.
            end
            Pop.
            Push v_t.
            Push p_i.
        end
    else if p_i is adjacent to v_t **then** {Fig. 1.21b}
        begin
        while $t > 0$ and v_t is not reflex **do**
        begin
            Draw diagonal $p_i \to v_{t-1}$.
            Pop.
        end
        Push p_i.
end

The stack contents as the algorithm processes the polygon shown in Fig. 1.22 are shown in Table 1.2. The algorithm ends when p_i is adjacent to both v_0 and v_t. Rather than insert special code to handle this case, we permit the redundancy of drawing one diagonal [(17, 16) in the above example] that is superfluous.

We now establish that each diagonal output by the algorithm lies entirely within the polygon. Consider first the diagonal (p_i, v_1) in Fig. 1.21a, which is drawn by the first **while** loop of the algorithm. It forms a triangle $T = (v_0, v_1, p_i)$. None of the vertices $v_2, \ldots, v_t$ can lie inside of T, since

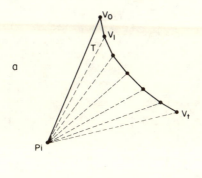

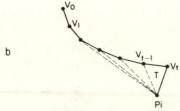

Fig. 1.21. Triangulation algorithm cases: p_i is adjacent to the stack bottom (a) or to the stack top (b).

the reflex angles at those vertices (stack property (3)) force them to lie on the opposite side of $v_0 v_1$ as p_i. Every p_j with $j > i$ has smaller y-coordinate than p_i, so none of these can lie in T. We have thus established that T cannot contain any vertex of P_i. It still could happen that T is crossed by an edge of P_i without any vertices being interior. But this is not possible because $v_0 p_i$ and $v_0 v_1$ are boundary edges of P_i. Therefore, (p_i, v_1) is an internal diagonal. Now the remaining diagonals output by the first **while** loop are internal by the same argument (or by induction).

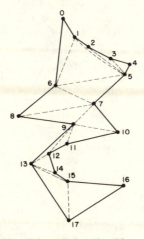

Fig. 1.22. Triangulation algorithm example.

Table 1.2

i	Stack (top$\rightarrow$)	Diagonals Drawn
2	0 1	
3	0 1 2	
4	0 1 2 3	
5	0 1 2 3 4	$(5,3)\,(5,2)\,(5,1)$
6	0 1 5	$(6,5)\,(6,1)$
7	5 6	$(7,6)$
8	6 7	$(8,7)$
9	7 8	$(9,7)$
10	7 9	$(10,9)$
11	9 10	$(11,9)$
12	9 11	$(12,9)$
13	9 12	$(13,12)$
14	12 13	$(14,13)$
15	13 14	$(15,13)$
16	13 15	
17	13 15 16	$(17,16)\,(17,15)$

Consider second the diagonal (p_i, v_{t-1}) in Fig. 1.21b, drawn by the second **while** loop. Let T be the triangle (v_{t-1}, v_t, p_i). The vertices $v_0, \ldots, v_{t-2}$ are above T and p_j for $j > i$ are below. So no vertex of P_i is inside T. And again, no edge of P_i can cross T since $v_t v_{t-1}$ and $v_t p_i$ are boundary edges of P_i. Thus the diagonal (p_i, v_{t-1}) is internal. The remaining diagonals are internal by the same argument.

Finally, we argue that the four stack properties are maintained by the algorithm. Only p_i and v_t are pushed onto the stack, and when both are pushed they are pushed in the correct vertical order. Thus the vertices are in decreasing order by y-coordinate (1). The vertices form a chain (2) because either (a) the stack is reset to two adjacent vertices (Fig. 1.21a) or (b) by induction (Fig. 1.21b). The internal angles are reflex (3) because p_i is only pushed when v_t is reflex in the second **while**. And finally, p_i is either adjacent to v_0 or v_t (4) because the montonicity of P_i guarantees that p_i has a (unique) neighbor above it, and in the chain $v_0, \ldots, v_t$, only v_0 and v_t do not have all their neighbors accounted for.

Concerning time complexity, each vertex is pushed at most twice on the stack, once as p_i and once as v_t. Examination of the code shows that for each Push there is a corresponding Pop, and thus the algorithm requires $O(n)$ time. Together with the $O(n \log n)$ algorithm for partitioning a polygon into monotone pieces, which adds on $O(n)$ additional edges, this yields the claimed $O(n \log n)$ overall time complexity.

The algorithm has been presented as merely producing diagonals, without the adjacency information contained in the dual graph of the triangulation. It is not difficult, however, to modify the algorithm to produce the complete graph structure for each monotone piece, and then to stitch together the graphs from the pieces, without increasing the time complexity. With this graph structure available, Avis and Toussaint's divide-and-conquer coloring algorithm may be replaced by a straightforward linear recursive graph traversal.

Recent Triangulation Algorithms

In this section we review four recent triangulation algorithms. The algorithms will only be sketched and no proofs will be given; often the authors themselves have only published sketches of their algorithms. Our main point is to illustrate the variety of approaches available.

Plane Sweep Algorithm of Hertel and Mehlhorn. The algorithm presented in the previous two sections uses a plane sweep to partition into monotone pieces, then sweeps over each piece to triangulate it. It is natural to wonder if the triangulation cannot be done during the same sweep that performs the partitioning. Hertel and Mehlhorn showed that indeed a plane sweep algorithm can be constructed (Hertel and Mehlhorn 1983). Moreover, their algorithm is not a trivial merging of the algorithms of Lee and Preparata and of Garey *et al.*; for instance, Hertel and Mehlhorn's algorithm achieves a complete triangulation in a single forward pass, whereas the monotone partitioning algorithm requires a reverse pass as well.

The plane sweep algorithm runs in $O(n \log n)$ time: $O(n \log n)$ to sort the vertices for the sweep, and $O(n)$ instances of data structure updates, each costing $O(\log n)$, so no asymptotic advantage has been gained over the Garey *et al.* algorithm. What makes the Hertel and Mehlhorn approach noteworthy is that they can modify it to achieve $O(n + r \log r)$ time, where r is the number of reflex vertices of the polygon. Since r can be as large as $n - 3$, this is no gain in the worst case, but it could be a significant gain in practice. Moreover, it was one of the first hints that *perhaps* better than $O(n \log n)$ might be achievable.

Two changes are made to achieve this new bound. First, the sweep line stops only at the r reflex vertices (and $O(r)$ other vertices that we will not specify here) rather than at all n vertices. Thus only $O(r)$ vertices need to be sorted. Second, the sweep line breaks into pieces, some of which may lag behind others. The data structure representing the state of the polygon "at" this now crooked sweep line is only of size $O(r)$, so that processing each of the $O(r)$ "event" vertices costs $O(\log r)$ each. Of course, $O(n)$ is still needed to output the $n - 3$ diagonals. The result is an $O(n + r \log r)$ algorithm.

Chazelle's Polygon Cutting Theorem. We remarked earlier that a naive implementation of the proof of the triangulation theorem results in an inefficient triangulation algorithm. The next algorithm we will discuss is in some sense a sophisticated implementation of the same idea. But rather than depending on the triangulation theorem, it depends on Chazelle's Cutting Theorem. We will present a specialized version of his more general result (Chazelle 1982):

THEOREM 1.4 [Chazelle 1982].   After $O(n \log n)$ preprocessing, it is possible to find, in $O(n)$ time, a diagonal that divides the polygon into two pieces P_1 and P_2 that satisfy $|P_1| \leq |P_2| \leq (2/3)|P| + 2$ (where $|Q|$ indicates the number of vertices of Q).

We must have that $|P_1| + |P_2| = |P| + 2$. Solving this equation for $|P_2|$ and substituting into the inequality shows that the theorem implies that $(1/3)|P| \leq |P_1|$. Thus the cutting theorem says that a preprocessed polygon can be divided into nearly equal-sized pieces in linear time. This immediately leads to a recursive algorithm for triangulating a polygon: namely, find a cutting diagonal as guaranteed by the theorem, and recurse on the two pieces. If the polygon has fewer than seven vertices, stop the recursion (as the theorem may result in fewer than three vertices in P_1) and triangulate by some brute-force method. Because the search for a cutting diagonal is linear, we have the recurrence relation $T(n) \leq 2T(2n/3) + O(n)$ for the time complexity, whose solution is $O(n \log n)$.

Sinuosity Algorithm of Chazelle and Incerpi.   The only supralinear step in the Garey *et al.* algorithm is partitioning into monotone pieces, which costs $O(n \log n)$. Chazelle and Incerpi have shown how the monotone partitioning can be improved to $O(n \log s)$, where s is the "sinuosity" of the polygon (defined below) (Chazelle and Incerpi 1983, 1984). The sinuosity may be $O(n)$, but it is "usually" very small. Their algorithm works by first finding a "trapezoidization" of the polygon, from which it is easy to derive a monotone partition. Indeed, Lee and Preparata's algorithm discussed in the previous section can be viewed as computing a trapezoidization.

The *trapezoidization* $Tr(P)$ of a polygon P is obtained by drawing a horizontal line through every vertex, extended to the point where it first crosses to the exterior of the polygon. Figure 1.23 shows an example. The horizontal lines partition the polygon into trapezoids, or triangles, which can be considered degenerate trapezoids. Each trapezoid T is "supported" on its top and bottom sides by a vertex of P. The vertices v of P that violate monotonicity in the y-direction are those that lie on the interior of a horizontal segment. Connecting each such v to the unique w that is the other support vertex for T partitions P into pieces monotone with respect to y. This is also illustrated in Fig. 1.23.

Chazelle and Incerpi compute the trapezoidization of a polygon by divide-and-conquer. To do this, they first note that a trapezoidization may be defined for any simple, oriented polygonal path, or a chain: it does not have to be a closed polygon. The horizontal partition lines are simply permitted to run to infinity if they meet no obstruction.

Given a polygon P defined by the vertices $p_1, \ldots, p_n$ in counterclockwise order, let P_1 be the chain $p_1, \ldots, p_{\lfloor n/2 \rfloor}$ and P_2 the chain $p_{\lfloor n/2 \rfloor + 1}, \ldots, p_n$.

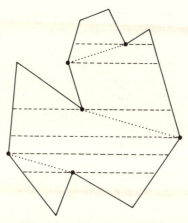

Fig. 1.23. A trapezoidization (dashed lines) leads to a monotone partitioning with the addition of diagonals to "internal" vertices (dotted).

The divide-and-conquer algorithm recursively computes $Tr(P_1)$ and $Tr(P_2)$, and then merges these two into $Tr(P)$. Obviously all the cleverness is embodied in the merge procedure.

Consider the example of Fig. 1.24. Starting from $v_1 = w_1$, the merge processing walks along the chains $v_1, \ldots, v_m$ and $w_1, \ldots, w_m$ simultaneously, stitching together the trapezoids to obtain the trapezoidization for their union. The process has many similarities to merging two sorted lists, but it is of course much more complicated. We will skip the details, and just note one important point: it is possible for the processing to take "short-cuts." For example, one can jump from v_a to v_b on P_1 without examining any of the vertices in between, as P_2 never crosses the $v_a v_b$ line.

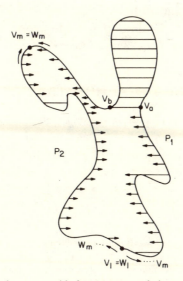

Fig. 1.24. Stitching together trapezoids from separate chains to form a trapezoidization.

We now define the *sinuosity* of a polygonal path $p_1, \ldots, p_k$. Assume for simplicity that no two adjacent vertices have the same y-coordinate. As i moves from 1 to $k-1$, the ray R through $p_i p_{i+1}$ may pass the horizontal (positive x-axis) either counterclockwise (ccw) or clockwise (cw). The path is called *spiraling* if R never passes the horizontal cw twice in a row, and *antispiraling* if it never passes ccw twice in a row. Here by "twice in a row" we mean two successive horizontal crossings, independent of the number of chain vertices between these crossings. Thus a spiraling path winds ccw, with perhaps some cw movements of less than 360°, and an antispiraling path winds cw. It is easy to partition a simple polygon into maximal spiraling and antispiraling chains in linear time. The number of chains is somewhat (±1) dependent on the starting position. The maximum number of chains over all starting positions for a polygon P is defined as the *sinuosity s* of P. For example, the polygon in Fig. 1.25 has $s = 1$: it is a spiral.

Chazelle and Incerpi have established that (a) the horizontal decomposition of any spiraling or antispiraling chain can be computed in linear time using shortcuts, and (b) that this leads to an $O(n \log s)$ algorithm for triangulating a simple polygon of sinuosity s. This result lent further credence to the long-standing conjecture that $O(n \log n)$ is not the lower bound on triangulation.

Triangulation Algorithm of Tarjan and Van Wyk. The conjecture just mentioned was finally settled by Tarjan and Van Wyk, who found an $O(n \log \log n)$ algorithm for triangulation (Tarjan and Van Wyk 1986). As one might suspect from a problem so resistant to solution, their algorithm is rather complex. It would take us very far afield into current data structure theory to explain the algorithm in detail, so we will only sketch it at a high level.

They start with the same observation used by Chazelle and Incerpi (and made independently in (Fournier and Montuno 1984)): triangulation is linear-time reducible to trapezoidization—that is, a triangulation may be

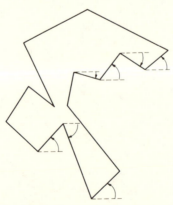

Fig. 1.25. A polygon with sinuosity 1: there are no two successive clockwise transitions across the horizontal.

constructed from a trapezoidization in linear time. Again similar to (Chazelle and Incerpi 1983), Tarjan and Van Wyk construct the trapezoidization by divide-and-conquer. But they divide the polygon, not chains. At any stage of the algorithm, a set S of subpolygons of P are maintained. A polygon P' is removed from S, and a vertex v_{cut} of P' is selected. A horizontal line L is drawn through v_{cut}, and P' is partitioned into pieces that lie above and below L. This is a complicated step, and requires a novel use of "finger search trees" (Brown and Tarjan 1980). The points at which P' crosses L are found in the order in which they occur in a traversal of the boundary of P', which is (in general) not the same as their left-to-right sorted order along L. The intersection points can, however, be sorted in linear time. This is another complicated step, and one of the keys to the algorithm's efficiency. The linear sorting depends on the points forming a "Jordan sequence" (Hoffman *et al.* 1985). After splitting and sorting, all those pieces that are triangles or trapezoids are output; those that are neither are added to S, and the process repeats.

Although it is unclear at this writing if this algorithm is of practical utility, its theoretical impact is felt throughout computational geometry, since so many algorithms depend on triangulation. Even improving on $O(n \log \log n)$ would be a major theoretical advance. The fundamental question of whether a linear-time triangulation algorithm is achievable remains open at this writing.

1.4. CONVEX PARTITIONING

We saw in the preceding sections algorithms whose performance was measured as a function of a variable (r and s) other than n, the number of vertices of the polygon. This suggests asking Klee's original art gallery question, but requesting the answer as a function of something besides n. As a convex n-gon only needs 1 guard, not $\lfloor n/3 \rfloor$, it makes sense to use a variable that is a more accurate measure of the "shape" of the polygon. In this section we investigate the art gallery question as a function of r, the number of reflex vertices of the polygon.

We first note that r can be as large as $n - 3$; see Fig. 1.26. This figure

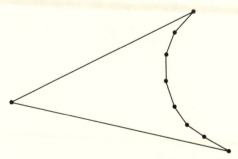

Fig. 1.26. Of a polygon's n vertices, as many as $n - 3$ may be reflex.

shows that r no more captures the "shape" of the polygon than n does, since only one guard is needed for this polygon regardless of the size of r. Nevertheless, the pursuit of this issue will draw us into the important topic of convex partitioning.

1.4.1. Theorems

Necessity

Superficially it appears that perhaps no more than roughly $r/2$ guards are ever necessary to see the interior of a polygon of r reflex vertices, but the "shutter" examples in Fig. 1.27 demonstrate that in fact r guards are sometimes necessary.

Sufficiency

Intuition suggests that placing a guard at each reflex vertex suffices to cover any polygon with $r > 1$ reflex vertices. That this is indeed the case can be established by Chazelle's "naive" convex partitioning (Chazelle 1980).

LEMMA 1.5 [Chazelle 1980].   Any polygon can be partitioned into at most $r + 1$ convex pieces.

Proof.   The proof is by induction. The lemma is clearly true when $r = 0$. In the general case, draw a ray from a reflex vertex bisecting the internal angle up to its first intersection with the polygon's boundary. This ray divides the polygon into two polygons with r_1 and r_2 reflex vertices, respectively. $r_1 + r_2 \leq r - 1$, since the ray resolved at least one reflex vertex (it may have resolved another at its point of contact with the boundary). Applying the induction hypothesis yields $r_1 + 1 + r_2 + 1 \leq r + 1$ convex pieces.   □

Fig. 1.27.   "Shutter" shapes show that r guards can be necessary.

THEOREM 1.5 [O'Rourke 1982].   *r* guards are occasionally necessary and always sufficient to see the interior of a simple *n*-gon of $r \geq 1$ reflex vertices.

Proof.   Necessity has already been established. For sufficiency, apply Chazelle's naive convex partition lemma. Each convex piece must have at least one reflex vertex on its boundary. Thus guards placed on every reflex vertex see into each convex piece.   □

We now turn to a discussion of algorithms for finding convex partitionings.

1.4.2.   Algorithms for Convex Partitioning

It is rather easy to compute the naive convex partition in $O(rn) = O(n^2)$ time as follows (Chazelle 1980). For each reflex vertex, intersect every edge of the polygon with the bisection of the reflex angle. Connect the reflex vertex to the closest intersection point. Chazelle shows how this speed can be improved to $O(n + r^2 \log(n/r))$ time, and I believe a plane-sweep algorithm can achieve $O(n \log n)$, but we will not present the details.

Because at most two reflex vertices can be resolved by a single cut, the minimum number of convex pieces into which a polygon may be partitioned is $\lceil r/2 \rceil + 1$. Thus, if an *optimal* partitioning results in *OPT* pieces, $OPT \geq \lceil r/2 \rceil + 1$. The naive partition achieves no more than $r + 1 \leq 2OPT$ pieces in $O(n^2)$ time. We will discuss two more algorithms, one faster but with a poorer performance ratio, and one slower but optimal.

The first results from an observation of Hertel and Mehlhorn (1983).

THEOREM 1.6 [Hertel and Mehlhorn 1983].   Any triangulation of a polygon can be converted into a convex partitioning of no more than $2r + 1$ pieces by removing diagonals.

Proof.   Let *d* be an internal diagonal of the triangulation incident with a vertex *v*. Call *d* *essential* for *v* if its removal would result in a non-convex interior angle at *v*. Then a reflex vertex cannot have more than two essential diagonals incident to it: an angle smaller than 360° cannot be partitioned into more than three intervals such that adjacent intervals span more than 180°. If each reflex vertex does have exactly two essential diagonals, and no two reflex vertices share essential diagonals, then $2r$ of the triangulation diagonals cannot be removed, resulting in a partition into $2r + 1$ convex pieces.   □

Note that $2r + 1 \leq 4OPT$. Although the performance ratio is lower, the algorithm implied by the theorem runs in $O(n \log \log n)$ time: $O(n \log \log n)$ for triangulation, and linear time for removal of inessential diagonals.

Finally, we briefly mention Chazelle's remarkable optimal algorithm (Chazelle 1980; Chazelle and Dobkin 1985). Construction of an optimal convex partition requires the introduction of "Steiner points": points that

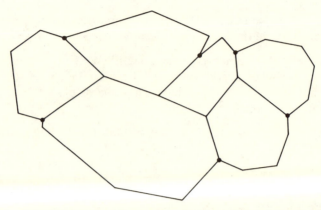

Fig. 1.28. An optimal convex partition may require interactions between the cuts resolving several reflex vertices.

are not vertices of the original polygon.[1] Such points were introduced by the naive partitioning, but in a very controlled manner. The situation for optimal partitions is more complicated, as illustrated in Fig. 1.28. This complexity leads one to believe that perhaps the problem is NP-hard, and indeed, we will see in Chapter 9 that many minimal partition problems are NP-hard. Nevertheless, Chazelle was able to obtain an $O(n^3)$ *optimal* algorithm using dynamic programming, and much else besides. His description fills 97 pages (Chazelle 1980), and we will make no attempt to summarize it here.

Convex partitions will be revisited for three-dimensional polyhedra in Chapter 10.

---

1. Convex partitions without Steiner points are discussed in Greene (1983).

2

ORTHOGONAL POLYGONS

2.1. INTRODUCTION

In this chapter we consider *orthogonal polygons,* an important subclass of polygons that yield many interesting partitioning and art gallery theorems. An orthogonal polygon is one whose edges are all aligned with a pair of orthogonal coordinate axes, which we take to be horizontal and vertical without loss of generality.[1] Thus the edges alternate between horizontal and vertical, and always meet orthogonally, with internal angles of either 90° or 270°. Orthogonal polygons are useful as approximations to polygons; and they arise naturally in domains dominated by Cartesian coordinates, such as raster graphics, VLSI design, or architecture.

The orthogonal art gallery theorem was first formulated and proved by Kahn, Klawe, and Kleitman in 1980 (Kahn *et al.* 1983). It states that $\lfloor n/4 \rfloor$ guards are occasionally necessary and always sufficient to see the interior of an orthogonal art gallery room. Thus the constrained nature of an orthogonal polygon permits covering with three-fourths as many guards as are needed for unrestricted polygons. Several different proofs of this theorem have been discovered, and several associated algorithms developed. As Fisk's proof of the unrestricted art gallery theorem eclipsed Chvátal's original proof, so Kahn *et al.*'s proof has been eclipsed by simpler proofs. But, as with Chvátal's proof, the original proof still retains considerable interest in its own right. So we will start with Kahn *et al.*'s proof, which establishes a beautiful partitioning result that is as important for orthogonal polygons as triangulation is for polygons: namely, that every orthogonal polygon may be partitioned by diagonals between vertices into convex quadrilaterals. The next section concentrates on establishing this theorem, from which the orthogonal art gallery theorem follows easily.

---

1. These polygons commonly have been called "rectilinear" polygons in the literature, but Grünbaum pointed out to me that "rectilinear" has the well-established meaning "characterized by straight lines," so that *every* polygon is rectilinear. Other terms used include "isothetic" and "rectanguloid."

2.2. KAHN, KLAWE, KLEITMAN PROOF

2.2.1. Convex Quadrilateralization

That a polygon can be partitioned with diagonals into triangles is almost obvious, perhaps because connecting any two vertices that can see one another is a valid first step in forming a triangulation: no care is required. Such is not the case with convex quadrilateralization: considerable care is required. Grouping pairs of triangles from a triangulation is *not* sufficient, as shown by Fig. 2.1a: no pairing of triangles in the illustrated triangulation leads to a convex quadrilateralization. I believe the main difference is the difficulty of finding "orthogonal ears." This is illustrated in Fig. 2.1b. It is natural to consider the quadrilaterals $(1, 2, 9, 10)$, $(3, 4, 5, 6)$, and $(6, 7, 8, 9)$ as "ears," but removing them leaves the non-convex quadrilateral $(2, 3, 6, 9)$. The unique convex quadrilateralization of this polygon is shown in Fig. 2.1c, which shows that $(6, 7, 8, 9)$ is not an ear, although $(1, 2, 9, 10)$ and $(3, 4, 5, 6)$ are. In general, convex quadrilateralization is not unique, as demonstrated in Fig. 2.2.

Henceforth we will shorten "convex quadrilateralization" to "quadrilateralization"; the only quadrilateralizations that will be used in this book are convex quadrilateralizations.

The concept that plays the role of an "ear" is what Kahn *et al.* call a "tab." To define this, we must first study the *neighbor* relation. Let P be an orthogonal polygon. Call a horizontal edge of P a *top* edge if the interior of P lies below it, and a *bottom* edge if the interior lies above it; *left* and *right* edges are defined similarly. A top edge T and a bottom edge B are *neighbors* if:

(a) T and B can see one another (that is, there are points t and b on T and B, respectively, such that tb is never exterior to P),

(b) there is no bottom edge B' higher than B such that T can see B', and

(c) there is no top edge T' lower than T such that B see T'.

Note that the neighbor relation is symmetric by definition. Not every

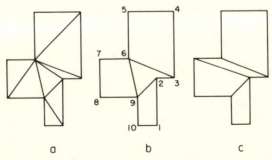

Fig. 2.1. Neither triangle pairing (a) nor ear removal (b) can lead to the unique quadrilateralization (c).

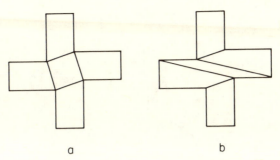

Fig. 2.2. Quadrilateralization is not unique.

horizontal edge has a neighbor, but if it does, it is clearly unique. So the relation matches certain pairs of top and bottom edges; see Fig. 2.3 for examples. We will see later that there must be at least one pair of neighboring edges in any orthogonal polygon.

A *tab* is a pair of neighboring edges connected to each other by a vertical edge. In Fig. 2.3a, (ab, cd) and (ef, gh) are tabs. What makes tabs important for convex quadrilateralization is that they can only be quadri-lateralized in one way: in Fig. 2.3a, the quadrilaterals $abcd$ and $efgh$ must be part of any convex quadrilateralization. This will be proved in Lemma 2.3.

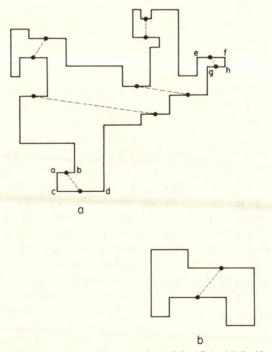

Fig. 2.3. Neighboring top and bottom edges; (ef, cd) and (ef, gh) are tabs.

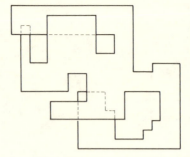

Fig. 2.4. An orthogonal polygon lying on several levels.

Unfortunately, it is not true that every orthogonal polygon has a tab; Fig. 2.3b shows an example that does not. Moreover, the concept can obviously be extended to define vertical tabs, but it is not even true that every orthogonal polygon must have either a horizontal or a vertical tab: Fig. 2.2 provides a counterexample. We will see below that Kahn *et al.* were forced to use a more complex structural characterization to achieve their result.

We now proceed with the proof. It is long and complicated. The proof is inductive, showing that any orthogonal polygon is reducible to a "smaller" one, which is convexly quadrilateralizable by the induction hypothesis. It is shown that any orthogonal polygon has at least one of three structural features:

(1) neighboring edges that do not form a tab;
(2) a "good" tab; or
(3) a "tab pair."

(These terms will be defined later.) The presence of these features is the "hook" that allows the reduction: for polygons without holes, the reduction amounts to cutting the polygon into two pieces, convexly quadrilaterizing each, then suturing the two quadrilateralizations together at the cut to form a convex quadrilateralization of the original.

The proof is remarkably general: it not only holds for orthogonal polygons, but also for orthogonal polygons with orthogonal holes, and also for orthogonal polygons that self-overlap in such a way that they can be considered to lie on several levels connected by "ramps." Figure 2.4 shows an example. A precise technical definition of the class is: a orthogonal polygon on a Riemann surface corresponding to a function with singularities outside of itself. We note that the triangulation theorem could be similarly extended to the analogous class of unrestricted polygons.

Geometric Lemmas

The first lemma permits degeneracies to be ignored. Define an orthogonal polygon to have its vertices in *general position* if no two vertices have the same horizontal or vertical coordinate. In the remainder of the section we will often shorten "orthogonal polygon" to "polygon" when there is no possibility of confusion.

LEMMA 2.1. A polygon P that is *not* in general position has the same quadrilateralization as any "nearby" P' that *is* in general position.

Proof.[2] Consider a sequence of orthogonal regions with the same number of edges as P, all in general position, that converge to P; distance between regions is measured by the Hausdorff metric. Since there are only finitely many quadrilaterizations of these regions, each region in the "tail" of the sequence must have the same convex quadrilaterization. Since convexity is closed under taking limits, this quadrilaterization must also be a convex quadrilaterization for P.   □

We will follow (Kahn *et al.* 1983) in first demonstrating the reductions, and then establishing the structural characterization that guarantees reducibility. We first need a geometric fact about neighboring edges. If $a = (a_x, a_y)$ and $b = (b_x, b_y)$ are two points, let $a\#b$ be the point (a_x, b_y), and let $\square(a, b)$ be the rectangle or box with vertices a, b, $a\#b$, $b\#a$. Figure 2.5 illustrates these definitions. If H and V are a horizontal and vertical edge, respectively, then $H\#V$ represents the point on the intersection of the lines containing H and V.

LEMMA 2.2. Let T and B be neighboring top and bottom edges of a polygon P. Then there is a left edge L left of both T and B, whose top endpoint is at least as high as T and whose bottom endpoint is at least as low as B, and a right edge R with analogous properties, such that $\square(L\#B, R\#T)$ is completely interior to P.

Proof. Since T and B are neighbors, a point t on T sees a point b on B. We can clearly chose these to be interior points of T and B. For any point p interior to P, define the left-bounding edge to be the first vertical edge hit by a horizontal leftward ray from p. Choose L to be the rightmost of the left-bounding edges for the points of tb (we will see below that all the points of tb have the same left-bounding edge, L).

Assume without loss of generality that t is left of b as illustrated in Fig. 2.6. L must be to the left of t, since otherwise, if L were between t and b, T

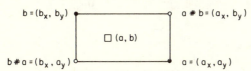

Fig. 2.5. Definition of the " $\#$ " and "$\square$" symbols.

---

2. This proof assumes mathematical knowledge not used elsewhere in the book; it may be skipped without loss of continuity.

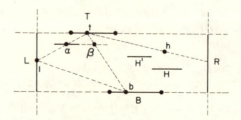

Fig. 2.6. If T and B are neighbors, then $\square$ ($L \neq B$, $R \neq T$) is empty.

would see some bottom edge above the top of L, and so above B, contradicting the neighborliness of T and B (this claim is justified in more detail in Kahn *et al.* (1983)).

Let l be any point on L between T and B. Then l must be visible to both t and b. For suppose otherwise: then there must be a point α of P on tl that blocks visibility. Let β be the point on tb horizontal from α, as illustrated in Fig. 2.6. Then somewhere between α and β there must be a vertical edge of P, which is the left-bounding edge for β, contradicting the fact that L is the rightmost left-bounding edge.

Therefore L must have its top at or above T, for otherwise T could see a bottom edge higher than B, contradicting the neighbor relation. Similarly, L's bottom must be at or below B. Exactly analogous arguments establish the same properties for R, the leftmost right-bounding edge.

Finally, we show that $Q = \square(L\#B, R\#T)$ is empty. Any vertical edge that intersects the interior of Q must have an endpoint in Q, for otherwise it would block the visibility of t for either L or R. So we can restrict discussion to horizontal edges. Let H be a horizontal edge that intersects Q. Draw a line of visibility from t to L or R (say R) such that it passes above H at some point h, as illustrated in Fig. 2.6. Let H' be the horizontal edge of P that minimizes the vertical distance to a point on th [H' may be the same as H]. Then H' is a bottom edge visible to T from t, contradicting the neighbor relation. $\square$

This geometric fact implied by the neighbor relation leads to the crucial property of tabs.

LEMMA 2.3. If ab and cd are the horizontal edges of a tab, then any quadrilaterization must include the quadrilateral $abcd$.

Proof. Lemma 2.2 establishes that the situation is as illustrated in Fig. 2.7;

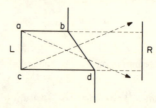

Fig. 2.7. A tab (ab, cd) forces the inclusion of quadrilateral $abcd$.

here $L = ac$. Any vertex visible to a, aside from b, c, and d, must lie below d. But connecting a to such a point means that c cannot be part of any convex quadrilateral. Similar arguments show that connecting c to any point above b blocks a from being part of a convex quadrilateral. Thus the quadrilateral $abcd$ is necessary. □

This is the key to the reductions: once a tab is isolated, the local quadrilaterization is known. We now proceed to describe the three reductions, after which the conditions supporting the reductions will be established.

The Three Reductions

We have yet to describe the quantity that is reduced by the reductions, and that forms the counter for the induction proof. A simple count of the number of vertices is not adequate because the reductions do not necessarily reduce the number of vertices. However, they either reduce the number of vertices or the number of holes. This suggests defining an orthogonal polygon P_1 of h_1 holes and n_1 vertices as *smaller* than P_2 with h_2 and n_2 holes and vertices if (1) $h_1 < h_2$, or (2) $h_1 = h_2$ and $n_1 < n_2$. Thus, for polygons without holes, "smaller" just means fewer vertices. Finally, define a polygon to be *reducible* if, whenever every smaller polygon P' is quadrilateralizable, then so is P.

LEMMA 2.4. If P has a pair of neighboring edges that do *not* form a tab, then P is reducible.

Proof. Let the top edge $T = ab$ and the neighboring bottom edge $B = cd$ with a to the left of c. Let $b' = d\#b$ and $c' = a\#c$ as illustrated in Fig. 2.8b.

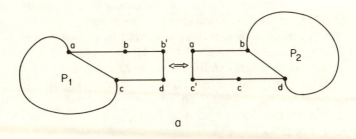

a

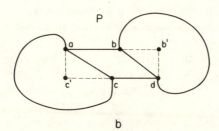

b

Fig. 2.8. Reduction for non-tab neighboring edges ab and cd.

Note that the rectangle $R = \square(a, d) = \square(c', b')$ is empty. Modify P to a multilevel polygon P' by introducing two tabs, one formed by the vertices a, b', d, c, and the other by the vertices d, c', a, b. In the special case when P has no holes, P' consists of two separate pieces P_1 and P_2, as illustrated in Fig. 2.8a. In any case, if P' is disconnected, then both P_1 and P_2 are smaller than P, since each has no more holes than P but fewer vertices. We claim that if, on the other hand, P' is connected, then P' has fewer holes than P, and so is smaller. This claim may be established by the following argument.

Let τ be a point immediately above T and β a point immediately below B. Both τ and β are exterior to P, since T is a top edge and B a bottom edge. Now τ and β are in the same connected component of the exterior of P', as they may be connected by a path that skirts either of the new tabs. But τ and β cannot be in the same connected component of the exterior of P: since P' is connected, there must be a path within P that encircles either τ or β, so that the cutting performed to make P' does not disconnect. Therefore, the reduction has reduced the number of holes of P by 1, and therefore P' is smaller.

Now assume the induction hypothesis: that all polygons smaller than P are quadrilateralizable; this guarantees that the reduced P' is quadrilaterizable. By Lemma 2.3, each of the introduced tabs can be quadrilaterized in just one way, as shown in Fig. 2.8a: $ab'dc$ and $bac'd$ must be included. Now, in P, replace these two quadrilaterals by $abdc$ as shown in Fig. 2.8b, and otherwise use the remainder of the quadrilateralization of P'. The result is a quadrilateralization of P. We have shown therefore that P is reducible, establishing the lemma. $\square$

The second reduction is based on the presence of certain types of tabs. This reduction is more complicated, and requires several definitions. Call a tab an *up tab* if its bottom edge extends horizontally further than its top edge, and a *down tab* if its top extends further than its bottom. Of the two bounding vertical edges guaranteed for a tab by Lemma 2.2, one connects the top to the bottom edge; call the other the *facing edge* of the tab. The top endpoint of the facing edge is called the *step point* and the adjacent horizontal edge the *step edge* for an up tab; for a down tab the step point and edge are at the bottom of the facing edge. These definitions are illustrated in Fig. 2.9.

Although tabs can be quadrilaterized in just one way, the mere presence of a tab does not lead immediately to a reduction. We classify tabs as either *good* or *bad*, depending on whether they do or do not lead to a reduction. Let ab and cd be the top and bottom edges of an up tab, and s its step point, as in Fig. 2.9. Then an up tab is *bad* if (1) its step edge is a bottom edge, and (2) $\square(b, s)$ is empty. These conditions are illustrated in Fig. 2.9. A *good tab* is one that is not bad. Thus a good up tab is one either whose step edge is a top edge, or whose step edge is a bottom edge but there is an edge within $\square(b, s)$, and therefore necessarily a top edge. We will see below that the presence of a top edge in $\square(b, s)$ permits the polygon to be cut near the tab in such a way as to establish reducibility.

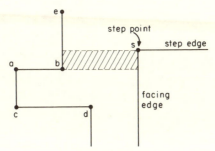

Fig. 2.9. Definitions of tab components; the tab (*ab, cd*) is bad.

LEMMA 2.5. If *P* has a good tab, then *P* is reducible.

Proof. Assume that the tab is an up tab; the argument for a down tab can be obtained by turning every figure upside-down. Let the vertices be labeled as in Fig. 2.9: *ab* and *cd* are the top and bottom edges of the tab, *e* is adjacent to *b*, and *s* is the step point of the tab. Since the tab is good, either some edge intersects the interior of $\square(b, s)$, or the step edge is a top edge. In the former case let *xy* be the lowest edge that intersects $\square(b, s)$, and in the latter let *xy* be the step edge. In either case, let *x* be left of *y*.

The analysis proceeds with two cases: *x* is left of *b*, in which case *x* must also be above *e* (Fig. 2.10a), or *x* is right of *b*, in which case it may be above or below *e* (Figs. 2.10b and 2.10c). In all three figures, it may be that *y = s* so that the step edge is a top edge.

Case 1 (x is left of b (Fig. 2.10a).). Replace *xy* and the chain *e, b, a, c, d* with two tabs, one down tab defined by the chain *y, b#y, b#c, d*, and one left horizontal tab defined by the chain *x, y, y#b, b, e*. Call the modified polygon *P'*. If *P* has no holes, then these alterations separate *P* into two polygons P_1 and P_2, as illustrated in Fig. 2.11a; otherwise the tabs overlap on different levels in *P'*.

Assume that any polygon smaller than *P* can be quadrilateralized. If *P* has no holes, then *P'* is clearly smaller, as both P_1 and P_2 have fewer vertices. If *P* has holes, then *P'* has one fewer hole. This can be seen by considering two exterior points τ and β, with τ above *xy* and β below *cd*; the argument is identical to that used in Lemma 2.4. Thus in either case *P'* is smaller and can therefore be quadrilateralized. It will be easier to assume

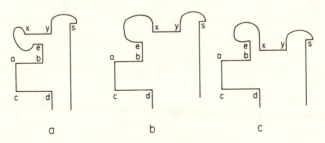

Fig. 2.10. Three good tab cases.

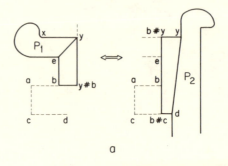

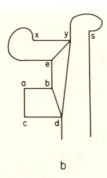

Fig. 2.11. Good tab reduction for Fig. 2.10a.

henceforth that P has no holes, although the argument is identical in the general case. By Lemma 2.3, the introduced tabs may only be quadrilateralized in one way: the quadrilateral $(y, y\#b, b, e)$ is included in P_1 and $(y, b\#y, b\#c, d)$ is included in P_2, as illustrated in Fig. 2.11a. Note that the diagonal ey cuts off P_1 and yd cuts off P_2 in such a manner that the two quadrilateralizations can be put together as shown in Fig. 2.11b: the tab quadrilaterals are removed and replaced by $yebd$, and $abcd$ is added. The result is a quadrilateralization of P, establishing that P is reducible.

Case 2 (x is right of b (Figs. 2.10b and 2.10c).). The two situations illustrated in Figs. 2.10b and 2.10c are handled with the same reduction; we will use the case where x is above e (Fig. 2.10b) as illustrated. The replacements made are the same as in Case 1, but the argument is a bit different. Perform the same alterations as in Case 1, resulting, when P has no holes, in P_1 and P_2 as illustrated in Fig. 2.12a. As in Case 1, P' is smaller, and so can be quadrilateralized. The tab introduced to P_2 requires the inclusion of the quadrilateral $(y, b\#y, b\#c, d)$, just as in Case 1, but $(y, y\#b)$ and eb are no longer neighbors in P_1, and so do not form a tab. Nevertheless, we claim that either the diagonal ey or bx is a part of any quadrilaterization of P_1.

Suppose to the contrary that $y\#b$ lies on more than one quadrilateral. Then a diagonal from $y\#b$ must either (1) go to the left of eb, blocking b

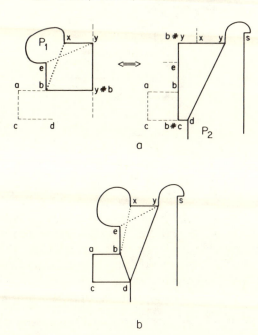

Fig. 2.12. Good tab reduction for Fig. 2.10b.

from being a vertex of any quadrilateral, or (2) go above xy, blocking any quadrilateral from containing y. Both (1) and (2) follow from the fact that $\square(b, y)$ is empty, since xy was chosen to be the lowest edge that intersects $\square(b, s)$.

Thus either $(e, y, y\#b, b)$ or $(b, x, y, y\#b)$ is in the quadrilateralization of P_1. In the former case, we make the same replacements as in Case 1: replace the end quadrilaterals in P_1 and P_2 with *yebd*. In the latter case replace with *ydbx*. In both cases add *abcd*. The result is a quadrilateralization of P, illustrated in Fig. 2.12b, establishing that P is reducible. $\square$

The third and final reduction depends on the presence of a tab pair: an up tab U and a down tab D such that the step edge of U is the bottom edge of D and the step edge of D is the top edge of U. Thus, as shown in Fig. 2.13b, the tabs "face" one another without intervening edges. Reduction is comparatively straightforward in this case.

LEMMA 2.6. If P contains a tab pair, then P is reducible.

Proof. Let ab, cd form the up tab, and fg, hi form the down tab, as illustrated in Fig. 2.13b. Move ab up to form the tab $(a\#f, f)$, cd, and move fg down to form the tab $(b, g\#b)$, hi. If P' is disconnected, then two pieces P_1 and P_2 (Fig. 2.13a) are both smaller than P. If P' is connected, then P' has one less hole than P, as can be seen by considering paths from an exterior point λ just left of ac and an exterior point ρ just right of ig. Thus

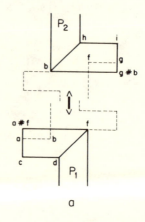

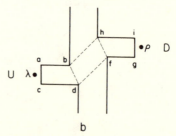

Fig. 2.13. Tab pair reduction.

P' is smaller. The induction assumption then guarantees that each is quadrilateralizable, and Lemma 2.3 ensures the introduced tabs have a unique quadrilateralization, as shown in Fig. 2.13a. These can be replaced by *abcd, bdfh,* and *hifg* in *P*, producing a quadrilateralization of *P* (Fig. 2.13b), and establishing that *P* is reducible. □

We now have established that if any one of the three structural features is present in *P*, then *P* is reducible—that is, the quadrilateralization theorem can be established by induction. We now turn to proving that in any orthogonal polygon, at least one of the three structures is present. The proof is by contradiction: we show that if *P* is irreducible, and therefore contains no instances of the three reducible structures, then *P* must have an infinite number of edges.

An important tool in the proof will be an association of every horizontal edge *E* with a tab $tab(E)$ as follows. If *E* is a top edge, define $n(E)$ to be the highest bottom edge below *E* that is visible to *E*; if *E* is a bottom edge, $n(E)$ is the lowest top edge above *E* visible to *E*. Clearly $n(E)$ is well-defined for any *E*, so it may be composed an arbitrary number of times. Note that if $n(n(E)) = n^2(E) = E$, then *E* and $n(E)$ are neighbors. Since *P* has a finite number of edges, the sequence E, $n(E)$, $n^2(E), \ldots, n^k(E), n^{k+1}(E), n^{k+2}(E), \ldots$ must be finite. Since visibility is

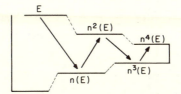

Fig. 2.14. The chain induced by $n(E)$ leads to $tab(E)$.

symmetric it must be the case that $n^{i+2}(E)$ falls between or at the heights of $n^i(E)$ and $n^{i+1}(E)$: otherwise $n^{i+1}(E)$ would map to $n^i(E)$, which would be closer and visible by symmetry. Therefore, the sequence cannot terminate with $n^i(E) = n^j(E)$ with $j - i > 2$; it must terminate with $n^k(E) = n^{k+2}(E)$ for some k, as illustrated in Fig. 2.14. As we observed above, this implies that $n^k(E)$ and $n^{k+1}(E)$ are neighbors. Because we are assuming that P is irreducible, it cannot have any neighboring edges that do not form a tab, by Lemma 2.4. Therefore, $n^k(E)$ and $n^{k+1}(E)$ form a tab, which is designated as $tab(E)$. Moreover, since an irreducible polygon cannot contain a good tab by Lemma 2.5, $tab(E)$ must be a bad tab.

We now prove that the relationship between E and $tab(E)$ illustrated in Fig. 2.14 is the only possible configuration.

LEMMA 2.7.   Let E be a horizontal edge, $tab(E)$ its tab, and F the facing edge of $tab(E)$. Then if E is a top edge, E falls horizontally between F and the top edge of $tab(E)$, and if E is a bottom edge, between F and the bottom edge of $tab(E)$.

Proof.   Without loss of generality let the tab $tab(E)$ be an up tab with top edge $n^{k+1}(E)$ and bottom edge $n^k(E)$ as illustrated in Fig. 2.15, and consider the top edge $n^{k-1}(E)$. If it overlaps horizontally with $n^{k+1}(E)$, then it must see a bottom edge A that is higher than $n^k(E)$, and if it extends left of F, then it must see a bottom edge B that is higher than $n^k(E)$.[3] The same argument can be applied to $n^{k-2}(E)$, and so on, backwards to E. $\square$

So far we have not explored the implications of the fact that since P is irreducible, each $tab(E)$ must be a bad tab. The next lemma depends crucially on this constraint.

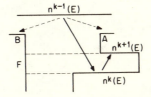

Fig. 2.15. E falls between F and the top edge of $tab(E)$.

---

3. See Kahn *et al.* (1983) for a detailed proof of these claims.

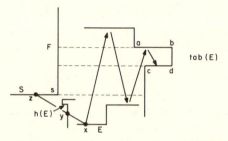

Fig. 2.16. There must exist a bottom edge $h(E)$ in the illustrated situation.

LEMMA 2.8. Suppose P is irreducible and that E is a bottom edge such that $tab(E)$ is a down tab not containing E. Then there is a bottom edge $h(E)$ that is not part of a down tab.

Proof. Let the top and bottom edges of the tab $tab(E)$ be ab and cd, and let F be the facing edge, s the step point, and S the step edge, as illustrated in Fig. 2.16. Since $tab(E)$ is a bad tab, (1) S is a top edge, and (2) $\square(s, c)$ is empty. The second condition implies that E is below S. Now E cannot see S, since $tab(E)$ must fall between E and $n(E)$. Thus a line xz from E to S must intersect an edge of P. Let y be the intersection closest to x. Clearly the edge through y cannot be a bottom edge, since x sees y, nor can it be a top edge, for the same reason that E cannot see S. So there must be a vertical edge through y. Let $h(E)$ be the horizontal edge adjacent to the upper end point of this edge. If $h(E)$ were a top edge, then either x sees it or one even lower, contradicting the fact that $abcd$ is $tab(E)$ and F faces this tab. Thus $h(E)$ is a bottom edge. However, $h(E)$ could not be the bottom edge of a down tab, for then x could either see the top of this tab, or some edge even lower. $\square$

Application of this lemma repeatedly will show that irreducible polygons must have an infinite number of bottom edges. We must also employ the restriction that irreducible polygons cannot contain a tab pair.

LEMMA 2.9. If P is irreducible, then P has an infinite number of edges.

Proof. Suppose to the contrary that P has a finite number of edges. Then, as described previously, the sequence $E, n(E), n^2(E), \ldots$ must lead to a tab U, which we can assume without loss of generality to be an up tab. Let ab be the top edge of the highest up tab U of P, and let S be U's step edge. We seek to establish that there is a bottom edge E that is above ab and not part of $tab(E)$; then Lemma 2.8 will be applied to obtain a contradiction.

Because U is a bad tab, its step edge S must be a bottom edge. Now, since S is above ab, $tab(S)$ is above U, and since U is the highest up tab, $tab(S)$ is a down tab. So if S is not part of $tab(S)$, then S can serve as E. So assume that S is the bottom edge of the down tab $tab(S)$. Let d be the step point of U, e the upper endpoint of the vertical edge incident to b, f the step point of $tab(S)$, and let E be the horizontal edge meeting e. U and $tab(S)$

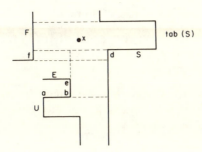

Fig. 2.17. U is the highest up tab, and S its step edge.

cannot form a tab pair (since P is irreducible), so $f \neq b$. Since U is a bad tab, $\square(b, d)$ is empty, which implies that E is a bottom edge. Since $tab(S)$ is also a bad tab, $\square(d, f)$ is empty, so e must be lower than f. These relationships are illustrated in Fig. 2.17.

We now show that E is not part of $tab(E)$. Suppose to the contrary that E is the bottom edge of $tab(E)$, and let T be its top edge. Since $tab(E)$ must be a down tab, there is a point x of T strictly between b and d horizontally. x must be above S since $\square(b, d)$ is empty, and it must be below the top of $tab(S)$, since otherwise E and T would not be neighbors. But then x lies within the rectangle determined by $tab(S)$, guaranteed to be empty by Lemma 2.2. This contradiction establishes that E is not part of $tab(E)$.

Now we may apply Lemma 2.8 to E (since $tab(E)$ is a down tab) to obtain a bottom edge $h(E)$ above E that is not part of a down tab. Since again $tab(h(E))$ must be a down tab, $h(E)$ is not part of $tab(h(E))$, and the lemma is again applicable. Proceeding in this manner we obtain an infinite sequence of distinct edges $E, h(E), h^2(E), \ldots$, thus establishing that P has an infinite number of edges. $\square$

We can summarize the argument in the following theorem.

THEOREM 2.1 [Kahn, Klawe, and Kleitman 1980].   Every orthogonal polygon P (with or without holes) is convexly quadrilateralizable.

Proof.   By Lemma 2.1 it suffices to consider polygons whose vertices are in general position. The basis of the induction proof is established by a rectangle, which is itself a convex quadrilateral. Assume then that all polygons smaller than P can be quadrilateralized. Lemma 2.9 establishes that P must contain an instance of at least one of the following structures:

(1)   A pair of neighboring edges that do not form a tab.
(2)   A good tab.
(3)   A tab pair.

Lemmas 2.4, 2.5, and 2.6 show that each of these features permits P to be reduced to a smaller P' in such a way that a quadrilateralization for P' (available by the induction hypothesis) extends to a quadrilateralization for P. $\square$

2.2.2. The Orthogonal Art Gallery Theorem

With Theorem 2.1 available, an easy proof of $\lfloor n/4 \rfloor$ sufficiency for coverage of an orthogonal polygon without holes is possible along the same lines as Fisk's proof of $\lfloor n/3 \rfloor$ sufficiency for general polygons.

THEOREM 2.2 [Kahn, Klawe, and Kleitman 1980]. $\lfloor n/4 \rfloor$ guards are sometimes necessary and always sufficient to cover the interior of an orthogonal polygon of n vertices.

Proof. Necessity is established by the orthogonal version of Chvátal's comb example: one guard is needed for each tong in Fig. 2.18.

For sufficiency, construct a graph G from a quadrilateralization of P by adding both diagonals to each quadrilateral, as illustrated in Fig. 2.19. Although it is not immediately obvious, G is planar, and therefore 4-colorable. We can establish 4-colorability without invoking the Four Color Theorem as follows.

Let $\bar{Q}$ be the dual of the quadrilateralization of P: each node of $\bar{Q}$ corresponds to a quadrilateral, and two nodes are connected by an arc if their quadrilaterals share a side. Then $\bar{Q}$ must be a tree, for if it contained a cycle, this would imply that P has a hole. Now proceed by induction. Remove any leaf quadrilateral q, leaving the tree $\bar{Q}'$. Since q has degree 1, it may be removed by cutting along a single diagonal d of the quad- rilateralization. Four-color $\bar{Q}'$ by the induction hypothesis, and reattach q to $\bar{Q}'$. Two of q's vertices are assigned different colors at the reattachment points, the endpoints of d, and the other two vertices of q can be assigned the remaining two colors.

Fig. 2.18. Orthogonal version of Fig. 1.2 establishes $\lfloor n/4 \rfloor$ necessity.

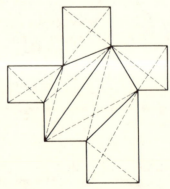

Fig. 2.19. A 4-colorable graph derived from a quadrilateralization by adding all quadrilateral diagonals.

Since the quadrilaterals cover P and are convex, placing guards at the vertices assigned the least frequently used color will cover the interior of P. As this color must be used no more than $\lfloor n/4 \rfloor$ times, the theorem is established. □

Note that the quadrilaterals clipped in this proof are "orthogonal ears"; thus every orthogonal polygon has at least two such ears, providing an orthogonal counterpart to Theorem 1.3.

We will see in Section 2.5 below that the powerful quadrilateralization theorem is not necessary to prove $\lfloor n/4 \rfloor$ sufficiency, but it does seem to be an essential tool in many other proofs. We now turn to an algorithm for constructing a convex quadrilateralization.

2.3. SACK'S QUADRILATERALIZATION ALGORITHM

2.3.1. Introduction

The proof presented in the preceding section does not immediately lead to an efficient algorithm. The first such algorithm is due to Sack (1984), and although it has been superseded to a certain extent by Lubiw's algorithm (Section 2.4), it remains interesting because it is an exact parallel of Lee and Preparata's monotone partitioning algorithm (Section 1.3.2). In addition, when supplemented by proofs of correctness, it can be seen as an alternative proof of the quadrilateralization theorem. Most of the proofs will only be sketched in this section; the reader is referred to Sack's thesis (Sack 1984) for more thorough proofs.

His algorithm factors the problem into three subproblems: partitioning into monotone polygons, quadrilateralization of monotone polygons, and quadrilateralization of "pyramids." This latter problem (first analyzed in Sack and Toussaint (1981)) is solved repeatedly during the quadrilateralization of a monotone polygon. We will describe the algorithm "bottom up," starting with pyramids.

2.3.2. Pyramid Quadrilateralization

Define a (vertical) *histogram* as an orthogonal polygon with one horizontal edge (the base) equal in length to the sum of the lengths of all the other horizontal edges (Edelsbrunner *et al.*, 1984). A (vertical) *pyramid* is then defined as a vertical histogram that is monotone with respect to the vertical direction.[4] It is easily seen that a pyramid must consist of two (perhaps empty) "staircases" as illustrated in Fig. 2.20. It is not surprising that these highly specialized polygons are easy to quadrilateralize.

Label the reflex vertices on the left staircase $l_1, \ldots, l_{a-1}$ from top to

---

4. This is equivalent to being horizontally *convex*, which requires that the polygon meet every horizontal line in a single segment.

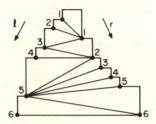

Fig. 2.20.   Quadrilateralization of a pyramid by list merging.

bottom, and label the left endpoint of the pyramid base l_a. Similarly let $r_1, \ldots, r_{b-1}$ be the reflex vertices in the right staircase sorted by height, and let r_b be the right endpoint of the base.

Now merge the two sorted lists of vertices; for the example in Fig. 2.20 the result is

$$l_1 l_2 r_1 l_3 l_4 r_2 r_3 r_4 r_5 l_5 r_6 l_6$$

Finally, for each vertex l_i in the list, draw a diagonal to the next r_j in the list, and similarly for each r_j, draw a diagonal to the next l_i. We will show that this procedure quadrilateralizes the pyramid in linear time. First we present a more formal description of the algorithm.

Algorithm 2.1 (Pyramid Quadrilateralization)
   (1)   Form two lists $l_a, \ldots, l_2, l_1$ and $r_b, \ldots, r_2, r_1$, sorted bottom to top, of the reflex vertices in the left and right staircases, with l_a and r_b the endpoints of the base.
   (2)   Merge these two sorted lists; call the result L.
   (3) $target \leftarrow \text{head}(L)$.
         $L \leftarrow \text{tail}(L)$.
         while L not empty **do**
         begin
             if head(L) on same staircase as $target$
                 then $target \leftarrow \text{head}(L)$
                 else output diagonal (head(L), $target$)
             $L \leftarrow \text{tail}(L)$.
         end

It is clear that this algorithm only requires linear time: the stairway lists can be constructed (1) in linear time, merging (2) takes only linear time, and the **while** loop (3) removes an element with each pass, and so also consumes just linear time.

We now turn to correctness. Each pair of adjacent reflex vertices on one staircase is connected to a common vertex on the other staircase. Thus the pieces of the induced partition are quadrilaterals. All the convex vertices are included in these quadrilaterals, and every reflex vertex is the source for a diagonal. Thus the quadrilaterals cover the polygon. It only remains to show that the quadrilaterals are convex.

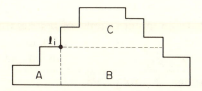

Fig. 2.21. l_i is connected to a vertex in B.

Let l_i be a reflex vertex on the left stair, as illustrated in Fig. 2.21, and let r_j be one of the target vertices on the right stair to which it is connected by the algorithm. Since r_j is on the right stair, it cannot be in region A of the figure. Since r_j is later in the list L than l_i, it is lower and cannot be in region C. Thus r_j is in region B, and so the concavity at l_i is "broken." Since every reflex concavity is broken, the resulting quadrilaterals are all convex. This completes the proof of correctness.

In the next section we will need a slightly stronger result. Define a *pseudo-pyramid*[5] as a monotone pyramid whose horizontal step edges may be slanted—that is, non-horizontal but sloping upwards maintaining monotonicity—and whose base edge may be sloped in either direction as long as both endpoints are below the lowest reflex vertex; see Fig. 2.22. It is easy to establish that Algorithm 2.1 also works for pseudo-pyramids, and we will use this result in the next section.

2.3.3. Orthogonal Monotone Quadrilateralization

Sack's monotone quadrilateralization algorithm makes a single pass over the polygon from top to bottom (the polygon is assumed to be monotone with respect to the vertical). Let the horizontal edges encountered in such a pass be $e_1, \ldots, e_n$, with e_1 highest. The algorithm will sometimes treat one of the diagonals it outputs as one of the e_i, a slanted horizontal edge. In either case, the action taken depends on whether e_i is a top edge or a bottom edge. Top edges are pushed onto a stack, forming the non-vertical edges of a pseudo-pyramid. Bottom edges cause one or two diagonals to be output, and perhaps the pyramid algorithm to be called to quadrilateralize the pyramid contained in the stack.

Edges will be identified as touching the left, the right, or both chains. Of

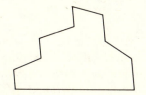

Fig. 2.22.   A pseudo-pyramid.

---

5. Sack's nomenclature is "worn-pyramid."

two edges a and b touching the left chain only, a is said to extend *further inside* than b if a's right endpoint is right of b's right endpoint; the term is similarly defined for edges touching the right chain only.

The algorithm is presented next, followed by an example and analysis.

Algorithm 2.2 (Monotone Quadrilateralization).
Sort horizontal edges from top to bottom; let $e_1, \ldots, e_n$ be the result.
Push e_1 onto stack S.
$i \leftarrow 2$
while S not empty **or** $i \neq n$ **do**
begin
  if $i = n$ **then**
    begin
      Push e_i on S.
      Call pyramid algorithm for S.
      exit.
    end.
  case e_i
  (1) top segment: Push e_i on S.
                       $i \leftarrow i + 1$
  (2) bottom segment: $e \leftarrow$ Pop S.
                  case e
           (A) e and e_i touch same chain:
                Join other ends of e and e_i by diagonal d.
                if e touches both chains **or** e extends further inside
                than e_i
                  then
                    begin
                        Push d on S.
                        $i \leftarrow i + 1$
                    end
                  else $e_i \leftarrow d$ {NB: i is not incremented}
          (B) e and e_i are on opposite chains:
                Join e and e_i with diagonals d_1 (higher) and d_2.
                Push d_1 on S.
                Call pyramid algorithm for S;
                Push d_2 on S;
                $i \leftarrow i + 1$
end

An example illustrating the execution of the algorithm is shown in Fig. 2.23; Table 2.1 shows the stack after processing e_i. Note that an upside-down pyramid is quadrilateralized directly, without calling the pyramid algorithm (e.g., e_1 through e_4); only pyramids with bases at the bottom are pushed onto the stack (e.g., diagonals I through K). This asymmetry makes it clear that the upright pyramids do not have to be handled with a special algorithm, but factoring the problem this way does make it easier to understand (and prove correct).

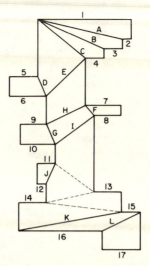

Fig. 2.23. A partition produced by the monotone quadrilateralization algorithm.

e_i	S
	Table 2.1
1	1
2	A
3	B
4	C
5	5 C
D	C
6	E
7	7 E
8	F E
9	9 F E
10	9 F E
G	F E
	H E (pyr)
11	I
12	11 I
13	J I
14	13 J I
15	14 13 J I
16	15 14 13 J I
	K 15 14 13 J I (pyr)
17	L
	17 L (pyr)

We now sketch an inductive proof of correctness; a more detailed proof may be found in Sack (1984). The induction hypothesis is the conjunction of these three statements:

(1) The stack S contains only the non-vertical edges of an upright pseudo-pyramid.
(2) No two edges in S contain points with the same y-coordinate.
(3) The next edge examined by the **while** loop, e_i, is connected by a vertical edge to the lowest edge of S on the same chain.

These statements are trivially true initially. If e_i is a top edge (Case 1), the stack is augmented, and by (3), this is a proper augmentation of a pyramid. Clearly statement (3) remains true, either because e_{i+1} is on the chain opposite that of e_i, or because e_{i+1} is directly connected to e_i by a vertical edge.

If e_i is a bottom edge on the same chain as the stack top e (Case 2A), then regardless of whether e touches both chains, or extends further inside than e_i, (3) guarantees that adding a single diagonal d will cut off a convex quadrilateral. If e extends further inside, then d represents a "wearing down" of the pyramid, and is properly pushed. Otherwise d acts just like a bottom edge. It is easily verified that in either case the truth of statements (2) and (3) is maintained.

If e_i is a bottom edge on the chain opposite that touched by the stack top e (Case 2B), then by properties (2) and (3), the region from the top of e to e_i is empty, and e_i and e can be connected by a pair of diagonals. The upper diagonal connects the two chains of the pyramid in S, and the stack is emptied by a call to Algorithm 2.1. The lower diagonal forms a new pyramid top.

This completes the proof of correctness. The algorithm clearly requires just linear time: sorting the horizontal edges can be accomplished by a linear merge of the edges in the two monotone chains, and the **while** loop makes at most as many passes as there are edges and diagonals, which is also linear. Finally, the pyramid algorithm is itself linear.

As with the generalization of pyramid to pseudo-pyramid, it will be important in the next section to generalize the class of polygons for which Algorithm 2.2 applies from orthogonal monotone to *pseudo-monotone* polygons. These are polygons that are:

(1) monotone with respect to the vertical,
(2) composed of vertical edges alternating with non-vertical edges, which must be either horizontal or upwardly slanting to satisfy (1),
(3) and such that the *shadow* of a slanted edge contains no vertices, where the shadow of a slanted edge is defined to be the set of points of the polygon visible to e by a horizontal line segment that is nowhere exterior to the polygon, but not including the endpoints of e.

This third requirement (similar to clause (2) of the induction hypothesis) is

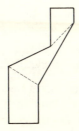

Fig. 2.24. A non-quadrilateralizable monotone polygon.

needed to avoid polygons such as the one shown in Fig. 2.24 that do not admit a convex quadrilateralization.

It is easily established that Algorithm 2.2 will work on pseudo-monotone polygons. The next section presents an algorithm for partitioning an orthogonal polygon into pseudo-monotone pieces.

2.3.4. Partitioning into Monotone Polygons

Define a *bottom peak* to be a bottom horizontal edge whose endpoints are both reflex vertices; define a *top peak* similarly for top edges. Then it is clear that an orthogonal polygon fails to be monotone with respect to the vertical direction precisely when it contains top or bottom peaks: these peaks play the role of up and down cusps in a general polygon (Section 1.3.2). Sack's algorithm is exactly analogous to Lee and Preparata's: the polygon is cut at each bottom peak by adding diagonals to the closest horizontal edge above it, and similarly for top peaks. The geometric lemma that permits the diagonals to be added is as follows.

LEMMA 2.10. Let *ab* be a bottom peak, and let *cd* be the lowest horizontal edge above *ab* that is partially visible to either *a* or *b*. Then:

(a) If *cd* is a top edge, then the rectangle bounded by *ab*, *cd*, and the facing edges of this neighboring pair (see Lemma 2.2), is empty. See Fig. 2.25a.

(b) If *cd* is a bottom edge, then *ab* and *cd* do not overlap horizontally, and the rectangle bounded by *ab*, the visible endpoint of *cd*, and the "facing" vertical edges, is empty. See Fig. 2.25b.

Proof. (Sketch).   Part (a) is equivalent to Lemma 2.2. For part (b), if *cd*

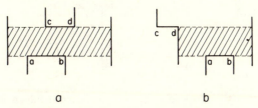

a   b

Fig. 2.25. Empty rectangles above bottom peaks.

and ab overlapped horizontally, then there would have to be an edge lower than cd and visible to a or b, contradicting the assumption that cd is the lowest. An argument similar to that used in Lemma 2.2 can be used to establish the emptiness of the rectangle illustrated in Fig. 2.25b. $\square$

Because the algorithm is so similar to Lee and Preparata's Algorithm 1.2, we will only present a high-level version here; a detailed version may be found in Sack (1984). The reason that Lee and Preparata's algorithm cannot be used without modification is that the monotone pieces resulting from their algorithm do not necessarily satisfy condition (3) in the definition of "pseudo-monotone."

Algorithm 2.3 (Pseudo-Monotone Partitioning of an Orthogonal Polygon).
Sort the horizontal edges, top to bottom; let $e_1, \ldots, e_n$ be the result.
for $i = 2$ **to** n **do**
    if e_i is a bottom peak
        then $e \leftarrow$ lowest horizontal or slanted edge above and visible to e_i.
        if e is a top edge
            then Join e and e_i into a convex quadrilateral
            else Join the visible endpoint of e to the closest endpoint of e_i.
        {Data structure manipulation here.}
    else if e_i is a top peak **then** {Similar to above.}

This algorithm makes a single pass over the polygon. The algorithm could be simplified by handling the bottom peaks on a top-to-bottom pass and the top peaks on a bottom-to-top pass (as is done in Algorithm 1.2), but we will maintain this more complicated form to simplify the correctness discussion. Note that the step that joins e and e_i into a convex quadrilateral is a special case of the first reduction (of neighboring edges that do not form a tab) in the Kahn, Klawe, Kleitman proof presented in the previous section.

An example of the partition created by the algorithm is shown in Fig. 2.26, where upward pointing arrows resolve bottom peaks, and downward arrows resolve top peaks.

We now argue that this algorithm partitions an orthogonal polygon into pseudo-monotone pieces in $O(n \log n)$ time. Assume as an induction hypothesis that all bottom and top horizontal peaks above a certain height

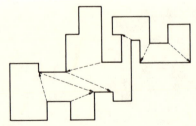

Fig. 2.26. A partition produced by the monotone partition algorithm.

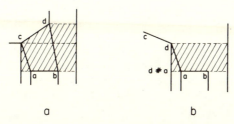

a   b

Fig. 2.27.   The diagonals chosen by the algorithm pass through empty (shaded) regions.

have been resolved by the algorithm, and that the resulting monotone chains above this height satisfy the pseudo-orthogonal criteria:

(1)   Vertical and slanted edges alternate.
(2)   The shadow of each slanted edge contains no vertices.

Consider now the next peak encountered, and assume it is a bottom peak $e_i = ab$ (the argument for a top peak is slightly different and will not be presented).

Let cd be edge e selected by the algorithm. There are two cases, illustrated in Fig. 2.27.

Case A (cd is a top segment).   Since cd satisfies condition (2) above, both c and d project horizontally to the same vertical edge. By a slight modification of Lemma 2.10, the entire shaded region of Fig. 2.27a is empty, and $abcd$ forms an internal convex quadrilateral.. Diagonals ac and bd satisfy both properties (1) and (2) of the induction hypothesis. Compare Fig. 2.8: in Fig. 2.27a, ab and cd also are non-tab neighboring edges.

Case B (cd is a bottom segment).   The situation is illustrated in Fig. 2.27b. Assume that the diagonal added by the algorithm is ad. This diagonal is easily seen to satisfy condition (2) of the induction hypothesis, but it does not satisfy condition (1), as now ad and dc are consecutive slanted edges. The solution is to replace a by $d\#a$ in the upper polygon. Then the upper polygon satisfies conditions for a pseudo-orthogonal monotone polygon, and can therefore be quadrilateralized by Algorithm 2.2. Is is possible to show (see Sack (1984)) that this algorithm will not use $d\#a$ as the endpoint of a diagonal, and that the unique quadrilateral that includes this vertex remains convex when $d\#a$ is replaced by a.

This completes our sketch of the correctness of Algorithm 2.3. Its time complexity is $O(n \log n)$ for the same reasons Lee and Preparata's has this bound: the initial sorting of the horizontal edges requires $O(n \log n)$, and there are $O(n)$ insertions and deletions into a dictionary data structure. I believe that Tarjan and Van Wyk's trapezoidalization algorithm mentioned in Section 1.3.2 can be used to improve the speed of Sack's algorithm to $O(n \log \log n)$.

2.4. LUBIW'S PROOF AND ALGORITHM

2.4.1. Introduction

In this section we present a clever and succinct proof of the convex quadrilateralization theorem due to Lubiw (1985). Her proof leads rather directly to another $O(n \log n)$ algorithm. In fact, we present two proofs: one for orthogonal polygons without holes, and one for those with holes. The latter obviously encompasses the former, but the proof for polygons without holes is so elegant that it deserves separate consideration.

Both proofs have the same structure, and depend on the following observation. From a quadrilateralization of an orthogonal polygon (with or without holes), remove one quadrilateral. What remains are perhaps several polygons each of which is quadrilateralizable. But these polygons are not (in general) themselves orthogonal. Thus there is a broader class of polygons beyond orthogonal to which the theorem applies; no one has characterized this class to date. Lubiw identified such classes for orthogonal polygons both with and without holes. For each member of the class, there is a quadrilateral whose removal results in smaller polygons within the same class. The quadrilateralization theorem follows immediately by induction.

Kahn, Klawe, and Kleitman's proof (Section 2.3) stays within the class of orthogonal polygons at all times; Lubiw's proof starts with a wider class more suited to the removal of quadrilaterals. The result is a simpler proof.

2.4.2. Orthogonal Polygons without Holes

Define the dual of a quadrilateralization of a polygon as in Section 2.2.2: a graph with a node associated with each quadrilateral, and an arc between two nodes if the corresponding quadrilaterals share a diagonal.[6] As previously mentioned, the dual graph of a quadrilateralization of a orthogonal polygon without holes is a tree, for the same reason that the dual of a triangulation of a polygon without holes is a tree (Lemma 1.3). Removal of one quadrilateral from a quadrilateralization of a polygon therefore disconnects the polygon into quadrilateralizable pieces, each of which is orthogonal except for one slanted edge. This observation motivates the following definition.

A *1-orthogonal polygon* is a polygon of no holes with a distinguished edge *e* called the *slanted edge,* such that the polygon satisfies four conditions:

(1) There are an even number of edges.
(2) Except for possibly *e,* the edges are alternately horizontal and vertical in a traversal of the boundary.
(3) All interior angles are less than or equal to 270°.
(4) The nose of the slanted edge contains no vertices.

---

6. These graphs will be studied further in the next chapter.

Fig. 2.28. The nose of a slanted edge.

The *nose* of a slanted edge e is the right triangle toward the inside of the polygon whose hypotenuse is e; the nose includes the interior of e but excludes the remainder of the boundary. See Fig. 2.28. Clearly the requirement that the nose not contain vertices implies that it is completely empty, since all other edges must be vertical or horizontal and could not intersect the nose without including their endpoint.

An orthogonal polygon is 1-orthogonal, where e may be any edge. Violation of any of the four conditions can lead to non-quadrilateralizable polygons, as is illustrated in Fig. 2.29.

THEOREM 2.3 [Lubiw 1985].   Any 1-orthogonal polygon P is convexly quadrilateralizable.

Proof.   The proof is by induction. If P has just four edges, then it has (perhaps after rotation by 90°) two horizontal edges and one vertical edge by (2). Regardless of the orientation of the slanted edge, P must be convex. This establishes the basis of the induction.

Assume now that P has more than four edges. We will show that there exists a *removable quadrilateral,* a convex quadrilateral whose removal disconnects P into smaller 1-orthogonal polygons.

Properties (1) and (2) jointly imply that the two edges adjacent to the slanted edge $e = ab$ are either both horizontal or both vertical. The interior angle requirement (3) then implies that one of the two situations illustrated in Fig. 2.30 holds (perhaps after rotation and/or reflection). In both cases, a

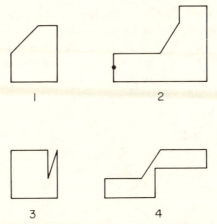

Fig. 2.29. Four unquadrilateralizable polygons, each violating one of the 1-orthogonal conditions.

Fig. 2.30. The slanted edge ab in standard orientation; the shading indicates the interior of the polygon.

top edge has b as its left endpoint. The removable quadrilateral has a and b as two of its vertices. We now specify the other two vertices c and d. Vertex c is the leftmost then highest vertex within the region R_1 shown in Fig. 2.31. R_1 is closed along the left and top, does not include the two left corners, and is open elsewhere. Since R_1 contains at least the vertex at the other end of the top edge E incident to b, c must exist. If c is not this other endpoint, then because it is leftmost, it is at the top of a vertical edge. Thus it is either at a corner as in Fig. 2.32a, or at the other end of E as in Figs. 2.32b and 2.32c.

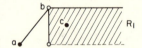

Fig. 2.31. Definition of vertex c and region R_1.

Corner d of the removable quadrilateral is specified according to two cases. Define region R_2 as shown in Fig. 2.33. It is closed on the top and right, excludes a and c, and is otherwise open. Define d to be, if it exists, the highest then rightmost vertex in R_2. If either of the situations illustrated in Fig. 2.32a or 2.32b obtains, then R_2 contains at least the vertex at the lower end of the vertical edge F incident to c, and so d is defined. In these cases, if $F \neq cd$, then because d is highest, it is at the top of a vertical edge, and because rightmost, it is at the right of a horizontal edge, and thus at a corner.

If the situation shown in Fig. 2.32c holds, however, d may be the left endpoint of a bottom edge G in R_2 (marked as d' in Fig. 2.34a) or R_2 may contain no vertex at all (Fig. 2.34b). In either of these situations, define the region R_3 as illustrated; it is closed on the left and bottom, excludes the two left corners, and is otherwise open. Now define d to be the leftmost then lowest vertex in R_3. Since R_3 includes at least the right endpoint of G, d must exist.

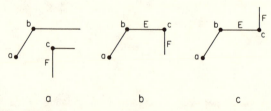

Fig. 2.32. Either c is at a corner (a) or at the other end of E (b and c).

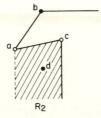

Fig. 2.33. Definition of vertex d and region R_2.

Having now defined vertices c and d under all circumstances, remove the quadrilateral *abcd*. First note that it is convex: the angle at b is convex because c is in R_1; the angle at a is convex because d is in R_2 or R_3; the angles at c and d are convex both when R_2 and R_3 are applicable.

Removal of *abcd* potentially leaves three polygonal regions, bounded by *bc, cd,* and *ad.* Each of these diagonals is clearly the only slanted edge in its respective polygon; thus condition (2) in the definition of 1-orthogonal is satisfied for each. Condition (3), that all angles are less than or equal to 270°, is easily seen to hold by examining the cases considered above, which are gathered in Fig. 2.35. That the nose of each slanted edge is empty (condition (4)) is guaranteed by choice of c as leftmost then highest, and the similar constraints on d. These constraints force the shaded regions in Fig. 2.35 to be empty. In all cases, the nose of each slanted edge is empty.

Finally, to prove that each remaining polygon has an even number of edges (condition (1)), we use the following clever counting argument of Lubiw. Define the endpoints of top, bottom, left, and right edges as partitioned into two types as specified in Fig. 2.36a. Endpoints of a slanted edge are given a type by the adjacent horizontal or vertical edges. It should be clear that each vertex of a 1-orthogonal polygon is assigned an unambiguous type by this scheme since, for example, a convex corner formed by a bottom and a left edge can only be a type 1 vertex. In any traversal of a 1-orthogonal polygon, the vertices alternate in type. Now note that a is type 1 and b is type 2 (Fig. 2.30); the cases shown in Fig. 2.35 show that c is always type 1 and d always type 2. Thus each of the diagonals *bc, cd,* and *ad* has both type 1 and type 2 endpoints (see Fig. 2.36b), and

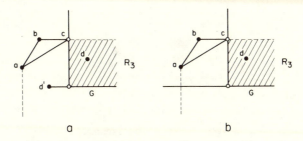

Fig. 2.34. Definition of vertex d and region R_3.

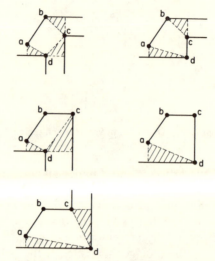

Fig. 2.35. The noses of the diagonals of the removable quadrilateral are all empty (shaded regions).

therefore the polygon pieces bounded by these diagonals maintain the type 1/2 alternation. Thus they must have an even number of vertices.

We have therefore shown that each of the pieces remaining is a 1-orthogonal polygon. Clearly they have fewer vertices than P, so the induction hypothesis guarantees they are quadrilateralizable. Joining their quadrilateralizations to *abcd* yields a quadrilateralization of P, establishing the theorem. □

An example of a quadrilateralization obtained by repeatedly removing the removable quadrilateral defined in this theorem is shown in Fig. 2.37. In the original polygon, edge 12 is chosen as the (degenerate) slanted edge. Rotations and reflections are often necessary to orient the slanted edge to match Fig. 2.30, but the procedure is entirely deterministic.

We now turn now to the more difficult case of orthogonal polygons with holes.

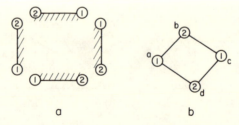

Fig. 2.36. Vertex types; the shading in (a) represents the polygon interior.

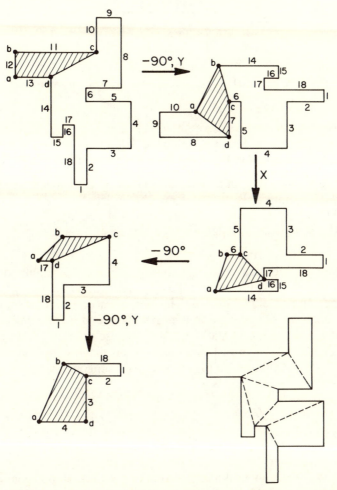

Fig. 2.37. Quadrilateralization by repeated deletion of a removable quadrilateral. The notation "$-90°$, Y" means that the figure is rotated 90° clockwise and then reflected in the Y-axis; the remaining arrow labels may be interpreted similarly.

2.4.3. Orthogonal Polygons with Holes

Because the dual of a quadrilateralization of a polygon with holes is not a tree, the removal of one quadrilateral may introduce more than one slanted edge into the remainder. For example, removal of any quadrilateral from the polygon shown in Fig. 2.38 introduces two slanted edges. Thus the class of 1-orthogonal polygons will not be sufficient to prove the more general theorem by the same technique.

Here Lubiw uses the same basic insight (independently) employed by Sack with his pseudo-pyramids and pseudo-monotone orthogonal polygons: if the horizontal edges of an orthogonal polygon are slanted, and some

Fig. 2.38. Removal of any quadrilatenral produces two slanted edges.

further conditions are satisfied, then the resulting polygon is still quadrilateralizable. This leads to the following definition:

A *pseudo-orthogonal* polygon is one that satisfies three conditions:

(1)   Every other edge in a traversal is vertical. The other edges are called
      slanted; note a slanted edge may be horizontal.
(2)   All interior angles are less than or equal to 270°.
(3)   The shadow of any slanted edge contains no vertices.

The *shadow* of an edge e is, as defined in Section 2.2, the horizontal
projection of e. For the precise purposes of her proof, Lubiw defines the
shadow to be open on the bottom if e is a left edge, and open on the top if a
right edge, and in either case not including e's endpoints; see Fig. 2.39.
Closing the open boundaries does not lead to unquadrilateralizable polygons, but the definition as stated leads to precise meshing of regions in the
proof. A horizontal edge is defined to have no shadow; thus all orthogonal
polygons (with or without holes) are pseudo-orthogonal.

Fig. 2.39. The shadow of an edge; the shading indicates the interior of the polygon

THEOREM 2.4 [Lubiw 1985].   A pseudo-orthogonal polygon P is convexly quadrilateralizable.

Proof.   The proof is by induction. If P has just four edges, then two must
be horizontal by (1), and regardless of the slant of the slanted edges, P is
convex. This establishes the basis step.

If P has more than four edges, then we show that P has a removable
quadrilateral: one whose removal leaves smaller polygons which are
themselves pseudo-orthogonal. Toward this end, define the *upper neighbor*
u of a vertex v as the lowest then rightmost vertex above v that is visible to
v, but not connected to v by a slanted edge, and strictly above v if v is on a
top edge.[7] Not every vertex has an upper neighbor: for example, a convex
corner at the junction of a top edge and a right edge has none.

We can now specify a removable quadrilateral. Throughout the remainder of the proof we will use $x < y$ to mean that x is lower than y, or they

---

7. These latter qualifications will not be needed in the proof, but only in the algorithm
correctness discussion to follow.

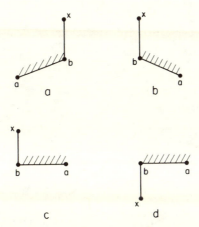

Fig. 2.40. b always has an upper neighbor; the shading indicates the interior of the polygon.

have the same height and x is right of y. Let ab with $a < b$ be a bottom edge, and let b's upper neighbor be c. If c is on a top edge cd, then ab and cd define a removable quadrilateral.

We must establish that this quadrilateral always exists. First we show that b always has an upper neighbor. If ab is not horizontal, then the vertical edge incident to b must be above b to satisfy the 270° requirement (2) (see Figs. 2.40a and 2.40b). The other endpoint of this edge guarantees that b has an upper neighbor. If ab is horizontal, then b is at the left. If the angle at b is convex (Fig. 2.40c) then the situation is as above. If the angle is reflex (Fig. 2.40d), then there clearly must be at least two vertices above and visible to b, so again b has an upper neighbor.

Second, we need to show that there is an ab as specified with b's upper neighbor on a top edge. Let ab with $a < b$ be the bottom edge with b maximum among all bottom edges with respect to "$<$". Thus b is the uppermost upper endpoint of all the bottom edges. Then b's upper neighbor c cannot be on a bottom edge. Since every vertex has a bottom or top (i.e., a slanted) edge incident to it by (1), c must be on a top edge.

Having shown that the quadrilateral always exists, we now show that it is removable. Let A be the set of points vertically between b and c, excluding those right of b and left of c, as illustrated in Fig. 2.41. Since c is the upper neighbor of b, A contains no vertices. Let d be the other end of the top edge containing c. If $d < c$, then it must be that $d < b$ to avoid A. But this would put b in the shadow of dc, violating condition (3). Thus we must have

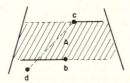

Fig. 2.41. The region A between b and its upper neighbor c.

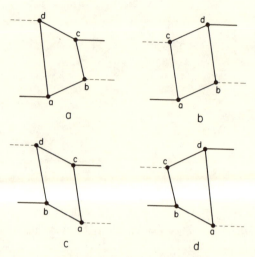

Fig. 2.42. The removable quadrilateral in all its orientations. The horizontal solid and dashed edges represent the closed and open boundaries of *B*.

$c < d$. This leads to four cases, as illustrated in Fig. 2.42. Let *B* be the union of *A* and the shadows of *ab* and *cd*. Then *B* is empty and so the quadrilaterals illustrated in the figure are each internal to *P*.

Next we show that the removable quadrilateral is convex. If *ab* is not horizontal, then the angle at *a* is clearly less than 180°, and the angle at *b* is less than 180° because the vertical edge incident to *b* must extend upwards to satisfy (2). If *ab* is horizontal, then both angles are less than 180° since *c* and *d* are both above *ab*. Exactly analogous arguments show that the angles at *c* and *d* are less than 180°, thereby establishing that the quadrilateral is convex.

Removal of the quadrilateral introduces two new slanted edges in each case of Fig. 2.42. Notice that in each case, the shadow of these slanted

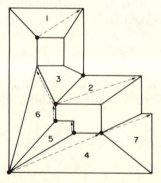

Fig. 2.43. Quadrilateralization by repeated deletion of removable quadrilaterals. The quadrilaterals are numbered in the order in which they are removed. The dashed arrows represent the upper neighbor relation.

edges is in B and so is empty, thus satisfying condition (3). Since vertical edges are incident to a, b, c, and d, the alternation of vertical and slanted is maintained (1). Finally, since angles less than or equal to 270° are being subdivided by the removal, condition (3) holds for the remainder. Thus the removal leaves pseudo-orthogonal pieces. Applying the induction hypothesis to these pieces, and merging the resulting quadrilateralizations with the removed quadrilateral, provides a quadrilateralization for P and establishes the theorem. □

An example of repeated application of the theorem to an orthogonal polygon with two holes is shown in Fig. 2.43. In the next section we show that this procedure can be implemented in $O(n \log n)$ time.

2.4.4. Lubiw's Algorithm

The proof in the preceding section leads to a surprisingly straightforward $O(n \log n)$ algorithm for quadrilateralizing a pseudo-orthogonal polygon. First, the upper neighbors of all vertices are found in $O(n \log n)$ time by a procedure nearly identical to Lee and Preparata's monotone partitioning algorithm (Section 1.3.2). Then quadrilaterals are removed as in Theorem 2.4 in linear time. The reason this simple approach works is the remarkable fact, proved by Lubiw, that the upper neighbors do not change when quadrilaterals are removed. If they did, recomputation would be necessary, and it would be very difficult to achieve $O(n \log n)$ time.

Because the algorithm is so simple and similar to others discussed previously, it will only be sketched. However, its correctness will be proved in detail.

The first step of the algorithm is to find the upper neighbor of every vertex. Note the similarity between the connection of a vertex to its upper neighbor and the connection of a cusp to the closest visible vertex above it that is used in Lee and Preparata's monotone decomposition algorithm, or Sack's algorithm 2.3. Upper neighbors may be found in a single plane sweep in the same way that all upward cusps can be cut in a single sweep. The details differ in only minor ways; see Lubiw (1985) for a precise exposition.

The second step of the algorithm is to make a list L of all bottom edges, sorted bottom to top by their uppermost then leftmost endpoint. This can be accomplished during the same sweep that computes upper neighbors.

The final step of the algorithm is to remove the uppermost edge ab in L, identify the upper neighbor c of its upper endpoint b, and remove the removable quadrilateral specified in Theorem 2.4. This bottom edge ab satisfies the conditions of the theorem because it is the highest bottom edge. Moreover, the (at most) two new bottom edges introduced by the removal of the quadrilateral are above all other bottom edges in L, and so are placed the end of L.

What remains to be established is that the upper neighbors computed in the first step remain valid throughout the execution of the algorithm. Lubiw's precise statement of this property is the following lemma.

LEMMA 2.11. Let P' result from P by repeated removal of quadrilaterals according to Theorem 2.4. Then if ab is a bottom edge of P' with $a < b$, the upper neighbor c of b in P' is the same as the upper neighbor of b in P.

Proof. Let bx be the vertical edge incident with b in P'. There are three possible relationships between a, b, and x, as illustrated in Fig. 2.40: x may be below b only if ab is horizontal (Fig. 2.40d); otherwise it must be above (Figs. 2.40a, 2.40b, and 2.40c). The vertical edge incident to a vertex is only removed with a quadrilateral when the vertex itself is removed; thus bx is also the vertical edge incident to b in P.

Let c be the upper neighbor of b in P. Let A be the union of the two shadows of the chord bc towards the left and right. Because c is an upper neighbor of b, A is devoid of vertices. The only way that c could *not* be the upper neighbor of b in P' is if the removal of some quadrilateral Q blocks the line of visibility bc. Since A is empty, such a Q must contain a vertex $y \leq b$ and a vertex $z \geq c$. If b itself is not a vertex of Q, then it falls within a shadow of one of Q's edges, inside the region B in the proof of Theorem 2.4, a contradiction. So b must be a corner of Q.

Consider now two cases. Suppose b is on the top edge forming Q. Then either b is at the right of a horizontal edge (Fig. 2.44a) or it is the highest endpoint of the top edge (Fig. 2.44b). Note that in the former case, the definition of upper neighbor implies that the left endpoint of the horizontal edge incident to b is *not* the upper neighbor of b, by requiring that the upper neighbor be strictly above b in this case. In either case, Q must lie below b, and there can be no vertex z of Q, $z \geq c$.

Finally, suppose b is on a bottom edge forming Q. Then examination of Fig. 2.42 shows that b is either removed or converted to a lowest vertex of a bottom edge. And once it is this type of vertex, further quadrilateral removals can only reduce the internal angle, keeping it lowest on a bottom edge, contradicting our assumption that it is highest on a bottom edge in P'.

Thus no such obstructing Q will be removed by the algorithm, and therefore the upper neighbor relation remains fixed throughout.   □

As with Sack's algorithm, I believe Tarjan and Van Wyk's trapezoidalization algorithm improves the speed of Lubiw's algorithm to $O(n \log \log n)$.

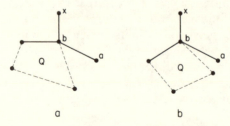

Fig. 2.44. Removal of Q cannot block b from its upper neighbor.

2.5. PARTITION INTO L-SHAPED PIECES[8]

Although the convex quadrilateralization theorem is deep and beautiful, it is not the only means of proving that $\lfloor n/4 \rfloor$ guards are sufficient to cover an orthogonal polygon, nor the only avenue for placing the guards in $O(n \log n)$ time. In this and the succeeding section, a different proof and algorithm are offered, based on a partition into L-shaped pieces rather than convex quadrilaterals. In this section we reprove the orthogonal art gallery theorem (Theorem 2.2), using the L-shaped partition introduced in O'Rourke (1983b).

2.5.1. Main Inductive Argument

The proof is phrased in terms of r, the number of reflex vertices of the orthogonal polygon, rather than n, the total number of vertices. This rephrasing is justified because there is a fixed relationship between r and n:

LEMMA 2.12. In an orthogonal polygon of n vertices, r of which are reflex, $n = 2r + 4$.

Proof. Let c be the number of vertices at which the internal angle is $\pi/2$; clearly, $n = c + r$. Since the sum of the internal angles of a simple polygon is $(n - 2)\pi$, and since the angle at each reflex vertex is $3\pi/2$,

$$(n - 2)\pi = c(\pi/2) + r(3\pi/2).$$

Solving for c and substituting into $n = c + r$ yields $n = 2r + 4$. $\square$

Since $\lfloor n/4 \rfloor = \lfloor (2r + 4)/4 \rfloor = \lfloor r/2 \rfloor + 1$, Theorem 2.2 can be stated as follows:

THEOREM 2.5 $\lfloor r/2 \rfloor + 1$ guards are necessary and sufficient to cover the interior of an orthogonal polygon of r reflex vertices.

The "comb" example (Fig. 2.18) establishes occasional necessity; an alternate sufficiency proof follows.

Define a *cut* of an orthogonal polygon as an extension of one of the two edges incident to a reflex vertex through the interior of the polygon until it first encounters the boundary of the polygon (see Fig. 2.45). A cut "resolves" its reflex vertex in the sense that the vertex is no longer reflex in either of the two pieces of the partition determined by the cut. Clearly a cut does not introduce any reflex vertices. The induction step of the proof cuts the polygon in two, and applies the induction hypothesis to each half. This will yield the formula of the theorem if a cut can be found such that at least one of the halves contains an odd number of reflex vertices. The only difficult part of the proof is establishing that such an odd-cut always exists. This sketch will now be formalized.

---

8. An earlier version of this section appeared in O'Rourke (1983b), © 1983 Birkhaüser Verlag.

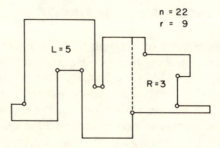

Fig. 2.45. A cut partitions a polygon into two pieces of L and R reflex vertices; since the cut resolves one reflex vertex, $r = L + R + 1$.

Proof of the Theorem

The theorem is clearly true for $r \leq 1$: a single guard suffices. So assume that $r \geq 2$ and that the theorem holds for all $r' < r$. Consider now two cases.

Case 1 (There exists a cut that resolves two reflex vertices). This case occurs when two reflex vertices can "see" one another along a vertical or horizontal line. Cut the polygon in two along this line, and let L and R be the number of reflex vertices in the two pieces produced. Since $r = L + R + 2$, the formula to be proved is

$$\lfloor r/2 \rfloor + 1 = \lfloor (L + R + 2)/2 \rfloor + 1 \geq \lfloor L/2 \rfloor + \lfloor R/2 \rfloor + 2.$$

Applying the induction hypothesis to each half yields a coverage of both polygons (and so the entire original polygon) with $\lfloor L/2 \rfloor + 1 + \lfloor R/2 \rfloor + 1$ guards, which, by the above calculation, is less than or equal to the formula to be established.

Case 2 (No two reflex vertices can see one another along a vertical or horizontal line). Lemma 2.17 below will establish that in this case, there exists an *odd-cut*: a cut such that one of the two pieces has an odd number of reflex vertices. Let such a cut be chosen, and let L and R be the number of reflex vertices in the halves, with R odd. As one reflex guard is resolved by the cut, $r = L + R + 1$. The formula of the theorem can therefore be written as

$$\lfloor r/2 \rfloor + 1 = \lfloor (L + R + 1)/2 \rfloor + 1 \geq \lfloor L/2 \rfloor + \lfloor (R - 1)/2 \rfloor + 2.$$

Applying the induction hypothesis to each half yields coverage by $\lfloor L/2 \rfloor + 1 + \lfloor (R - 1)/2 \rfloor + 1$ (since R is odd), which, by the above calculation, is less than or equal to the formula to be proved. $\square$

2.5.2. Existence of Odd-Cuts

The existence of odd-cuts will now be established. First note that an odd-cut may not exist if reflex vertices can see one another along horizontal or vertical lines (see Fig. 2.46), but that this falls under Case 1 of the proof

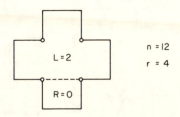

Fig. 2.46. A polygon that does not admit an odd-cut, but that permits a single cut to resolve two reflex vertices.

above. Therefore, in this section it will be assumed that the vertices of the polygon are in "general position" in the sense that no cut can resolve two reflex vertices. Second note that the existence of an odd-cut is trivial if r, the total number of reflex vertices, is even: any cut partitions the reflex vertices according to $r = L + R + 1$, so one of L or R must be odd and the other even. When r is odd, either L and R are both even or both odd; the task is to show that a cut can be found such that they are both odd. Finally note that a horizontal odd-cut does not always exist: Fig. 2.47 shows an example with $r = 5$. In this case, only a vertical odd-cut exists. Thus cuts in both directions must be considered; call a horizontal cut an *H-cut* and a vertical cut a *V-cut*.

The proof depends on a particular orthogonal partitioning of the polygon, which will now be defined for H-cuts. Call a reflex vertex *H-isolated* if the other endpoint of its incident horizontal edge is not reflex, and otherwise call it a member of an *H-pair*. Partition the polygon by forming an H-cut at each reflex vertex that is a member of an H-pair (see Fig. 2.48); the only reflex vertices not resolved in this partitioning are H-isolated vertices. This decomposition is a partition into pieces monotone with respect to the y axis, as was used in Section 2.3. It will be proved that either an H-odd-cut exists or there is precisely one H-isolated vertex. The proof depends on a rather close analysis of the structure of this partition, which will be explored in terms of its region adjacency graph, called its *H-graph*.

Each piece of the partition corresponds to a node of this graph, and node A is connected by an arc directed to node B iff (1) A and B are adjacent pieces, separated by an H-cut, and (2) the H-pair corresponding to the H-cut lies on the boundary of the A piece. See Fig. 2.48. The following lemma classifies the nodes according to their incident arcs.

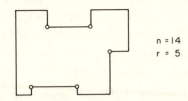

Fig. 2.47. A polygon that has no horizontal odd-cut.

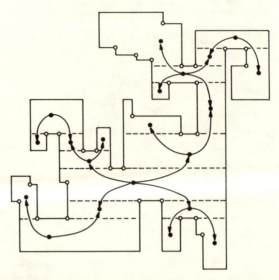

Fig. 2.48. The H-graph associated with a polygon records region adjacency in the partitioned formed by cutting at each H-pair member.

LEMMA 2.13.   The H-graph corresponding to the above defined partition of an orthogonal polygon can have just four types of nodes (see Table 2.2).

Table 2.2

Name	Total Degree	Incoming Arcs	Outgoing Arcs
leaf	1	1	0
branch	3	1	2
source	2 or 4	0	2 or 4
sink	2	2	0

Proof.   The general position assumption prevents a single cut linking two reflex vertices. Thus each region can have at most two H-pairs and therefore four H-cuts on its boundary. Thus the degree of a node is less than or equal to 4. The definition of "arc" implies that a node cannot have just one outgoing arc. Thus a degree 1 node must be a leaf. A degree 2 node can have two outgoing (source) or two incoming (sink) arcs; one outgoing arc is not possible. A degree 3 node must be a branch, again because one outgoing is not possible. A degree 4 node must have two H-pairs on its boundary, which implies that all four arcs are outgoing.   □

It will now be shown that the graph for a polygon that does *not* admit an H-odd-cut must have a very special structure.

LEMMA 2.14.   If a polygon's H-graph contains a sink node, then it admits an H-odd-cut.

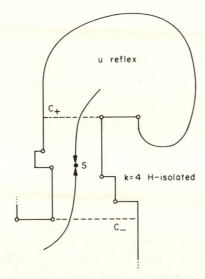

Fig. 2.49. A sink region S always permits an odd-cut.

Proof. Let S be the region corresponding to a sink node, and let C_+ and C_- be the upper and lower H-cuts on the boundary of S. Let S contain k H-isolated vertices, and let the total number of reflex vertices in the portion of the original polygon above C_+ (not including the vertex forming C_+) be u. See Fig. 2.49.

If u is odd, then C_+ is an H-odd-cut. If u is even, a cut at the highest H-isolated vertex in S (if $k > 0$) or C_- (if $k = 0$) is an H-odd-cut. □

Thus, if a polygon does not admit an H-odd-cut, it cannot have any sink nodes. This implies that such a graph has just a single source node, as two source nodes can only interlink via sinks. Thus the graph is a tree with a source root node, and otherwise binary directed towards the leaves.

LEMMA 2.15. If a polygon does not admit an H-odd-cut, then it has exactly one H-isolated vertex located in its sole source region.

Proof. First it will be shown that all leaf and branch nodes must be devoid of H-isolated vertices. The proof is by induction on the number of arcs to the nearest leaf node, which we call the *frontier distance*.

Suppose some leaf L contains $k > 0$ H-isolated reflex vertices. Let C be the H-cut corresponding to its single incoming arc (see Fig. 2.50). Then if k is odd, C is an odd-cut, and if k is even, then the H-isolated vertex in L closest to C is an odd-cut. This establishes the basis of the induction.

Suppose now that all leaf and branch nodes with frontier distance $d' < d$ have no H-isolated vertices, and consider a branch node B at distance d. Let C be the H-cut corresponding to its single incoming arc, and let $k > 0$ be the number of H-isolated vertices in B. If k is odd, then C is an odd-cut, since by the induction hypothesis none of the descendants of B have any

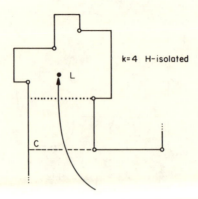

Fig. 2.50. If a leaf region L has $k > 0$ H-isolated vertices, then it admits an H-odd-cut.

H-isolated vertices, and otherwise the reflex vertices come in H-pairs. If k is even, then the H-isolated vertex in B closest to C can form an odd-cut.

Finally, it will be shown that the single source region S must have exactly one H-isolated vertex to avoid an H-odd-cut. Suppose S contains an even number k of H-isolated vertices, and let C be a cut corresponding to one of S's outgoing arcs (see Fig. 2.51). Then C is an odd-cut, since it resolves one reflex vertex of an H-pair, and otherwise all other reflex vertices are either in the even k H-isolated vertices or they come in H-pairs. If k is odd and greater than 1, then the second closest one to C forms an odd-cut. Thus there must be exactly one H-isolated vertex. □

Clearly Lemmas 2.13–2.15 holds for V-cuts as well as H-cuts. Thus, if a polygon does not admit an H-odd-cut nor a V-odd-cut, then it must have a single H-isolated vertex h and a single V-isolated vertex v, both located in source regions of the H- and V-graphs, respectively. That these conditions are impossible to achieve is shown by the following lemma.

LEMMA 2.16. A polygon of $r \geq 3$ reflex vertices cannot have exactly one H-isolated vertex in a region corresponding to a source node of its H-graph, and exactly one V-isolated vertex in a region corresponding to a source node of its V-graph.

Proof. Let h and v be the H- and V-isolated vertices, respectively. All reflex vertices besides h and v (there is at least one such since $r \geq 3$) are

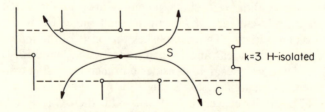

Fig. 2.51. A source region S admits an H-odd-cut if it contains $k \neq 1$ H-isolated vertices.

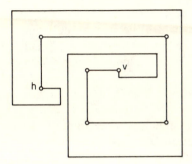

Fig. 2.52. Reflex vertices that are members of both H- and V-pairs form a spiral chain whose end-points are either H- or V-isolated.

members of both an H-pair and a V-pair, else they would be isolated. This implies that they are all adjacent, forming a contiguous chain of reflex vertices. This chain cannot close upon itself without forming a hole, contradicting the assumption that the polygon has no holes. The polygon is therefore a *spiral* (having a single concave chain) whose endpoints are h and v (see Fig. 2.52). But then h is in a leaf region of the H-graph and v in a leaf region of the V-graph, contradicting the requirement that they be located in source regions. □

The existence of odd-cuts is now established:

LEMMA 2.17. An orthogonal polygon with an odd number $r \geq 3$ of reflex vertices, no two of which can see one another along a vertical or horizontal line, admits an odd-cut.

This completes the proof of Theorem 2.5.[9] This proof easily extends to "multi-level" orthogonal polygons connected by ramps, as used in Theorem 2.1, but it does not immediately extend to orthogonal polygons with holes. This latter case will be considered in Chapter 5.

2.6. ALGORITHM TO PARTITION INTO L-SHAPED PIECES[10]

The proof described in the previous section does not translate directly into an algorithm, because of the difficulty of finding odd-cuts. Nevertheless, we now show that, with the addition of a few new ideas, it can be implemented to run in $O(n \log n)$ time. Application of the new trapezoidalization algorithm reduces the time to $O(n \log \log n)$. We will assume throughout that the polygon is in general position; this is the hard case, as was pointed out in Section 2.5.2.

---

9. A somewhat simpler proof along similar lines was offered in Mannila and Wood (1984). As this book was being revised a third, even simpler proof was published (Györi, 1986).
10. An earlier version of this section appeared in Edelsbrunner *et al.* (1984), © 1984 Academic Press.

At a coarse level, the algorithm is very simple. First the polygon is preprocessed to detect which horizontal cuts are odd-cuts. Then it is partitioned at every such horizontal odd-cut. Finally, guards are placed in each of the resulting pieces. This will achieve coverage with $\lfloor r/2 \rfloor + 1$ guards.

The simplicity of this procedure results from care applied at two critical junctures. First, it is easier algorithmically to make an odd-cut in a polygon with an odd number r of reflex vertices than in one with an even number. The reason, which will be detailed below, is that no updating of the preprocessed computations are necessary for each cut when the number of reflex vertices is odd. We therefore take the counterintuitive step of complicating the polygon by introducing a new reflex vertex if r is even; the bound of $\lfloor r/2 \rfloor + 1$ is clearly unaffected.

The second critical juncture arises when all horizontal odd-cuts have been made, and only vertical odd-cuts remain. As previously mentioned, the polygon must then have a restricted structure, and guard placement is nearly trivial. This is fortunate, as otherwise the preprocessing step might have to be repeated with each oscillation between horizontal and vertical cuts.

These claims are justified in the following section.

2.6.1. The Algorithm

The algorithm for locating $\lfloor r/2 \rfloor + 1$ guards in an orthogonal polygon of n vertices, r of which are reflex, consists of six distinct steps:

(1) If r is even, then add an additional reflex vertex.
(2) Perform a plane sweep to find all horizontal cuts.
(3) Traverse the boundary once, labeling the parity of the cuts.
(4) Partition the polygon at each horizontal odd-cut.
(5) For each resulting piece, place a guard at every other reflex vertex.
(6) Remove the extra reflex vertex, if introduced in step (1).

Each of these steps will now be described in detail and justified.

Add Reflex Vertex: $O(n)$

If r is even, then $\lfloor (r+1)/2 \rfloor + 1 = \lfloor r/2 \rfloor + 1$, so the addition of a reflex vertex is justified. The reason for doing so was alluded to above and will be expanded on below. The extra reflex vertex can be added in linear time as follows. Choose an arbitrary convex vertex $v = (x, y)$. Find the smallest non-zero horizontal and vertical separations Δx and Δy from x and y to other vertices by examining the coordinates of each of the $O(n)$ vertices. Delete vertex v and replace it with three others as illustrated in Fig. 2.53. Since no edges of the polygon can cross the rectangle with corners (x, y) and $(x + \Delta x/2, y + \Delta y/2)$, clearly this "dent" maintains the simplicity of the polygon. That it does not interfere with visibility will be shown later.

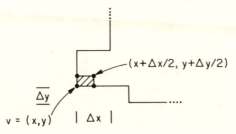

Fig. 2.53. A reflex vertex introduced by removing a "chip" from the polygon at a convex vertex v.

Plane Sweep for Horizontal Cuts: $O(n \log n)$ *or* $O(n \log \log n)$

Each reflex vertex determines a unique horizontal cut. The goal of this step is to find each horizontal cut and to insert a new "artificial" vertex into the circular list of vertices representing the polygon at the end of each cut, doubly linking each reflex vertex with its associated artificial vertex. This data structure then serves as input to step (3) of the algorithm.

The locations of the artificial vertices are found by a sweep of a horizontal line from top to bottom over the polygon. This is a standard plane sweep, and is nearly identical to the monotone partitioning algorithm of Lee and Preparata (Algorithm 1.2), or to that used in Sections 2.3 and 2.4. The vertical edges of the polygon are sorted by their maximum y coordinate. At each position of the sweep line H, a data structure S holds all those vertical edges pierced by H, organized left to right. When H moves down and encounters a reflex vertex v, the vertical edge hit by v's horizontal cut is available in S as adjacent to the vertical edge whose top or bottom is v (see Fig. 2.54). After computing the coordinates of the corresponding artificial vertex, a vertical edge is either inserted or deleted from the data structure S, depending on whether v is the top or the bottom of a vertical edge. The data structure can be chosen to support $O(\log n)$ insertion and deletion time, which leads to $O(n \log n)$ time overall. Since these horizontal cuts are precisely what the trapezoidalization algorithm of Tarjan and Van Wyk constructs (Section 1.3.2), use of that algorithm instead of a plane sweep reduces the time complexity of this step to $O(n \log \log n)$. As this is the only step that might be supra-linear, the entire algorithm is $O(n \log \log n)$.

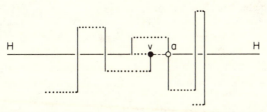

Fig. 2.54. When the sweep line H hits a reflex vertex v, the artificial vertex a on its cut lies on a vertical edge adjacent to v's edge in S.

Boundary Traversal to Compute Cut Parity: $O(n)$

The next step is to determine which of the horizontal cuts are odd-cuts—that is, have an odd number of reflex vertices to one side or another. As the total number of reflex vertices r is known, finding the number to one side of a cut determines the number to the other side. The number to one side of each cut can be found in a single boundary traversal of the polygon as follows.

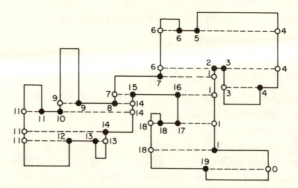

Fig. 2.55. Labels on reflex (solid dots) and artificial vertices (open circles) are generated in a counterclockwise scan of the boundary, incrementing the label counter at each reflex vertex.

Distinguish three types of vertices: convex, reflex, and artificial. Start at an arbitrary vertex, initialize a counter to zero, and proceed counterclockwise around the polygon. If the next vertex is convex, do nothing; if the next vertex is artificial, label it with the counter value; if the next vertex is reflex, increment the counter value and label the vertex with this new value (see Fig. 2.55). As soon as both end points of a cut are labeled, the number of reflex vertices k to one side is determined by the difference between the two labels. When the artificial vertex of a cut is encountered second, then the exact difference of the labels is k; when the reflex vertex is second, then k is the difference less 1 (see Fig. 2.56).

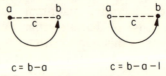

$$c = b - a \qquad\qquad c = b - a - 1$$

Fig. 2.56. The labels a and b assigned to the two ends of a cut determine the number of reflex vertices c to one side by their difference or difference less 1.

It is not actually necessary to compute the *number* of reflex vertices to each side, as only the parity is needed. Thus each reflex and artificial vertex can be labeled as even or odd during the traversal, and the parity of the cuts determined by straightforward modification of the rules above.

Cut at Each Horizontal Odd-Cut: $O(n)$

The goal of the fourth step is to cut the polygon at each horizontal odd-cut; the remaining pieces will then be easy to cover with guards. The only

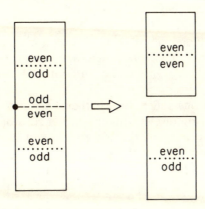

Fig. 2.57. Partitioning at an odd-cut can either flip or leave the parity of other cuts unchanged when the total number of reflex vertices is even.

potential difficulty with this step is that, after a particular cut is made, the parities computed in the previous step may no longer be correct for the cuts in the two pieces. For example, Fig. 2.57 shows that a particular odd-cut can either leave the parity of other cuts unchanged, or it could flip their parity, depending on whether the odd number of reflex vertices is inside the portion including the cut or not. However, note that the situations in Fig. 2.57 can only arise when the total number of reflex vertices r is even. When r is odd, then there is only one type of odd-cut: a cut that has an odd number of reflex vertices to *each* side. Partitioning the polygon at such an odd-cut leaves the parity of the cuts in each half unchanged (see Fig. 2.58).

Since step (1) of the algorithm guarantees that r is odd, all the horizontal odd-cuts may be made without any updating to the parities computed in step (3). At the conclusion of this partitioning, we are left with several orthogonal polygons, all of which have only even horizontal cuts remaining.

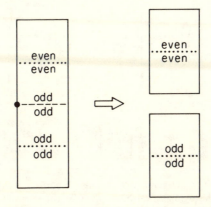

Fig. 2.58. If the total number of reflex vertices is odd, then partitioning at an odd-cut does not affect the parity of other cuts.

Guard Placement: $O(n)$

Consider now an orthogonal polygon with no horizontal odd-cuts. If it has no reflex vertices, then it is a rectangle and can be covered with a single guard placed anywhere within the interior. This satisfies the bound $\lfloor r/2 \rfloor + 1$ of the theorem.

If there is at least one reflex vertex, then Lemma 2.17 establishes that a vertical odd-cut exists. However, finding such a cut would require repetition of the previous four steps of the algorithm, and ultimately may lead to switching back to horizontal cuts again. Such oscillation and the computation it entails could be very expensive. Fortunately, polygons without horizontal odd-cuts have a special structure that makes guard placement easy.

It was proven in Section 2.5.2 that a polygon with only even horizontal cuts must appear as in Fig. 2.59: it is formed by two "histograms" joined at their bases. This structural restriction was stated in a different but equivalent terms in Lemma 2.15. More precisely, define a *vertical histogram* as in Section 2.3.2: an orthogonal polygon that has one horizontal edge (the base) equal in length to the sum of lengths of all the other horizontal edges. Then a polygon that has no horizontal odd-cuts must have a reflex vertex whose horizontal cut partitions the polygon into two vertical histograms (as in Fig. 2.59). Such a polygon clearly must have an odd number of reflex vertices.

Guards placed at every other reflex vertex from left to right will necessarily cover such a polygon. To see this, let the reflex vertices be $v_1, v_2, \ldots, v_k$ in sorted order from lowest x coordinate to highest; here k is odd. Make a vertical cut at $v_2, v_4, \ldots, v_{2\lfloor k/2 \rfloor}$. The polygon has now been partitioned into $\lfloor k/2 \rfloor + 1$ L-shaped pieces, each containing one reflex vertex (see Fig. 2.59). Place guards on $v_1, v_3, \ldots, v_{2\lfloor k/2 \rfloor + 1}$. This clearly covers the polygon with $\lfloor k/2 \rfloor + 1$ guards, achieving the bound of the theorem.

The sorting of the reflex vertices can be accomplished in linear time by

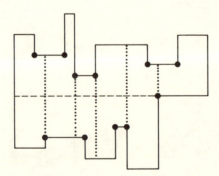

Fig. 2.59. Polygons with no horizontal odd-cuts have a horizontal cut (dashed) that paritition them into two vertical histograms, which can then be cut vertically into L-shaped pieces at every other reflex vertex.

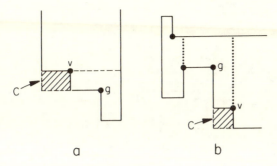

Fig. 2.60. The chip region C is visible to some guard g, regardless of whether a horizontal (a) or vertical (b) cut emanates from v.

merging the two histogram chains, which are necessarily already sorted. Once the order is determined, no vertical cuts need actually be made: the guards are simply assigned to every other reflex vertex. Note that after step (5) is completed, the polygon has been implicitly partitioned into L-shaped pieces; one of these may be modified to a rectangle in the final step discussed next.

Finally, we note that the same simple guard location procedure would work if the polygon were monotone with respect to the x axis. This is a wider class of shapes than the double histograms that result from step (5).

Replacement of Chip: $O(n)$

If an extra reflex vertex was introduced by removing a "chip" C at a convex corner of the polygon in step (1) of the algorithm (see Fig. 2.60), then returning the polygon to its original form will not require any more guards, nor even a movement of the existing guard locations.

Consider two cases. If the introduced reflex vertex v is assigned a guard during step (5), then retract the chip back to the original convex corner, and place the guard in that corner. Clearly the L-shaped region formerly covered by the guard at v is now a rectangle and covered by the guard in the corner. If v is not assigned a guard, then a cut was made at that vertex in the algorithm, either a horizontal cut in step (3) or a vertical cut (implicitly) in step (4). In either case, one of the two edges incident to v is a complete edge of an L-shaped region that has a guard g in it (see Fig. 2.60). This follows since the edges of the chip were chosen too small to be hit by any cuts. Clearly the guard g sees into C.

2.6.2. Discussion

We have assumed that no two reflex vertices of the polygon can see one another along a vertical or horizontal line. Lemma 2.17 depends on this assumption: without it a polygon may have no odd-cuts, either horizontal or vertical (Fig. 2.46). Fortunately this degeneracy is in our favor, so to speak, and is easy to handle.

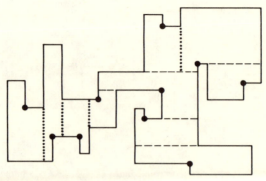

Fig. 2.61. Guards positioned in the polygon of Fig. 2.55. The dashed lines are the horizontal cuts made in step (4) of the algorithm, and the dotted lines are the vertical cuts implicit in step (5). Here $r = 19$, and $\lfloor r/2 \rfloor + 1 = 10$ guards are used.

If two reflex vertices see one another along a horizontal, this can be detected during the plane sweep, step (2) of the algorithm. Before commencing step (3), we can cut the polygon into pieces at each such horizontal. As established in Section 2.5.1, recursive application will achieve the desired bound, and each piece can be processed by the algorithm separately.

If two reflex vertices see one another along a vertical, one of the L-shaped regions formed by the implicit vertical cuts in step (5) may degenerate to a rectangle, but this in no way affects the execution of the analysis of the algorithm.

The guard locations chosen by the algorithm for the example used in Fig. 2.55 and the partition they induce, are shown in Fig. 2.61.[11]

---

11. I thank Carmen Castells and David Shallcross for implementing this algorithm.

3

MOBILE GUARDS

3.1. INTRODUCTION

In this chapter we explore an interesting variant of the art gallery problem suggested by Toussaint. Rather than modify the shape of the polygons as in the previous chapter, we modify the power of the guard. Specifically, each guard is permitted to "patrol" an interior line segment. Let s be a line segment completely contained in the closed polygonal region P: $s \subseteq P$. Then $x \in P$ is said to be seen by s, or is covered by s, if there is a point $y \in s$ such that the line segment $xy \subseteq P$. Thus x is covered by the guard if x is visible from some point along the guard's patrol path. This is the notion of *weak visibility* from a line segment introduced in Avis and Toussaint (1981b) (*strong visibility* requires x to be seen from every point of s), a concept further explored in Chapter 8.

The main reason that mobile guards are interesting is that they lead to some clean theorems, some difficult theorems, and to interesting open problems. Secondarily they connect to the important notion of edge visibility, to be discussed further in Chapters 7 and 8. A covering by mobile guards induces a partition into edge-visible polygons.

We present two long proofs in this chapter. The first establishes that $\lfloor n/4 \rfloor$ mobile guards are occasionally necessary and always sufficient to cover an n vertex polygon. The second proof, which is quite complex, establishes the equivalent result for orthogonal polygons: $\lfloor (3n + 4)/16 \rfloor$ mobile guards are necessary and sufficient. This latter quantity may seem ugly in comparison to the simpler fractions we have encountered so far, but there is a clean logic behind it, as revealed in Table 3.1. Mobile guards are more powerful than stationary guards: only 3/4's as many are needed, in both general and orthogonal polygons—the second column is 3/4 times the first. Moreover, orthogonal polygons are 3/4's easier to cover than general polygons: the second row is 3/4 times the first. Thus orthogonal polygons require about $(3/4)^2 \lfloor n/3 \rfloor$ mobile guards.

The first proof, presented in Section 3.2, is entirely combinatoric, following the outline of Chvátal's proof (Section 1.2.1). The second proof,

81

Table 3.1

Guard → Shape	Stationary	Mobile
General	$\lfloor n/3 \rfloor$	$\lfloor n/4 \rfloor$
Orthogonal	$\lfloor n/4 \rfloor$	$\lfloor (3n+4)/16 \rfloor$

presented in Section 3.3, is an instance where no reduction to combinatorics has been discovered, and complex geometric reasoning seems necessary. The chapter closes with a discussion of related results.

3.2. GENERAL POLYGONS[1]

We first define various types of guards, both geometric and combinatorial. Three geometric mobile guards types with different degrees of patrol freedom can be distinguished. An *edge guard* is an edge of P, including the endpoints. A *diagonal guard* is an edge or internal diagonal between vertices of P, again including the endpoints. A *line guard* is any line segment wholly contained in P. (Recall that P is a closed region.) Geometric guards are said to *cover* the region they can see.

The combinatorial counterparts of these guards are obtained by defining a *guard* in a triangulation graph T of a polygon P to be a subset of the nodes of T. Then a *vertex guard* in T is a single node of T, an *edge guard* is a pair of nodes adjacent across an arc corresponding to an edge of P, and a *diagonal guard* is a pair of nodes adjacent across any arc of T. The analog of covering is domination: a collection of guards $C = \{g_1, \ldots, g_k\}$ is said to *dominate* T if every triangular face of T has at least one of its three nodes in some $g_i \in C$.

The goal of this section is to prove that $\lfloor n/4 \rfloor$ combinatorial diagonal guards are sometimes necessary and always sufficient to dominate the triangulation graph of a polygon with $n \geq 4$ vertices. It is clear that if a triangulation graph of a polygon can be dominated by k combinatorial vertex guards, then the polygon can be covered by k geometric vertex guards. The implication is that a proof of the sufficiency of a $\lfloor n/4 \rfloor$ of combinatorial diagonal guards in a triangulation graph establishes the sufficiency of the same number of geometric diagonal and line guards in a polygonal region.

Necessity is established by the generic example due to Toussaint shown in Fig. 3.1: each 4 edge lobe requires its own diagonal guard.

---

1. An earlier version of this section appeared in O'Rourke (1983a), © 1983 D. Reidel.

Fig. 3.1. A polygon that requires $\lfloor n/4 \rfloor$ edge, diagonal, or line guards.

3.2.1. Sufficiency Proof

The proof is by induction and follows the main outlines of Chvátal's inductive proof (and Honsberger's exposition (Honsberger 1976)). Before commencing the proof, it will be convenient to establish certain facts that will be in various cases of the proof. The most important of these concerns "edge contractions." Let P be a polygon and T a triangulation graph for P, and let e be an edge of P, and u and v the two nodes of T corresponding to the endpoints of e. The *contraction* of e is a transformation that alters T by removing nodes u and v and replacing them with a new node x adjacent to every node to which u or v was adjacent.[2] Compare Figs. 3.2a and 3.2d. Note that an edge contraction is a *graph* transformation, not a polygon transformation: the geometric equivalent ("squashing" the polygon edge) could result in self-crossing polygons. Edge contractions are nevertheless useful because of the following lemma.

LEMMA 3.1. Let T be a triangulation graph of a polygon P, and T' the graph resulting from an edge contraction of T. Then T' is a triangulation graph of some polygon P'.

Proof. We construct a figure with curved edges corresponding to T', then straighten the edges to obtain P'.

Let P_t be the planar figure corresponding to the triangulation T, and let e be the edge contracted and u and v its two endpoints in P_t. Let the vertices to which u and v are connected by diagonals and edges be $y_0, \ldots, y_i$ and $z_0, \ldots, z_j$, respectively, with $y_0 = v$ and $z_0 = u$, and the remainder labeled according to their sorted angular order. See Fig. 3.2a. Note that $y_1 = z_1$ is the apex of the triangle supported by e.

Now introduce a new vertex x on the interior of e, and connect the y and z vertices to x by the following procedure. Connect y_1 to x; this can be done without crossing any diagonals because y_1 is the apex of a triangle on whose base x lies. Remove the diagonal (u, y_1). Connect y_2 to x within the region

---

2. Harary calls this transformation an *elementary contraction* (Harary 1969).

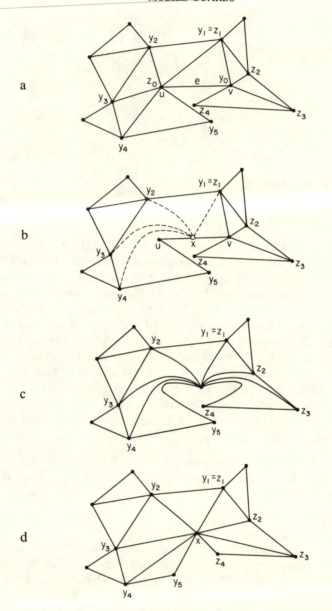

Fig. 3.2. If all the arcs in a triangulation graph (a) incident to u and v are made adjacent to x (b and c), the resulting graph may be deformed into a straight line graph (d).

bounded by (x, y_1, y_2, u); the line may need to be curved but again no crossings are necessary. Remove the diagonal (u, y_2). Continue in this manner (see Fig. 3.2b) until all the y's have been connected to x. Then apply a similar procedure to the z vertices. The result is a planar figure whose connections are the same as those of T'. See Fig. 3.2c.

Finally, apply Fáry's theorem (Giblin 1977): for any planar graph drawn in the plane, perhaps with curved lines, there is a homeomorphism[3] in the plane onto a straight-line graph such that vertices are mapped to vertices and edges to edges. Applying such a homeomorphism to the figure constructed above yields P', a polygon that has T' as one of its triangulations. See Fig. 3.2d. $\square$

The main use of this contraction result is the following.

LEMMA 3.2 Suppose that $f(n)$ combinatorial diagonal guards are always sufficient to dominate any n-node triangulation graph. Then if T is an arbitrary triangulation graph of polygon P with one vertex guard placed at any one of its n nodes, then an additional $f(n-1)$ diagonal guards are sufficient to dominate T.

Proof.   Let u be the node at which the one guard is placed, and let v be a node adjacent to u across an arc corresponding to an edge e of P. Edge contract T across e, producing the graph T' of $n-1$ nodes. By Lemma 3.1 T' is a triangulation graph, and so can be dominated by $f(n-1)$ diagonal guards. Let x be the node of T' that replaced u and v. Suppose that no guard is placed at x in the domination of T'. Then the same guard placements will dominate T, since the given guard at u dominates the triangle supported by e, and the remaining triangles of T have dominated counterparts in T'. Again compare Figs. 3.2a and 3.2d. If a guard is used at x in the domination of T', then this guard can be assigned to v in T, with the remaining guards maintaining their position. Again every triangle of T is dominated. $\square$

We note in passing that the same lemma holds for other types of guards, but we will only need to use it with diagonal guards. Intuitively, one can view this lemma as saying that one edge can be "squashed" out for guard coverage calculations if a guard is assigned to either of the edge's endpoints.

The next three lemmas establish special diagonal guard results for small triangulation graphs.

LEMMA 3.3.   Every triangulation graph of a pentagon $(n=5)$ can be dominated by a single combinatorial diagonal guard with one endpoint at any selected node.

Proof.   Let T be a triangulation graph of a pentagon, and let the selected node be labeled 1. It is easy to show that there are only five distinct triangulations. In each case, a single combinatorial diagonal guard (pair of adjacent nodes), with one end at node 1 can dominate the graph (see Fig. 3.3). $\square$

LEMMA 3.4   Every triangulation graph of a septagon $(n=7)$ can be dominated by a single combinatorial diagonal guard.

---

3. A *homeomorphism* is a continuous one-one onto mapping whose inverse is also continuous; intuitively it is a deformation without tearing or pasting—that is, it preserves topological properties.

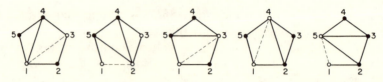

Fig. 3.3. A pentagon can be dominated by a single diagonal guard (shown dashed) with one end at node 1.

Proof. Let T be a triangulation graph of a septagon, and let d be an arbitrary internal diagonal. This diagonal partitions the seven boundary edges of T according to either $2 + 5 = 7$ or $3 + 4 = 7$; clearly the partition $1 + 6 = 7$ is not possible.

Case 1 $(2 + 5 = 7)$. Let $d = (1, 3)$. Then d supports another triangle T, either $(1, 3, 4)$, $(1, 3, 5)$, $(1, 3, 6)$, or $(1, 3, 7)$. Only two of these cases are distinct.

Case 1a $(T = (1, 3, 4))$. Then $(1, 4, 5, 6, 7)$ is a pentagon (see Fig. 3.4a). By Lemma 3.3, this pentagon can be covered with a single diagonal guard with one end of node 1. This guard dominates the entire graph.

Case 1b $(T = (1, 3, 5))$. Choose diagonal $(1, 5)$ for the guard (see Fig. 3.4b). Regardless of how the quadrilateral $(1, 5, 6, 7)$ is triangulated, all of T is dominated.

Case 2 $(3 + 4 = 7)$. Let $d = (1, 4)$. Then both ways of triangulating the quadrilateral $(1, 2, 3, 4)$ lead to situations equivalent to Case 1a above.   □

LEMMA 3.5 Every triangulation graph of an enneagon $(n = 9)$ can be dominated by two combinatorial diagonal guards such that one of their endpoints coincides with any selected node.

Proof. Let T be a triangulation graph of an enneagon, let the selected node be labeled 1, and let d be any internal diagonal with one end at 1. This diagonal partitions the boundary edges of T according to either $2 + 7 = 9$, $3 + 6 = 9$, or $4 + 5 = 9$.

Case 1 $(2 + 7 = 9)$. Let $d = (1, 3)$. The diagonal d supports another triangle T whose apex is at either 4, 5, 6, 7, 8, or 9. Only three of these cases are distinct.

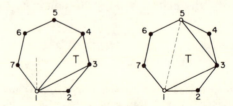

Fig. 3.4. A septagon can be dominated by a single diagonal guard.

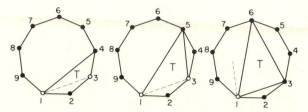

Fig. 3.5. A enneagon can be dominated by two diagonal guards, with one of their ends at node 1.

Case 1a $(T = (1, 3, 4))$. Dominate the septagon $(1, 4, 5, 6, 7, 8, 9)$ with one guard by Lemma 3.4, and use $(1, 3)$ for the second guard (see Fig. 3.5a).

Case 1b $(T = (1, 3, 5))$. Dominate the septagon $(1, 3, 5, 6, 7, 8, 9)$ with one guard by Lemma 3.4, and use $(1, 3)$ for the second guard (see Fig. 3.5b).

Case 1c $(T = (1, 3, 6))$. Dominate the hexagon $(1, 2, 3, 4, 5, 6)$ with one guard by Lemma 3.4, and dominate the pentagon $(1, 6, 7, 8, 9)$ with one guard whose endpoint is at 1 by Lemma 3.3 (see Fig. 3.5c).

Case 2 $(3 + 6 = 9)$. Let $d = (1, 4)$. If diagonal $(1, 3)$ is present, then we have exactly Case 1a above. Otherwise diagonal $(2, 4)$ is present, and one guard along $(1, 2)$ together with a guard for the septagon as in Case 1a suffices.

Case 3 $(4 + 5 = 9)$. Let $d = (1, 6)$. This is equivalent to Case 1c above. □

Finally we must establish the existence of a special diagonal that will allow us to take the induction step, just as Lemma 1.1 did for Chvátal's proof.

LEMMA 3.6. Let P be a polygon of $n \geq 10$ vertices, and T a triangulation graph of P. There exists a diagonal d in T that partitions T into two pieces, one of which contains $k = 5$, 6, 7, or 8 arcs corresponding to edges of P.

Proof. Choose d to be a diagonal of T that separates off a minimum number of polygon edges that is at least 5. Let $k \geq 5$ be this minimum number, and label the vertices $0, 1, \ldots, n - 1$ such that d is $(0, k)$. See Fig. 3.6. The diagonal d supports a triangle T whose apex is at t, $0 \leq t \leq k$. Since k is minimal, $t \leq 4$ and $k - t \leq 4$. Adding these two inequalities yields $k \leq 8$. □

With the preceding lemmas available, the induction proof is a nearly straightforward enumeration of cases.

THEOREM 3.1 [O'Rourke 1983]. Every triangulation graph T of a polygon of $n \geq 4$ vertices can be dominated by $\lfloor n/4 \rfloor$ combinatorial diagonal guards.

Proof. Lemmas 3.3, 3.4, and 3.5 establish the truth of the theorem for $5 \leq n \leq 9$, so assume that $n \geq 10$, and that the theorem holds for all $n' < n$. Lemma 3.6 guarantees the existence of a diagonal d that partitions T into

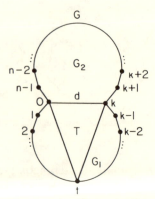

Fig. 3.6. The diagonal d separates G into two pieces, one of which (G_1) shares $5 \le k \le 8$ edges with G.

two graphs T_1 and T_2 where T_1 contains k boundary edges of T with $4 \le k \le 8$. Each value of k will be considered in turn.

Case 1 ($k = 5$ *or* 6). T_1 has $k + 1 \le 7$ boundary edges including d. By Lemma 3.4, T_1 can be dominated with a single diagonal guard. T_2 has $n - k + 1 \le n - 5 + 1 = n - 4$ boundary edges including d, and by the induction hypothesis, it can be dominated with $\lfloor (n-4)/4 \rfloor = \lfloor n/4 \rfloor - 1$ diagonal guards. Thus T_1 and T_2 together can be dominated by $\lfloor n/4 \rfloor$ diagonal guards.

Case 2 ($k = 7$). The presence of any of the diagonals $(0, 6)$, $(0, 5)$, $(1, 7)$, or $(2, 7)$ would violate the minimality of k. Consequently, the triangle T in T_1 that is bounded by d is either $(0, 3, 7)$ or $(0, 4, 7)$; since these are equivalent cases, suppose that T is $(0, 3, 7)$. The quadrilateral $(0, 1, 2, 3)$ has two distinct triangulations. Each will be considered separately.

Case 2a ($(1, 3)$ is included.). Dominate the pentagon $(3, 4, 5, 6, 7)$ with one diagonal guard with one end at node 3. This is possible by Lemma 3.3. This guard dominates all of T_1. Since T_2 has $n - 7 + 1 = n - 6$ boundary edges, it can be dominated by $\lfloor (n-6)/4 \rfloor \le \lfloor n/4 \rfloor - 1$ diagonal guards by the induction hypothesis. This yields a domination of T by $\lfloor n/4 \rfloor$ diagonal guards.

Case 2b ($(0, 2)$ is included.). Form graph T_0 by adjoining the two triangles $T = (0, 3, 7)$ and $T' = (0, 2, 3)$ to T_2 (see Fig. 3.7). T_0 has $n - 7 + 3 = n - 4$ edges, and so can be dominated by $\lfloor (n-4)/4 \rfloor = \lfloor n/4 \rfloor - 1$ diagonal guards by the induction hypothesis. In such a domination, at least one of the vertices of $T' = (0, 2, 3)$ must be a diagonal guard endpoint. There are three possibilities:

(0) If node 0 is a guard end, then T_0 can be extended to include $(0, 1, 2)$ without need of further guards.
(2) If node 2 is a guard end, then T_0 can again be extended to include $(0, 1, 2)$.

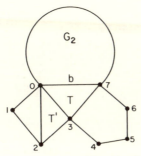

Fig. 3.7. G_0 is formed by adding T and T' to G_2.

(3) If node 3 is a guard end, then there are three possible locations for the other end of the guard. If the other end is at either node 0 or 2, then we fall into the two cases above. If the other end is at node 7, then replace the diagonal guard $(3, 7)$ with $(0, 7)$. Every triangle that was previously dominated is still dominated, and again T_0 can be extended to included $(0, 1, 2)$.

Thus all but the pentagon $(3, 4, 5, 6, 7)$ can be dominated with $\lfloor n/4 \rfloor - 1$ diagonal guards, and the pentagon only requires a single diagonal guard by Lemma 3.4, resulting in a total of $\lfloor n/4 \rfloor$ diagonal guards for all of T.

Case 3 $(k = 8)$. T_1 has $k + 1 = 9$ boundary edges, and so by Lemma 3.5, it can be dominated with two diagonal guards, one of whose endpoints is at node 0. Now T_2 has $n - k + 1 = n - 7$ boundary edges. By Lemma 3.2, the one guard at node 0 permits the remainder of T_2 to be dominated by $f(n - 7 - 1) = f(n - 8)$ diagonal guards, where the function $f(n')$ specifies a number of diagonal guards that are always sufficient to dominate a triangulation graph of n' nodes. By the induction hypothesis, $f(n') = \lfloor n'/4 \rfloor$. Therefore, $\lfloor (n - 8)/4 \rfloor = \lfloor n/4 \rfloor - 2$ diagonal guards suffice to dominate T_2. Together with the two allocated to T_1, all of T is dominated by $\lfloor n/4 \rfloor$ diagonal guards.   □

COROLLARY.   Any polygon P of $n \geq 4$ edges can be covered by $\lfloor n/4 \rfloor$ geometric diagonal or line guards.

Proof.   The diagonal guard result follows immediately from the theorem. Since diagonal guards are special cases of line guards, the same number of these more powerful guards clearly suffice.   □

3.2.2. Edge Guards

The above proof depends on the fortunate identity between the number of combinatorial and geometric diagonal guards necessary and sufficient to dominate and cover triangulation graphs and polygons, respectively. This identity is not known to hold for edge guards, however. No polygons are known to need more than $\lfloor (n + 1)/4 \rfloor$ *geometric* edge guards (see Fig. 3.8),

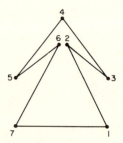

Fig. 3.8. A polygon of seven edges that requires two edge guards.

but triangulation graphs exist that require $\lfloor 2n/7 \rfloor = \lfloor n/3.5 \rfloor$ *combinatorial* edge guards (see Fig. 3.9). Thus it appears that a different proof technique is required in this case.

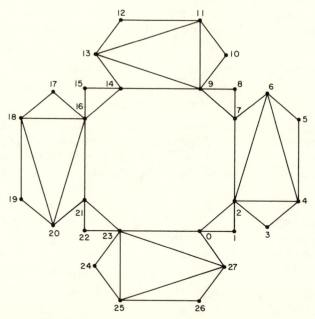

Fig. 3.9. A triangulation graph that requires two edge guards per seven edges. The central octagon may be triangulated arbitrarily.

3.3. ORTHOGONAL POLYGONS

In this section we present Aggarwal's proof that $\lfloor (3n+4)/16 \rfloor$ mobile guards are sufficient for covering an n vertex simple orthogonal polygon (Aggarwal 1984). The occasional necessity of this number of mobile guards is established by a connected series of swastika-like polygons, as shown in Fig. 3.10. The single swasktika shown in Fig. 3.10a with $n = 20$ requires four guards, one per arm; note that $(3 \cdot 20 + 4)/16 = 64/16 = 4$. Merging two

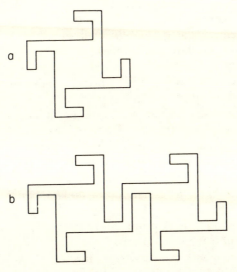

Fig. 3.10. Polygons that require $\lfloor(3n+4)/16\rfloor$ mobile orthogonal guards: (a) $n=20$ and $g=4$; (b) $n=36$ and $g=7$.

20-vertex swastika's together removes four vertices at the join, yielding $n=36$, as in Fig. 3.10b. This polygon requires seven guards, one for each of the six isolated arms, and one at the join; note that $(3\cdot36+4)/16=112/16=7$. Joining k swastikas results in an $n=16k+4$ vertex polygons that requires $3k+1$ guards; and note that $\lfloor(3n+4)/16\rfloor=3k+1$. The necessity for other values of n is established by attaching a spiral of the appropriate number of edges to one arm of a swastika. Figure 3.11 shows that a spiral addition of 6 edges requires one guard more than the swastika; a spiral addition of 12 edges requires two guards more. These are the critical additions; spirals with a different number of edges do not require a different number of guards.

This establishes the necessity of $\lfloor(3n+4)/16\rfloor$ guards. We now turn to sufficiency. Aggarwal's proof is at least superficially similar in structure to the proof for general polygons in the preceding section. The proof is by induction. A small number of quadrilaterals are cut off from the given polygon, these small number covered separately, and the remainder of the polygon handled recursively. The difficulties arise at the interface between

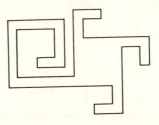

Fig. 3.11. Addition of a spiral establishes necessity for other values of n.

the quadrilaterals cut off and the remainder. In the previous section, interfacing required choosing the diagonal guard with one end at the interface, and applying the "edge-squashing" lemma (3.2) to reduce the number required in the remainder; in effect a guard is shared across the interface. In Aggarwal's proof, the delicacy of the interface requires a complex strategy to complete the induction proof.

Besides the increased complexity, the proof differs in two additional aspects from that of Theorem 3.1. First, it uses geometric constructions throughout, as opposed to reducing the geometric problem to a purely combinatorial one. It is unclear if this is essential; this point will be revisited in Section 3.4. Second, the remainder of the polygon is often modified and needs to be requadrilateralized. The proof of Theorem 3.1 maintained the same triangulation throughout. The combination of these differences result in a unique and complicated proof. It remains to be seen if a simpler approach can establish the same result.

Before commencing with the details, it may be helpful to sketch the main outline of the proof. It will be shown below in Lemma 3.8 that there is always a diagonal d in any quadrilateralization of an orthogonal polygon that cuts off 2, 3, or 4 quadrilaterals. If four quadrilaterals are cut off by d, then properties of quadrilateralizations of orthogonal polygons permit only two essentially different cases, and the induction carries through with a bit of sharing in the vicinity of d. If three quadrilaterals are cut off by d, then there are five distinct cases to handle, only one of which requires extensive sharing at the interface. Finally, if two quadrilaterals are cut off by d, then there are seven cases, most of which require sharing, some rather complicated. All the sharing is accomplished through one complex lemma (3.21). In all cases it will be shown that applying the induction hypothesis to the remainder of the polygon, taking into account any interface sharing, results in $\lfloor (3n+4)/16 \rfloor$ guards. We assume throughout that the polygon is in "general position" in that no two vertices can be connected by a vertical or horizontal line that does not intersect the boundary of the polygon.

We will first discuss structural properties of orthogonal polygons that will be used throughout the remainder of the section. Then we will establish the lemmas used to share at the interface, and finally prove the theorem.

3.3.1. Properties of Orthogonal Polygons

We will conduct the argument in terms of the number of quadrilaterals q in a quadrilateralization of the polygon rather than in terms of the number of vertices n. Our first two lemmas relate these quantities.

LEMMA 3.7. For any quadrilateralization of an orthogonal polygon of n vertices into q quadrilaterals, $n = 2q + 2$.

Proof. The sum of the interior angles of an orthogonal polygon of n vertices is $180(n-2)$ degrees. But since there are q quadrilaterals, each of 360 degrees, $360q = 180(n-2)$, or $n = 2q + 2$.   □

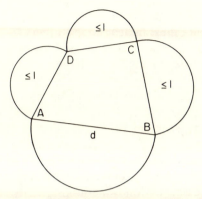

Fig. 3.12. Diagonal d cuts off a minimum number of quadrilaterals that is at least 2.

The same lemma holds for any quadrilateralizable polygon, even those that are not orthogonal.

Since q is fixed for any polygon, we will sometimes say "the number of quadrilaterals in P" rather than "the number of quadrilaterals in any quadrilateralization of P."

Applying this lemma to the sufficiency bound of $\lfloor(3n + 4)/16\rfloor$ shows that it is equivalent to $\lfloor(3q + 5)/8\rfloor$. It is in this form that the bound will appear throughout the proof.

The following lemma is the equivalent of Lemma 3.6.

LEMMA 3.8. Let P be an orthogonal polygon and Q a quadrilateralization of P. There exists a diagonal d in Q that partitions P into two pieces, one of which contains $q = 2, 3,$ or 4 quadrilaterals of Q.

Proof. Choose d to be a diagonal of Q that separates off a minimum number of quadrilaterals that is at least 2. Let $q \geq 2$ be this minimum. Let $ABCD$ be the quadrilateral supported by $d = AB$ towards the piece with q quadrilaterals; see Fig. 3.12. The number of quadrilaterals in the BC, CD, and DA regions illustrated in the figure is each less than 2—that is, less than or equal to 1—otherwise q would not be minimal. Therefore, $q \leq 4$. □

It will often be useful to use the dual of a quadrilateralization. Let every quadrilateral of a quadrilateralization Q be a node of a graph $\bar{Q}$, where two nodes are adjacent in $\bar{Q}$ iff their corresponding quadrilaterals share a diagonal.[4] The following is immediate (compare Lemma 1.3).

LEMMA 3.9. For any quadrilateralization Q of an orthogonal polygon, the dual $\bar{Q}$ is a tree with each node of degree no more than 4.

As an application of this observation, we can obtain an alternate proof of Lemma 3.8. Choose any root r for $\bar{Q}$, and let x be a leaf at maximum

---

4. As mentioned in Chapter 1, this is the graph theoretic "weak dual," weak because no node is assigned to the exterior face.

distance from r, and let y be the parent of x. Then all of the nodes adjacent to y not on the ry path must be leaf nodes; otherwise there would be a path longer than rx. Thus the diagonal of y that crosses the ry path cuts of 2, 3, or 4 quadrilaterals, depending on whether y is of degree 2, 3, or 4, respectively.

One of the main tools used throughout the proof is a cut, a tool previously used in Section 2.5. A *cut* L in an orthogonal polygon P is a maximal interior line segment in P (maximal in the sense that any line segment properly containing L contains a point exterior to P) that contains an edge and a reflex vertex of P. L partitions P into two or three pieces, depending on whether it contains one or two reflex vertices respectively; see Fig. 3.13. In either case, the following holds.

LEMMA 3.10. The sum of the number of quadrilaterals in the pieces defined by a cut L of P is equal to the number of quadrilaterals in P.

Proof. Suppose L partitions P into two pieces P_1 and P_2 as in Fig. 3.13a. Let P, P_1, and P_2 have n, n_1, and n_2 vertices and q, q_1, and q_2 quadrilaterals, respectively. Then $n_1 + n_2 = n + 2$, as L introduces one new vertex, counted in each of P_1 and P_2. Lemma 3.7 shows that

$$q_1 + q_2 = \frac{n_1 - 2}{2} + \frac{n_2 - 2}{2} = \frac{n - 2}{2} = q.$$

If L partitions P into three pieces as in Fig. 3.13b, then L can be considered as a combination of two "half" cuts, each resolving just one reflex vertex. The first partitions P into two pieces, and the second partitions one of the pieces into two, resulting in three pieces. Applying the result just established for two pieces yields the lemma for three pieces.   □

We now present a series of lemmas detailing the relationship between a diagonal of a quadrilateralization and the local structure of the polygon; henceforth "diagonal" means diagonal of a quadrilateralization. Recall that the *orientation* of an edge is horizontal or vertical. We will say that edges a and b are *to the same side* of d if they are in the same piece of P partitioned off by d; note that a and b may be in opposite half-planes defined by d but still to the same side.

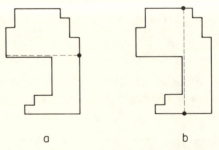

a   b

Fig. 3.13.   A cut partitions a polygon into two (a) or three (b) pieces.

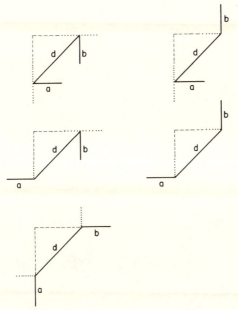

Fig. 3.14. The five possible arrangements when a and b have opposite orientations. The dotted lines represent possible orientations of the edges to the other side of d; the dashed lines indicate an added right angle that forms a subpolygon.

LEMMA 3.11. Let a and b be edges of P adjacent and to the same side of a diagonal d. Then a and b have the same orientation.

Proof. Without loss of generality orient d with positive slope with the polygon P_1 containing a and b below. Assume for contradiction that a and b have different orientations. Then there are five distinct possible combinations of a and b: hanging up, down, left, or right from the endpoints of d, as shown in Fig. 3.14. The other three possible combinations force a and b to not be to the same side of d. We can derive a contradiction in two ways. First note that in all five cases, addition of a right angle above d produces a new orthogonal polygon P'; perhaps it will be necessary to put this new angle on a different "level" as defined in Section 2.2, but this will not affect the angle sums. Let q_1 be the number of quadrilaterals in P_1. Then the sum of the internal angles of P' is $360q_1 + 180$. But this implies that P' is not quadrilaterizable, in contradiction to Theorem 2.1.

For a second proof, recall Lubiw's scheme of assigning "types" to each vertex of an orthogonal polygon such that they alternate type 1 and type 2 in a traversal of the boundary (Section 2.4.2, especially Fig. 2.36). In all five cases of Fig. 3.14, d connects two vertices of the same type. Thus the strict alternation is destroyed, and P_1 has an odd number of vertices. But this contradicts the assumption that P_1 is quadrilateralizable, since any polygon partitioned into quadrilaterals must have an even number of vertices. □

Because no internal angle of a quadrilateral can be greater than 270°

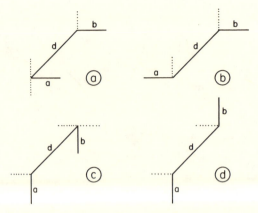

Fig. 3.15. The four possible arrangements of a and b when d is in its standard orientation. The dotted lines indicate the possibilities for the edges adjacent to d and to a and b.

(since all are subangles of either 90° or 270°), only four configurations are possible for d, a, and b, as illustrated in Fig. 3.15. We will raise this observation to a lemma for later reference.

LEMMA 3.12.   The only configurations possible for a diagonal d and its two adjacent edges a and b to one side (perhaps after rotation and reflection to orient d with positive slope) are those shown in Fig. 3.15.

Although not needed for the proof of the art gallery theorem, we now turn our attention to characterizing the quadrilateral trees of orthogonal polygons. This is accomplished by showing that Lemma 3.12 restricts the configuration possible for a quadrilateral of a specific degree to a finite set of possibilities, and that only certain configurations can "mate" with one another as adjacent quadrilaterals. We start by showing that a degree 4 quadrilateral can have only one configuration. A *configuration* is defined by the orientations of the edges of the polygon adjacent to each vertex of a quadrilateral, and the type (convex/reflex) of the vertices.

Let a reflex vertex whose exterior angle is in the first quadrant (between the positive x and positive y axes) be called type 1, in the second quadrant (between the positive y and the negative x axes), type 2, and similarly for type 3 and 4.

LEMMA 3.13.   Let $ABCD$ be a quadrilateral of degree 4 in $\bar{Q}$ for any orthogonal polygon P. Then A, B, C, and D are each reflex vertices of P, of types 1, 2, 3, and 4 in counterclockwise order.

Proof.   Assume to the contrary that at least A is convex. Without loss of generality let A be a lower left corner as illustrated in Fig. 3.16a. Then Fig. 3.15a shows that edge a' forces b and b' to have the orientations shown at B; b' forces c and c' as shown at C; and c' forces d and d' at D. But now d' lies inside $ABCD$, contradicting the assumption that $ABCD$ is an internal quadrilateral.

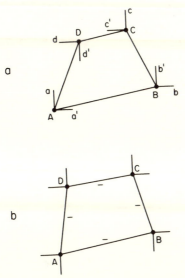

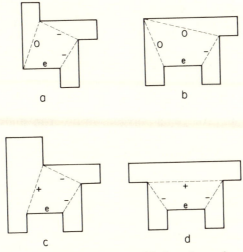

Fig. 3.16. If A is convex (a), d' is forced to be internal to $ABCD$; if A is reflex (b), the degree 4 quadrilateral has a unique configuration.

Now let A be a type 3 reflex vertex. Following the same logic as above forces the configuration shown in Fig. 3.16b, establishing the lemma. $\square$

The possible configurations proliferate for quadrilaterals of smaller degree, but the proofs proceed the same way, repeatedly applying the constraints imposed by Lemma 3.12, and will only be sketched.

LEMMA 3.14. A quadrilateral of degree three can have just one of the four configurations shown in Fig. 3.17.

Fig. 3.17. The four configurations possible for a degree 3 quadrilateral.

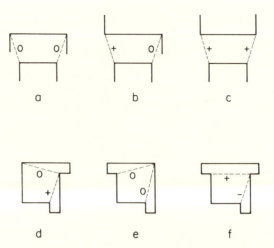

Fig. 3.18. The six configurations possible for a degree 2 quadrilateral.

Proof. Let e be the edge of the quadrilateral shared with the polygon. It is easily shown using Lemma 3.12 that both endpoints of e cannot be convex. If one endpoint is convex and the other reflex, Fig. 3.17a is forced. If both are reflex, three configurations are possible, shown in Figs. 3.17b–3.17d. □

The $+$, $-$, and 0 markings in Figs. 3.16 and 3.17 (and in the figures to follow) will be explained later.

LEMMA 3.15. A quadrilateral of degree 2 can have just one of the six configurations shown in Fig. 3.18.

Proof. If the two edges shared with the polygon are non-adjacent, then the three configurations shown in Figs. 3.18a–3.18c are possible. If the shared edges are adjacent, then the three configurations shown in Figs. 3.18d–3.18f are possible. □

LEMMA 3.16. A quadrilateral of degree 1 can have just one of the two configurations shown in Fig. 3.19.

This completes the classification of the possible configurations of the quadrilaterals in an orthogonal polygon. In order to study which configurations can mate with one another, we introduce the concept of "charge" on a diagonal. Let a and b be edges to the same side and adjacent to a diagonal d

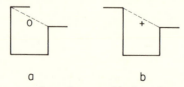

Fig. 3.19. The two configurations possible for a degree 1 quadrilateral.

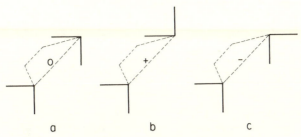

Fig. 3.20. Definitions of the three diagonal charges.

of a quadrilateral. If a and b lie in the same half-plane determined by d, then we will say they have the same *parity*; otherwise they have opposite parity. Thus in Figs. 3.15a and 3.15c, a and b have the same parity, and in Figs. 3.15b and 3.15d they have opposite parity. The *charge* on a diagonal d of a quadrilateral q, with respect to q, is 0 if the adjacent edges to both sides of d have the same parity (Fig. 3.20a), + if the adjacent edges to the q side have the same parity, and the adjacent edges to the opposite side of d have opposite parity (Fig. 3.20b), and − if the adjacent edges to the q side have opposite parity, and those to the opposite side of d have the same parity (Fig. 3.20c). Note that charge is defined with respect to a quadrilateral, so that each diagonal has a charge defined on either side.

LEMMA 3.17. The net charge on any diagonal in a quadrilateralization of an orthogonal polygon must be zero: the charges must be 0/0, +/−, or −/+.

Proof. This is immediate from the definition of charge: a 0 charge on one side is a 0 from the other side, and a + charge on one side is a − from the viewpoint of the other side. □

For the purpose of determining which configurations of quadrilaterals can mate with one another, each configuration can be reduced to a square symbol labeled with charges. The symbols corresponding to the configurations established in Lemmas 3.13–3.16 are displayed in Fig. 3.21 in the same order in which they appear in Figs. 3.16–3.19. We will refer to these symbols as, for example, [3b], meaning the b symbol for a degree 3 quadrilateral as displayed in Fig. 3.21. All quadrilateral trees of orthogonal polygons can be constructed by gluing these symbols together such that each diagonal is uncharged.

We may finally state and prove the characterization theorem.

THEOREM 3.2 [O'Rourke 1985]. A tree is a quadrilateral tree for a simple orthogonal polygon iff no node has degree greater than 4, and the tree contains no path connecting two degree 4 nodes by a sequence of zero or more degree 3 nodes—that is, the path degree sequence (4 3* 4) does not occur.

Proof. It is immediate that two degree 4 nodes cannot be adjacent, since

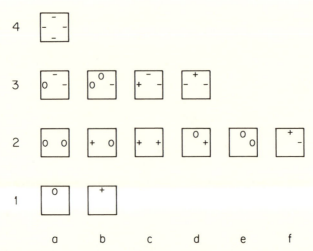

Fig. 3.21. Symbols for all possible quadrilateral configurations. The numbers to the left indicate the degree of the quadrilaterals, the letters below distinguish different configurations.

the symbol [4] has a negative charge on every diagonal. The degree sequence (4 3 3 3...) can be achieved by mating [4] with the + charge of either [3c] or [3d], and then mating − / + again with either [3c] or [3d], and so on. But it is clear that the last degree 3 quadrilateral in such a sequence has two − diagonals free, neither of which can mate with [4]. Thus the degree sequence (4 3 ... 3 4) cannot occur in the quadrilateral tree of any orthogonal polygon.

Now we show that any tree that does not contain a (4 3* 4) path can be realized as the quadrilateral tree of an orthogonal polygon, by assigning square symbols to each node such that all diagonals are uncharged. Assign to each degree 4 node the only choice, [4]. For each connected subtree S composed of degree 3 nodes, distinguish two cases. If S is adjacent to a [4], assign [3c] to each node in S, aligning the charges to balance. This will leave only − charges on the unmatched diagonals of S. If S is not adjacent to a [4], assign one of the leaves [3a], and all the other nodes of S [3c] as in the first case. Now there is one unmatched 0 diagonal, and the remaining unmatched diagonals are negatively charged. The important point is that no unmatched diagonal has a + charge. Next assign each degree 1 node adjacent to a negative diagonal [1b], and all others [1a]. Note that a degree 1 node will not be adjacent to a + charge by construction. Finally assign the degree 2 nodes one of the symbols to cancel the charges appropriately. Since the only charge configuration not available with degree 2 nodes is one with two negative diagonals, this will always be possible as long as a degree 2 node does not have to mate with two positive diagonals. But by construction, all free diagonals are either 0 or −. This completes the construction and the proof. □

The construction procedure is illustrated in Fig. 3.22. Figure 3.22a shows a tree that does not contain the forbidden degree sequence, and Fig. 3.22b

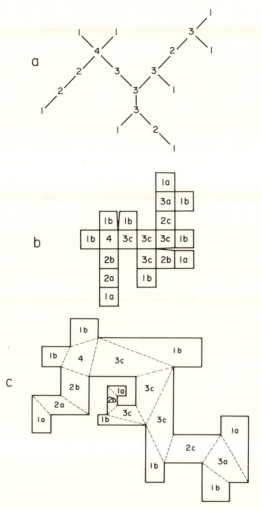

Fig. 3.22. A non-forbidden tree (a), a selection of symbols matching the tree degrees (b), and an orthogonal polygon realizing the symbols (c).

shows the symbols assigned by the construction, glued together appropriately to cancel charges. Finally Fig. 3.22c shows an orthogonal polygon that results by replacing the symbols by their corresponding configurations. It is clear that there are many options in the transition from the symbols to the actual polygon, but the transition is always possible by adjusting the lengths of the edges to avoid overlap, in a manner similar to the local scale changes used in Culberson and Rawlins (1985).

3.3.2. Sharing Lemmas

In this section we develop three "sharing lemmas" similar in spirit to Lemma 3.2 in the proof for general polygons in Section 3.2. They all have

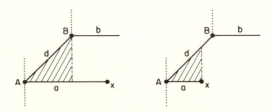

Fig. 3.23. The partial shadow of a diagonal.

the following flavor: "Suppose the induction hypothesis holds, and we are given a polygon with one (or more) guards placed in particular locations 'free.' Then an additional X guards suffice for total coverage." Here X will always be just the right amount to establish the induction hypothesis. I am calling these "sharing" lemmas because in effect they are sharing "fractional" guards across the induction dividing diagonal.

The induction hypothesis that is the premise of these lemmas is:

Induction Hypothesis (IH). Any orthogonal polygon with $q' < q$ quadrilaterals may be covered with $\lfloor (3q' + 5)/8 \rfloor$ mobile orthogonal guards.

First we present a specialized geometric lemma that will be needed in the proofs of the sharing lemmas. Let a and b be the two edges adjacent to and to the same side of a diagonal d, with the same parity. Thus we have either Fig. 3.15a or 3.15c. These situations are clearly identical after rotation and reflection, and we will henceforth consider just Fig. 3.15a. In this situation, define the *partial shadow* of d to be the closed triangular region defined by d, a, and a vertical line through either x, the right endpoint of a, or through the vertex incident to d and b, whichever is leftmost. See Fig. 3.23.

LEMMA 3.18. The partial shadow of a diagonal in a quadrilateralization of an orthogonal polygon is empty.

Proof. The partial shadow is only defined in the situation illustrated in Fig. 3.23. Let A be the vertex incident to d and a as shown. Assume the shadow is not empty, and let e be the leftmost vertical edge in the shadow. Then A and e must be part of a quadrilateral Q. But there is no vertex that can serve as the fourth for Q: it cannot lie to the right of e, for then Q would be non-convex; it cannot lie collinear with e, for then our general position assumption is violated; nor can it lie to the left of e, since e is leftmost. □

The following lemma is almost the direct analog of Lemma 3.2.

LEMMA 3.19. If P is a polygon of q quadrilaterals with one guard placed along a convex edge e (one whose endpoints A and B are both convex vertices), then assuming IH, P can be covered with an additional $\lfloor [3(q-1) + 5]/8 \rfloor$ guards.

Proof. The proof is by induction on q. The lemma is clearly true when $q = 1$. Assume it is true for $q' < q$. Let $Q = ABCD$ be the quadrilateral

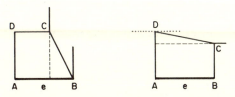

Fig. 3.24. If $ABCD$ has degree 1 and e is guarded, one quadrilateral may be removed.

containing $e = AB$. The proof proceeds by cases depending on the degree of Q. If $deg(Q) = 1$, it follows easily; $deg(Q) = 2$ requires more work; and $deg(Q) = 3$ is not possible.

Case ($deg(Q) = 1$). Either BC (or symmetrically DA) or CD is the sole internal diagonal of Q. In either situation, illustrated in Fig. 3.24, a cut through C partitions P into a covered rectangle and a polygon of $q - 1$ quadrilaterals by Lemma 3.10. Applying IH establishes the lemma.

Case ($deg(Q) = 2$). The internal diagonals of Q are either adjacent or not.

Case 2.1 (Non-adjacent Diagonals) The only situation possible is shown in Fig. 3.25a, corresponding to Fig. 3.18a. The two cuts illustrated partition P into 3 pieces, a rectangle bound by the cuts, and two orthogonal polygons P_1 and P_2 of, say, q_1 and q_2 quadrilaterals. By Lemma 3.10, $q_1 + q_2 + 1 = q$. Now note that the guard along e is a guard between two convex vertices in

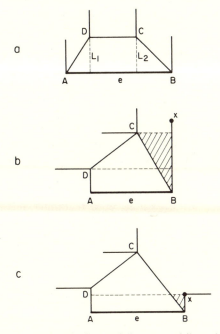

Fig. 3.25. If $ABCD$ has degree 2 and e is guarded, one quadrilateral may be removed, either by induction (a), or by removal of a rectangle (b and c).

each of P_1 and P_2. Since $q_1 < q$ and $q_2 < q$, the induction hypothesis for this lemma applies. Therefore, P can be covered with

$$\lfloor [3(q_1 - 1) + 5]/8 \rfloor + \lfloor [3(q_2 - 1) + 5]/8 \rfloor$$

additional guards. Tedious analysis shows that this is less than or equal to $\lfloor [3(q - 1) + 5]/8 \rfloor$, establishing the lemma.

Case 2.2 (Adjacent Diagonals).   Only Fig. 3.18d is possible, which we will further partition into the two cases shown in Figs. 3.25b and 3.25c. Let BC and CD be the diagonals of Q; C must be above D. The two figures are distinguished by whether x, the upper endpoint of the vertical edge incident to B, is higher or lower than D. In the former case (Fig. 3.25b), a cut through D, and in the latter case (Fig. 3.25c), a cut through x, is guaranteed by the emptiness of the partial shadow of BC (Lemma 3.18) to partition P into a covered rectangle and a polygon of $q - 1$ quadrilaterals. Applying IH establishes the lemma.

That the case $deg(Q) = 3$ is not possible is immediate from the possible configurations shown in Fig. 3.17: e is not a convex edge in any of the possible configurations.   □

The next sharing lemma in effect "squashes out" two quadrilaterals.

LEMMA 3.20.   If P is a polygon of q quadrilaterals with two guards placed on consecutive convex edges AB and BC, then assuming IH, P can be covered with an additional $\lfloor [3(q - 2) + 5]/8 \rfloor$ guards.

Proof.   The proof is similar to the preceding one. The structural possibilities are clearly the same as in that proof, but with BC here playing the role of AB there. Let Z, A, B, C, D, and E be consecutive vertices on the boundary of P. Let Q be the quadrilateral including BC; Q is not necessarily $ABCD$.

Case 1 ($deg(Q) = 1$).   Either $Q = ABCD$ with AD the internal edge (Fig. 3.26a), or $Q = BCDE$ with BE the internal edge (Fig. 3.26b). In the first instance D is reflex, and a horizontal cut through it leaves a covered rectangle and a polygon of $q - 1$ quadrilaterals that satisfies Lemma 3.19. Applying that lemma establishes the result. In the second instance, E is reflex, and a vertical cut leaves a covered rectangle and a polygon of $q - 1$

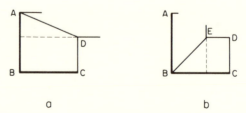

a   b

Fig. 3.26. If $ABCD$ has degree 1 and AB and BC are guarded, one quadrilateral may be removed.

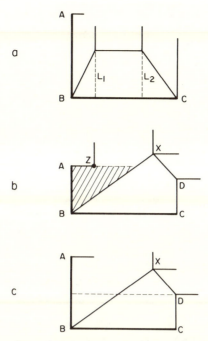

Fig. 3.27. If $ABCD$ has degree 2 and AB and BC are guarded, either induction applies (a), the situation is impossible (b), or a quadrilateral may be removed (c).

quadrilaterals that satisfies the induction hypothesis (and Lemma 3.19). In all cases, then, the result holds.

Case 2 ($deg(Q) = 2$). The same two cases apply as in Lemma 3.19.

Case 2.1 (Non-adjacent Diagonals.) The situations must be as in Fig. 3.27a. The two cuts L_1 and L_2 partition P into a covered rectangle, a polygon P_1 with q_1 quadrilaterals that satisfies the induction hypothesis, and a polygon P_2 of q_2 quadrilaterals that satisfies Lemma 3.19, where $q_1 + q_2 + 1 = q$. Applying both results yields coverage with

$$\lfloor [3(q_1 - 2) + 5]/8 \rfloor + \lfloor [3(q_2 - 1) + 5]/8 \rfloor$$

additional guards. A tedious analysis reveals this to be no larger than $\lfloor [3(q - 2) + 5]/8 \rfloor$ for $q \geq 2$.

Case 2.2 (Adjacent Diagonals) A cannot be a vertex of Q: Figs. 3.18d, 3.18e, and 3.18f do not permit three consecutive convex vertices. Therefore $Q = BCDX$, corresponding to Fig. 3.18d, with D reflex. Now if X is above A, as in Fig. 3.27b, Z is in the partial shadow of BX, a contradiction. So we are left with the situation shown in Fig. 3.27c. A cut through D establishes the result as in Case 1 (compare Fig. 3.26a). □

The last sharing lemma is the most complex. It takes the form: if certain sharing conditions hold, then the remainder of the polygon needs one full guard less than $\lfloor(3q+5)/8\rfloor$. The sharing conditions are rather complicated, but essentially the idea is to place two guards crossing each other orthogonally such that the previous two lemmas apply to the pieces of the resulting partition.

LEMMA 3.21. If P is a polygon of q quadrilaterals with a guard placed along a maximal segment L_1 that contains a polygon edge that is situated in P such that

(a) there are two cuts orthogonal to L_1 that partition off rectangles touching (and thereby covered by) L_1, and

(b) L_1 cuts the remainder (P with the two rectangles removed) into one or two (i.e., not three) pieces.

then assuming IH, P can be covered with an additional $\lfloor(3q+5)/8\rfloor - 1$ guards.

Proof. Note that L_1 is not necessarily a cut, but could be a convex edge. Let P_1 and P_2 be the two pieces separated by L_1 after removal of the two rectangles; P_2 may be empty. The premise of the lemma is a bit ungainly, but is composed to have two geometric consequences:

(1) If P_2 is not empty, there is at least one reflex vertex on L_1 in $P_1 \cup P_2$.

(2) L_1 lies on a convex edge of both P_1 and P_2.

We first support these claims. If L_1 is a cut, it partitions P into two or three pieces. If L_1 cuts P into three pieces, the premise can only be satisfied if the third piece is composed of one or both of the rectangles cut off, disallowing Fig. 3.28a for example. If L_1 cuts P into two pieces, then if the second piece is composed of one or both of the cut off rectangles, then P_2 is empty, as in

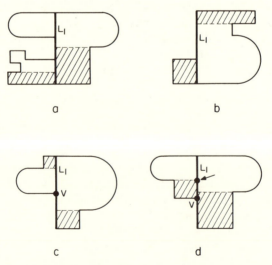

a　　　　　　　　　　　b

c　　　　　　　　　　　d

Fig. 3.28. The cut in (a) does not satisfy the conditions of the lemma; in (b), P_2 is empty; in (c) and (d), L_1 contains a reflex vertex.

Fig. 3.28b, for example. Let V be the reflex vertex on L_1 (the one in $P_1 \cup P_2$ in case there are two reflex vertices on L_1). Then either V is in $P_1 \cup P_2$, as in Fig. 3.28c, or there is at least one other reflex vertex on L_1 introduced by the orthogonal cuts, as in Fig. 3.28d. Finally, since L_1 is a supporting line for both P_1 and P_2, it constitutes a convex edge in each.

Let P_1 and P_2 have q_1 and q_2 quadrilaterals. Then $q_1 + q_2 = q - 2$ by Lemma 3.10. We now apply the previous two sharing lemmas to establish the claim.

By property (2), Lemma 3.19 applies to both P_1 and P_2, resulting in complete coverage with

$$\lfloor [3(q_1 - 1) + 5]/8 \rfloor + \lfloor [3(q_2 - 1) + 5]/8 \rfloor = \lfloor (3q_1 + 2)/8 \rfloor + \lfloor (3q_2 + 2)/8 \rfloor$$

additional guards. A tedious case analysis shows that this quantity is no greater than $\lfloor (3q + 5)/8 \rfloor - 1$ for all possible mod 8 residues of q_1 and q_2 *except* in the single case when both $q_1 \equiv 2 \pmod 8$ and $q_2 \equiv 2 \pmod 8$. We now concentrate on this "hard" case. Note that P_2 cannot be empty in this case.

Introduce a cut L_2 orthogonal to L_1 through the reflex vertex V guaranteed by property (1), and place a guard along L_2. L_2 must partition one of P_1 or P_2, say P_2, into two pieces P_2' and P_2'', with q_2' and q_2'' quadrilaterals; it may or may not partition P_1, as illustrated in Fig. 3.29. If L_2 partitions P_1, call the pieces P_1' and P_1'' with q_1' and q_1'' quadrilaterals. Now although $q_1' + q_1'' = q_1$ by Lemma 3.10, $q_2' + q_2'' = q_2 + 1$, since L_1 already resolved the reflex vertex V.

Note that the conditions for the application of Lemma 3.20 hold for both P_2' and P_2''; L_1 and L_2 both lie on convex edges in each. Therefore, all of P_2

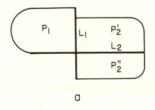

a

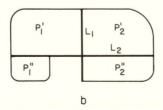

b

Fig. 3.29. The cut L_2 may (a) or may not (b) partition P_1.

can be covered with

$$g_2 = \left\lfloor [3(q_2' - 2) + 5]/8 \right\rfloor + \left\lfloor [3(q_2'' - 2) + 5]/8 \right\rfloor \tag{1}$$

guards. If L_2 does not partition P_1, then we apply Lemma 3.20 to P_1 to cover it with

$$g_1 = \left\lfloor [3(q_1 - 2) + 5]/8 \right\rfloor \tag{2}$$

guards. If L_2 does partition P_1, then Lemma 3.20 can be applied to P_1' above L_2, and Lemma 3.19 to P_1'' below L_2, resulting in

$$g_1' = \left\lfloor [3(q_1' - 2) + 5]/8 \right\rfloor + \left\lfloor [3(q_1'' - 1) + 5]/8 \right\rfloor \tag{3}$$

guards. Using the special case assumption that $q_1 = 8k_1 + 2$, (2) yields $g_1 = 3k_1$, and a case analysis and $q_1' + q_1'' = q_1$ shows that (3) implies $g_1' \leq 3k_1$. Therefore, $3k_1$ guards suffice for P_1 in either case. The assumption $q_2 = 8k_2 + 2$ and $q_2' + q_2'' = q_2 + 1$ leads to (1) to $g_2 \leq 3k_2$. Thus a total of $3(k_1 + k_2)$ guards suffice. Finally, $q = q_1 + q_2 = 8(k_1 + k_2) + 6$ implies that $\lfloor (3q + 5)/8 \rfloor - 2 = 3(k_1 + k_2)$, which together with the 1 guard placed on L_2, establishes the lemma. $\square$

3.3.3. Proof of Orthogonal Polygon Theorem

We have finally assembled enough lemmas to prove the main theorem.

THEOREM 3.3 [Aggarwal 1984]. $\lfloor (3q + 5)/8 \rfloor = \lfloor (3n + 4)/16 \rfloor$ mobile guards are sufficient to cover any orthogonal polygon P of q quadrilaterals and n vertices.

Proof.   The proof is by induction on q. If $q \leq 2$, then 1 guard clearly suffices. Assume now the induction hypothesis IH. Fix an arbitrary quadrilateralization of P. Lemma 3.8 established that there is a diagonal d that cuts off a minimal number k of 2, 3, or 4 quadrilaterals. These constitute the three cases of the proof, which we consider in reverse order.

Case $k = 4$.   Recall from the proof of Lemma 3.8 (see Fig. 3.12) that d must be a diagonal of a degree 4 quadrilateral Q, say $Q = ABCD$ with $d = DA$. Lemma 3.13 shows that A, B, C, and D must all be reflex vertices. Let A be left of and lower than D, which can be achieved without loss of generality by rotation and reflection. We can distinguish three cases, only two of which are real possibilities, depending on the horizontal sorting of B, C, and D. We will use the notation $X < Y$ to mean that point X is strictly left of point Y.

Subcase ($C < D$ (Fig. 3.30a)).   This case violates Lemma 3.11, as completion of the polygon between B and C as illustrated demonstrates.

Subcase ($C > D$ and $B < D$ (Fig. 3.30b)).   Place a guard on the vertical cut L_1 through D as illustrated. Then this cut satisfies the conditions of Lemma

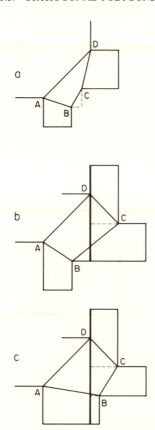

Fig. 3.30. If *ABCD* has degree 4, then either the situation is impossible (a), or Lemma 3.21 applies (b and c).

3.21, with P_2 empty. Applying that lemma yields coverage of P_1 with $\lfloor (3q + 5)/8 \rfloor - 1$ guards, which, together with the guard along L_1, establishes the theorem.

Subcase ($C > D$ and $B > D$ (Fig. 3.30c)). Again Lemma 3.21 applies with L_1 the vertical cut through *D*.

Case k = 3. The proof of Lemma 3.8 shows that *d* is a diagonal of a degree 3 quadrilateral *Q*. Let *Q* = *ABCD* with *d* = *DA*. Orient *d* as in Fig. 3.31a, and assume without loss of generality that the edges of *P'* adjacent to *d* are horizontal, with *A* reflex. (Figure 3.17 shows that at most one of *A, B, C, D* is convex, so one end of *d* is always reflex. If the other end is convex, *d* angles away from the reflex vertex as in Fig. 3.31a; if the other end is reflex, then either *d* angles away as in Fig. 3.31a, or it will after reflection in the *x* axis.) We distinguish five cases, depending mainly on which edge of *Q* is a polygon edge. In each case, Lemma 3.21 is invoked.

Subcase (*BC* is a polygon edge.) *BC* must be horizontal and below *A*,

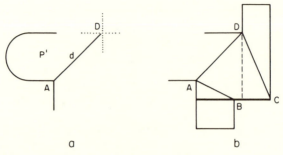

Fig. 3.31. The configuration when $k = 3$: the dotted edges in (a) represent the two possible orientations of the polygon edge at D. If BC is a polygon edge, Lemma 3.21 applies.

otherwise either Q is non-convex or Lemma 3.11 is violated. Consequently the parity of the horizontal edges adjacent to d in P' is the same, and the situation is as illustrated in Fig. 3.31b. A horizontal cut through B satisfies the conditions of Lemma 3.21 (with P_2 empty), and the theorem follows by placing a guard along the cut and applying Lemma 3.21.

Subcase (CD is a polygon edge). CD must be vertical to satisfy Lemma 3.11, and B must be left and below C since Q is convex. Regardless of the vertical placements of A, B, and C, a vertical cut through B satisfies Lemma 3.21. Figure 3.32 shows that in each of the three possible vertical sortings (A, C, B), (C, A, B), and (C, B, A), in a, b, c respectively, the theorem follows by placing a guard along the cut and applying Lemma 3.21.

Subcase (AB is a polygon edge).   Distinguish further subcases, depending on the location of C with respect to B and D.

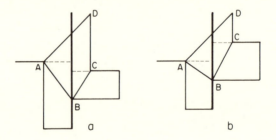

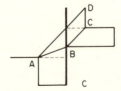

Fig. 3.32. If CD is a polygon edge, Lemma 3.21 applies.

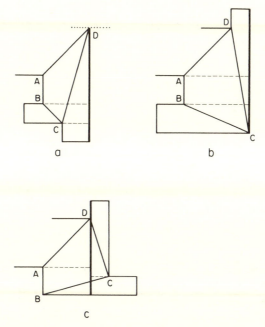

Fig. 3.33. If AB is a polygon edge, Lemma 3.21 applies in all cases.

Subsubcase (*C* is below *B* and left of *D* (Fig. 3.33a).). Let L_1 be the maximal vertical segment containing *D*. This satisfies Lemma 3.21, regardless of whether or not *D* is reflex.

Subsubcase (*C* is below *B* and right of *D* (Fig. 3.33b).). Let L_1 be the vertical edge containing *C*. This satisfies Lemma 3.21.

Subsubase (*C* is above *B* and left of *D*). This case violates Lemma 3.11 and so is not possible.

Subsubcase (*C* is above *B* and right of *D* (Fig. 3.33c).). Let L_1 be the maximal vertical segment containing *D*. This satisfies Lemma 3.21.

Case $k = 2$. Although this case is simplest in some sense, it requires the most extensive sharing, since so little is cut off by *d*. Fortunately, all the sharing is concentrated into Lemma 3.21. We partition the problem into two subcases, depending on whether the edges adjacent to *d* in P' have the same or opposite parity. Let $d = DA$ as usual, and let *A* be below *D* so that *A* is always reflex.

Subcase (Same Parity). Let *d* be oriented as in Fig. 3.34a. Place a guard along the vertical edge through *D* if *D* is convex (Figs. 3.34b and 3.34c), or along the first vertical edge hit by a horizontal cut through *A* (Fig. 3.34d). In all cases, Lemma 3.21 applies, with P_2 empty.

Subcase (Opposite Parity). Orient *d* as in Fig. 3.35a. That both *A* and *D*

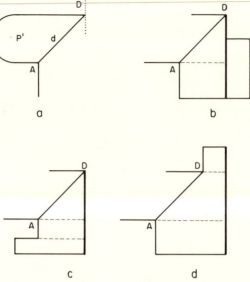

Fig. 3.34. When the edges adjacent to *d* have the same parity, Lemma 3.21 applies in all cases.

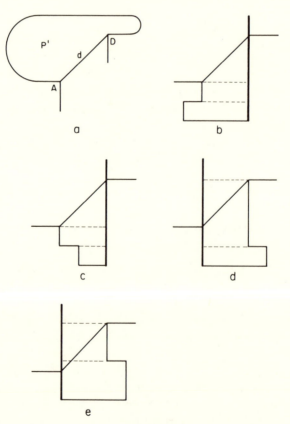

Fig. 3.35. When the edges adjacent to *d* have opposite parity, Lemma 3.21 applies in all cases.

are reflex with their adjacent edges oriented as shown can be seen by examination of Fig. 3.18. Of the four vertices in the chain counterclockwise between A and D, exactly one is reflex. If the first or second (counterclockwise from A) is reflex (Figs. 3.35b and 3.35c), a vertical cut L_1 through D satisfies the conditions of Lemma 3.21. If the third or fourth vertex from A is reflex (Figs. 3.35d and 3.35e), a vertical cut through A satisfies Lemma 3.21. In all cases, placing a guard along L_1 and applying Lemma 3.21 yields coverage by $\lfloor (3q+5)/8 \rfloor - 1 + 1$ guards, establishing the theorem.

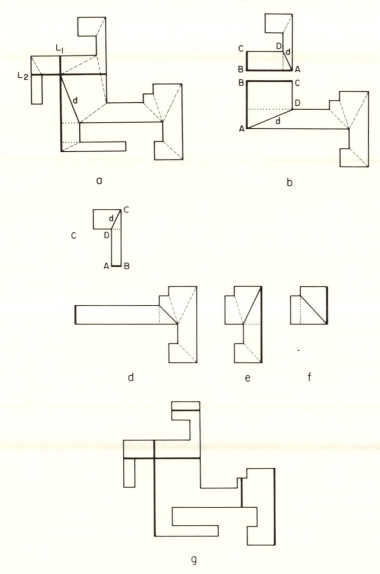

Fig. 3.36. An "execution" of the proof of Theorem 3.3 and the lemmas it invokes. The final guard placement is shown in (g).

We have exhausted all possibilities, and therefore the theorem is established.   □

The proof just presented is constructive, and therefore can be converted to an algorithm. The algorithm is highly inefficient, however, since requadrilateralization is implicitly required at almost every step. It will help understanding the proof if we step through a small example, tracking the proof through the various lemmas and "executing" them as procedures.

Consider the polygon shown in Fig. 3.36a. It has $n = 26$ vertices and $q = 12$ quadrilaterals. The theorem then says that six guards suffice; actually four suffice in this case. Using the quadrilateralization in Fig. 3.36a, d is a diagonal that cuts off a minimum number k of quadrilaterals; in this case, $k = 2$. Following the theorem, the $k = 2$ case (opposite parity: Fig. 3.35b reflected) invokes Lemma 3.21. In our particular case, the cut L_1 and the abutting rectangles are shown. L_1 partitions P into pieces with $q_1 = 2$ and $q_2 = 10$ quadrilaterals. This is the hard case of the lemma, and requires a second cut L_2 shown. Two non-trivial pieces remain, and for both Lemma 3.21 invokes Lemma 3.20, because there are guards on two consecutive convex edges (Fig. 3.36b). Both pieces fall under the same case of Lemma 3.20 ($deg(Q) = 1$: Fig. 3.26a reflected), both introducing a cut and invoking Lemma 3.19 for a guard along a single convex edge. Figure 3.36c shows the smaller piece. Lemma 3.19 makes a cut (following Fig. 3.24b) and applies the IH, which in this case is trivial since the remaining piece is a rectangle, which is assigned its own guard. Figure 3.36d shows the larger piece. Again Lemma 3.19 cuts and applies IH to the polygon shown in Fig. 3.36e. We are now back at the "top level" in the main theorem. In the quadrilateralization shown, d cuts off a minimum $k = 2$ quadrilaterals. The case here is the same parity one (Fig. 3.34c), and introduces a guard along the vertical edge shown. The top remainder is handled by Lemma 3.19, because the guard forms a convex edge. Lemma 3.19 then (unnecessarily in this case) invokes IH again, this time at the basis, and a guard is assigned to the rectangle in Fig. 3.36f. The resulting five guards assigned are shown in Fig. 3.36g.

3.4. Discussion

The guards used for the general polygon theorem (Theorem 3.1) are combinatorial: visibility is needed only at the two vertices at the endpoints of diagonals. The guards used for the orthogonal polygon theorem (Theorem 3.3) are geometric: visibility is required throughout their length. The guards used in the two theorems differ in other respects. Several features of the orthogonal guards are:

(1)   Visibility is required throughout the length of the guard.
(2)   Guards are oriented horizontal or vertical only.
(3)   Each guard can be chosen to include an edge of the polygon.
(4)   Visibility is only required orthogonal to the guard.
(5)   The patrols of two guards may pass through one another.

These were not conditions imposed on the problem, but rather those that "fell out" of Aggarwal's proof. It would be interesting to disallow the fifth condition above: do not permit the lines of two guards to cross. But the most interesting question concerning these qualifications on guard "power" is whether (1) is necessary: can the same result be achieved with combinatorial guards, as in the general polygon case?

Aggarwal has proven several other results on mobile guards (Aggarwal 1984). The most important is that for quadrilaterizable polygons—that is, those that can be partitioned into convex quadrilaterals, $\lfloor n/5 \rfloor$ guards are necessary and sufficient. Since $\lfloor n/5 \rfloor > \lfloor (3n + 4)/16 \rfloor$ for all $n > 20$, this result does not contradict Theorem 3.3. Despite Theorem 3.2, which characterizes the quadrilateral trees of orthogonal polygons, it remains an open problem to characterize those polygons that are quadrilateralizable. Aggarwal's proof of the $\lfloor n/5 \rfloor$ result differs in two ways from the proof of Theorem 3.3: first, it is entirely combinatorial, and second, it is much longer: at one point 93 separate cases are considered! Several other of his mobile guard results for specialized polygons will be discussed in the next chapter.

4

MISCELLANEOUS SHAPES

4.1. INTRODUCTION

Five generic shapes of polygons have been usefully distinguished in the literature: convex, orthogonal, star, spiral, and monotone.[1] Convex polygons obviously do not lead to interesting art gallery theorems, since the answer to most questions is 1, and orthogonal polygons were discussed in Chapter 2. In this chapter we cover the three "miscellaneous" shapes: star, spiral, and monotone. Other shapes could be considered—for example, orthogonal spiral—but highly specialized shapes do not lead to interesting theorems. The three shapes considered here have arisen in "practice," and each can be recognized in linear time.

We examine vertex guards (as a function of both n, the number of vertices, and r, the number of reflex vertices), edge, diagonal, and line guards. The results obtained are summarized in Table 4.1. Most of the results are easy to obtain (with one exception), and are often established by a single example.

Table 4.1

Guard Type	Star	Spiral	Monotone
vertex	$\lfloor n/3 \rfloor$	$\lfloor n/3 \rfloor$	$\lfloor n/3 \rfloor$
	$\lfloor r/2 \rfloor + 1$	$\lfloor r/2 \rfloor + 1$	$\lfloor r/2 \rfloor + 1$
edge	$\geq \lfloor n/5 \rfloor$		
diagonal	2	$\lfloor (n+2)/5 \rfloor$	
line	1		$\lfloor (n+2)/5 \rfloor$

---

1. Orthogonal is often called "rectilinear," and star is usually called "star-shaped" in the literature.

4.2. STAR POLYGONS

A *star polygon* P is a polygon that may be covered by a single guard: there is a point $x \in P$ such that every point of P is visible from x. The set of all points of P that can see every point of P is called the *kernel* of P. Thus a star polygon is one with a non-null kernel. It is easy to see that the kernel is the intersection of all the interior half-planes determined by the edges of P (*interior half-planes* are towards the left in a counterclockwise traversal of the boundary). Thus the kernel is convex. This characterization leads to an $O(n \log n)$ algorithm for constructing the kernel by using Shamos's half-plane intersection algorithm (Shamos 1978). Lee and Preparata showed, however, that the kernel can be constructed in $O(n)$ time (Lee and Preparata 1979). Thus the question of whether a given polygon is a star can be answered in linear time by checking if the kernel is empty. This linear-time recognition capability increases the usefulness of the star class.

Although every star polygon can be covered by one point guard, more interesting questions arise if restrictions are placed on the guard. If the guards are restricted to vertices only, then $\lfloor n/3 \rfloor$ are sometimes necessary, as can be seen by warping the "comb" example (Fig. 1.2) to a star "sun burst" shape shown in Fig. 4.1. Note that, aside from the spike apex, only the two vertices at the base of each spike can see the spike completely. That $\lfloor n/3 \rfloor$ is sufficient of course follows from Chvátal's theorem (Theorem 1.1).

In terms of the number of reflex vertices, a slight modification of Fig. 4.1, shown in Fig. 4.2, establishes the necessity of $\lfloor r/2 \rfloor + 1$ vertex guards. Sufficiency is established as follows. Let x be a point in the kernel. Connect x to every reflex vertex by a line segment, as illustrated in Fig. 4.3. Let y be a reflex vertex. Note that xy resolves the reflex vertex at y, leaving convex angles on either side. Thus the r "spokes" from x partition the polygon into r pieces, at least $r - 1$ of which are convex. There may be at most one piece non-convex at x. Suppose all pieces are convex. Then placing a guard at every second reflex vertex covers the polygon with $\lceil r/2 \rceil$ guards. If there is one non-convex piece, then cover it with two guards, one at each (former) reflex vertex on its boundary, and again place a guard at every second reflex vertex in the remainder. The result is coverage by $2 + \lceil (r - 3)/2 \rceil = \lceil (r + 1)/2 \rceil$ guards. Thus $\lceil (r + 1)/2 \rceil = \lfloor r/2 \rfloor + 1$ guards suffice in either case.

Fig. 4.1. A star polygon that requires $\lfloor n/3 \rfloor$ vertex guards.

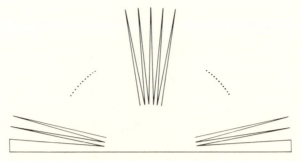

Fig. 4.2.   A star polygon that requires $\lfloor r/2 \rfloor + 1$ vertex guards.

Since r may be as large as $n - 3$ (see Fig. 1.26), this result may be worse than Chvátal's $\lfloor n/3 \rfloor$, but it is better whenever $r < 2\lfloor n/3 \rfloor - 2$.

For edge guards, the only result known is that at least $\lfloor n/5 \rfloor$ edge guards are necessary. This is established by another "sun burst" example due to Toussaint, shown in Fig. 4.4. In this figure, the endpoints of each edge on the lower semicircle are diametrically opposed to the vertices separating the spikes. Thus, if the spikes are long enough, the apex of each spike is visible from only one edge on the lower semicircle. For example, apex A in Fig. 4.4 is only visible to e. Of course, A is also visible from the edges adjacent to its two base vertices a and b. But the conclusion remains that each spike requires its own edge guard. The figure has $n = 5s$ vertices if there are s spikes, and therefore establishes that $s = \lfloor n/5 \rfloor$ edge guards are necessary. Whether this many edge guards is always sufficient remains an open problem.

Mobile guards are more powerful in star polygons. If the patrol is unrestricted (a *line* guard in the notation of the previous chapter), then clearly one guard suffices: just choose a line that intersects the kernel. If the patrol is restricted to vertex-to-vertex diagonals or edges (*diagonal* guards), then it may be that no diagonal intersects the kernel, as in Fig. 4.5. But if the kernel does not intersect any diagonal, then it must lie inside one triangle T of any triangulation. Then placing guards along any two sides of T will cover the entire polygon, since any line through the kernel must intersect the boundary of T in two locations, and at least one of these must lie on a side covered by a guard. That two diagonal guards are sometimes necessary is established by either of the polygons shown in Fig. 4.6, due to

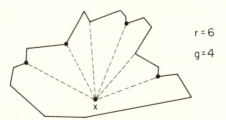

$r = 6$

$g = 4$

x

Fig. 4.3.   A partition of a star made by connecting a kernel point x to every reflex vertex.

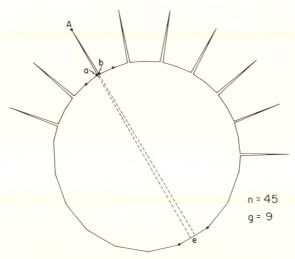

Fig. 4.4. A star polygon requiring $\lfloor n/5 \rfloor$ edge guards.

Shermer and Suri. In both figures, not all vertices are visible from any single diagonal. For example, in Fig. 4.6a, diagonal (4, 9) cannot see 2, and in Fig. 4.6b, diagonal (13, 14), cannot see 1 or 11.

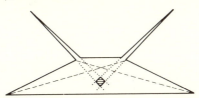

Fig. 4.5. No diagonal intersects the kernel (shaded).

The following theorem summarizes the results of this section.

THEOREM 4.1 [Toussaint 1982]. For coverage of a star polygon of n vertices and r reflex vertices, $\lfloor n/3 \rfloor$ and $\lfloor r/2 \rfloor + 1$ vertex guards are necessary and sufficient, $\lfloor n/5 \rfloor$ edge guards are necessary, and 2 diagonal guards are necessary and sufficient.

4.3. SPIRAL POLYGONS

A *reflex chain* of a polygon is a sequence of consecutive reflex vertices. A *spiral polygon* is a polygon with at most one reflex chain. Feng and Pavlidis studied decomposition of polygons into spiral pieces for its application to character recognition (Feng and Pavlidis 1975; Pavlidis and Feng 1977). Spiral polygons are easily recognized in linear time with a single boundary traversal.

Spiral polygons may require $\lfloor n/3 \rfloor$ vertex or point guards, although here the example is not a simple distortion of the comb shape. The generic example consists of $2k$ equally spaced vertices on the circumference of a circle, and k more vertices on a slightly larger concentric circle. See Fig. 4.7 for an instance with $k = 6$ and $n = 3k = 18$ vertices. There are $k + 2$ convex vertices and $r = 2k - 2$ reflex vertices. Let the vertices on the inner circle occur at multiples of α degrees; then the vertices on the outer circle occur at multiples of 2α. The outer radius is chosen close enough to the inner radius so that each convex vertex on the outer circle (not near either junction between the convex and reflex chains) can see just three vertices on the inner circle, and each reflex vertex on the inner circle can see just two vertices on the outer circle. Placing guards at each vertex on the outer circle, or every other vertex on the inner circle, both result in complete coverage with $k = \lfloor n/3 \rfloor$ guards. It is easily seen that no advantage is gained

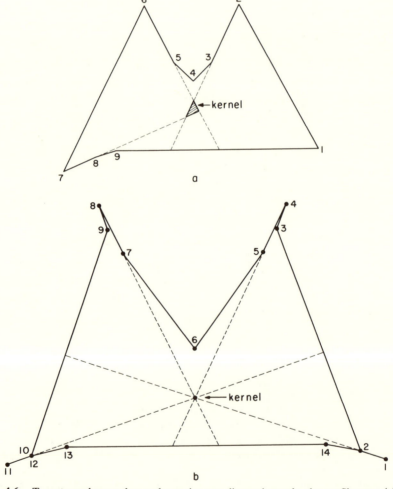

Fig. 4.6. Two star polygons that each require two diagonal guards, due to Shermer (a) and Suri (b).

by mixing guards on the outer and inner circle, or by placing guards on points other than vertices. This establishes that $\lfloor n/3 \rfloor$ point guards are necessary, and Chvátal's theorem gives sufficiency.

In terms of the number of reflex vertices r, the same example establishes $\lfloor r/2 \rfloor + 1$ necessity: $r = 2k - 2$, so $\lfloor r/2 \rfloor + 1 = k$. Sufficiency is established with Chazelle's "naive" convex partitioning, obtained by bisecting every reflex vertex, as shown in Fig. 4.8. The resulting $r + 1$ convex regions can be covered by guards placed at every other reflex vertex, and one additional guard for the last convex region if r is even—that is, $\lfloor r/2 \rfloor + 1$ guards always suffice.

Although the edge guard problem for spiral polygons has not been investigated, the diagonal guard problem has been solved: $\lfloor (n + 2)/5 \rfloor$ are necessary and sufficient. It is somewhat easier to understand the example that establishes necessity after seeing the sufficiency proof, so we will proceed with sufficiency first. It depends on two observations: a spiral polygon may be triangulated so that the dual to the triangulation is a path, and a five triangle polygon may always be covered by one diagonal guard. The first observation is proved in the next lemma; the second observation is Lemma 3.4.

LEMMA 4.1.   There exists a triangulation of any spiral polygon whose dual is a path—that is, a tree with just two leaves.

Proof.   Let a spiral polygon have c convex and r reflex vertices. The proof is by induction on c and r. The induction hypothesis is that every spiral polygon with $c' < c$ and $r' \le r$, or $c' \le c$ and $r' < r$, has a path triangulation dual such that the convex vertices a and b that are adjacent to the ends of the reflex chain are the apexes of the leaf triangles.

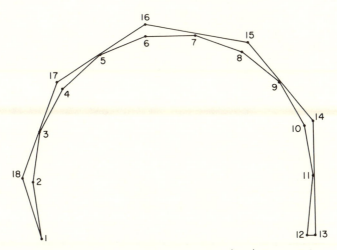

Fig. 4.7.   A spiral polygon that requires $\lfloor n/3 \rfloor$ point guards.

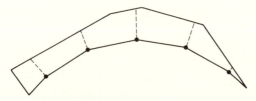

Fig. 4.8. A partition of a spiral polygon into $r + 1$ convex pieces.

If $r = 0$, then P is a convex polygon, every triangulation is possible, and the additional clause of the hypothesis hold vacuously. If $r = 1$, or if $c = 3$ (which is its minimum value), then the basis for the induction is established by the triangulations shown in Figs. 4.9a and 4.9b, respectively.

Assume now that the induction hypothesis holds. Let x be the reflex and y the convex vertex adjacent to a, the convex vertex defined in the hypothesis. Then it is clear that x must be able to see y. Cut off the triangle xay, forming a new spiral polygon P' with c' convex and r' reflex vertices. There are two cases to consider, depending on whether the new angle at x is reflex or convex.

Case 1 (x is reflex in P' (Fig. 4.10a).)   Then $c' = c - 1$ and $r' = r$; y becomes a' in P'.

Case 2 (x is convex in P' (Fig. 4.10b).).   Then $c' = c$ and $r' = r - 1$; x becomes a' in P'.

In either case the induction hypothesis applies, yielding a path with xy an edge of a leaf triangle. Attaching a node for xay to this yields a path for P satisfying the induction hypothesis. □

We can now prove the claimed sufficiency theorem easily. Let a spiral polygon have n vertices, and chose a triangulation whose dual is a path of $t = n - 2$ nodes as guaranteed by the above lemma. By Lemma 3.4, a septagon may always be covered by one diagonal guard. Thus each five triangles in the path may be covered by one diagonal guard. This yields a total coverage by $\lceil t/5 \rceil = \lceil (n - 2)/5 \rceil = \lfloor (n + 2)/5 \rfloor$ guards.

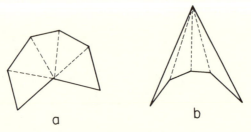

Fig. 4.9. Path triangulations of spiral polygons with one reflex vertex (a) and three convex vertices (b).

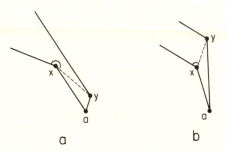

Fig. 4.10. Cutting off an ear from a spiral.

Necessity of this many guards is established by constructing a spiral polygon that only has one triangulation, whose dual is a path. This may be accomplished with $n = 10k + 3$ vertices, with $5k + 2$ convex and $5k + 1$ reflex, arranged as illustrated in Fig. 4.11 for $k = 1$. It should be clear that the only triangulation of this polygon is the one shown. Coverage of five triangles by one guard is then the best possible, and since there are $t = n - 2 = 10k + 1$ triangles, $\lceil t/5 \rceil = \lfloor (n + 2)/5 \rfloor$ guards are necessary.

These results on spiral polygons are summarized in the following theorem (Aggarwal 1984).

THEOREM 4.2 [Aggarwal 1984]. For a cover of a spiral polygon of n vertices, r of which are reflex, $\lfloor n/3 \rfloor$ and $\lfloor r/2 \rfloor + 1$ point guards are necessary and sufficient, and $\lfloor (n + 2)/5 \rfloor$ diagonal guards are necessary and sufficient.

4.4. MONOTONE POLYGONS

The results known for monotone polygons match those for spiral polygons exactly, suggesting that they are in some sense equally restrictive classes. Necessity for point and mobile guards follows by noting that the critical spiral polygons (Figs. 4.7 and 4.11) are also monotone if the reflex angles are chosen close to 180°. Also, of course, the comb example is monotone. The sufficiency proofs, however, are different. That $\lfloor r/2 \rfloor + 1$ vertex guards

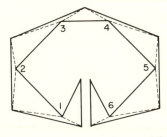

Fig. 4.11. A spiral polygon requiring $\lfloor (n + 2)/5 \rfloor$ diagonal guards.

suffice is easily established by drawing a horizontal line through every reflex vertex (assuming the axis of monotonicity is vertical). This partitions the polygon into $r + 1$ convex pieces, each with a reflex vertex on its boundary. Placing guards at every other reflex vertex in a vertical sort establishes that $\lceil (r + 1)/2 \rceil = \lfloor r/2 \rfloor + 1$ guards suffice.

The sufficiency proof for $\lfloor (n + 2)/5 \rfloor$ mobile guards is the only one amongst these specialized results that is difficult. The interested reader is referred to Aggarwal's thesis (Aggarwal 1984), which contains a 15-page proof. The guards used in his proof are not always diagonal guards, so the result is only established for line guards. In summary we have this theorem.

THEOREM 4.3 [Aggarwal 1984].   For a cover of a monotone polygon of n vertices, r of which are reflex, $\lfloor n/3 \rfloor$ and $\lfloor r/2 \rfloor + 1$ point guards are necessary and sufficient, and $\lfloor (n + 2)/5 \rfloor$ line guards are necessary and sufficient.

Finally we mention again that Preparata and Supowit found a linear-time algorithm for computing the set of directions with respect to which a polygon is monotone (Preparata and Supowit 1981).

5

HOLES

5.1. INTRODUCTION

One of the major open problems in the field of art gallery theorems is to establish a theorem for polygons with holes. A *polygon with holes* is a polygon P enclosing several other polygons $H_1, \ldots, H_h$, the holes. None of the boundaries of $P, H_1, \ldots, H_h$ may intersect, and each of the holes is empty. P is said to bound a *multiply-connected* region with h holes: the region of the plane interior to or on the boundary of P, but exterior to or on the boundary of $H_1, \ldots, H_h$. (A polygon without holes is said, in contrast, to be *simply-connected.*) Similarly we define an *orthogonal polygon with holes* to be an orthogonal polygon with orthogonal holes, with all edges aligned with the same pair of orthogonal axes. For both general polygons with holes and orthogonal polygons with holes, a gap remains between the available necessity and sufficiency proofs. In this chapter we discuss these problems, and present partial results obtained by Aggarwal and Shermer.

Recall that the proof of Theorem 2.1 established that orthogonal polygons with holes may be convexly quadrilateralized. But we have yet to prove that arbitrary polygons with holes may be triangulated.

LEMMA 5.1. A polygon P with holes may be triangulated.

Proof. Let P have h holes and n vertices in total. The proof is by induction on h primarily, and n secondarily. Theorem 1.2 establishes the basis of the induction for $h = 0$. For the general case, let d be a completely internal diagonal, whose existence can be guaranteed by the same argument as used in Theorem 1.2: choose an arbitrary convex vertex v_2, with neighbors v_1 and v_3, on the outer boundary of P, and let $d = v_1 v_3$ if this is internal, and otherwise let $d = v_2 x$, where x is the closest vertex to v_2 measured perpendicular to $v_1 v_3$. If d has one endpoint on a hole, then it increases n by 2, but decreases h by 1. If d has both endpoints on the outer boundary of P, then it partitions P into two polygons P_i with $n_i < n$ vertices and $h_i \leq h$ holes, $i = 1, 2$. In either case, the induction hypothesis applies and establishes the theorem. $\square$

The number of triangles and quadrilaterals that result from triangulation and quadrilateralization are dependent on the number of holes:

LEMMA 5.2.   Let a polygon P with h holes have n vertices total, counting vertices on the holes as well as on the outer boundary. Then a triangulation of P has $t = n + 2h - 2$ triangles, and a quadrilateralization has $q = n/2 + h - 1$ quadrilaterals.

Proof.   Let the outer boundary of P have n_0 vertices, and let the ith hole have n_i vertices; thus $n = n_0 + n_1 + \cdots + n_h$. The sum of the interior angles of the outer boundary is $(n_0 - 2)180$ degrees; the sum of the exterior angles of the ith hole is $(n_i + 2)180$. Thus

$$180[(n_0 - 2) + (n_1 + 2) + \cdots + (n_h + 2)] = 180t$$

or $t = n + 2h - 2$. Since $q = t/2$, $q = n/2 + h - 1$.

The same result may be obtained with Euler's Theorem. There are $V = n$ vertices, $F = t + h + 1$ faces, one for each triangle and hole, plus the exterior face, and $E = (3t + n)/2$ edges, where three per triangle plus the boundary counts each edge twice. Then $V - E + F = 2$ yields $t = n + 2h - 2$ as above.   □

Throughout the remainder of the chapter, we will use n, h, t, and q to designate the quantities defined in this lemma and P to represent a polygon with holes (including the holes).

The best sufficiency result for both the general and the orthogonal problems is the following theorem.

THEOREM 5.1 [O'Rourke 1982].   For a polygon of n vertices with h holes, $\lfloor (n + 2h)/3 \rfloor = \lceil t/3 \rceil$ combinatorial guards suffice to dominate any triangulation, and for an orthogonal polygon, $\lfloor (n + 2h)/4 \rfloor = \lceil q/2 \rceil$ combinatorial guards suffice to dominate any quadrilateralization.

Proof.[1]   First we note that the equivalences of $\lceil t/3 \rceil$ and $\lfloor (n + 2h)/3 \rfloor$, and $\lceil q/2 \rceil$ and $\lfloor (n + 2h)/4 \rfloor$, follow directly from Lemma 5.2 by substitution. Thus this theorem is a direct extension of the sufficiency halves of Theorems 1.1 and 2.2, which established respectively that $\lfloor n/3 \rfloor = \lceil t/3 \rceil$ and $\lfloor n/4 \rfloor = \lceil q/2 \rceil$ guards suffice.

Given a polygon P with holes, triangulate it into t triangles; call the triangulation T. The plan of the proof is to "cut" the polygon along diagonals of the triangulation in order to remove each hole by connecting it to the exterior of P. It is clear that every hole must have diagonals in T from some of its vertices to either other holes or the outer boundary of P. Cutting along any such diagonal either merges the hole with another, or connects it to the outside. In either case, each cut reduces the number of holes by one. We are not quite finished, however, because we need to choose the cuts so that the result is a single polygon: it may be that a choice of cuts results in several disconnected pieces.

---

1. I have incorporated several ideas from Aggarwal (1984).

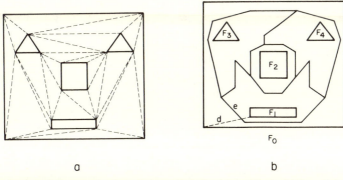

Fig. 5.1. A triangulation graph of a polygon with holes (a) and its dual (b): each hole in (a) is surrounded by a cycle in (b).

Let $\bar{T}$ be the (non-weak) dual of the triangulation. $\bar{T}$ is a planar graph of maximum degree three, which, in its natural embedding, has h bounded faces $F_1, \ldots, F_h$, one per hole of P. Let F_0 be the exterior unbounded face. Choose any face F_i that shares at least one edge e with F_0. There must be such a face because there must be a diagonal of T from the outer boundary to some hole, and the dual of this diagonal in $\bar{T}$, is e. Removal of e from $\bar{T}$ merges F_i with F_0 without disconnecting the graph. See Fig. 5.1 for an example. Note that removal of an edge in $\bar{T}$ is equivalent to cutting P along the corresponding diagonal of T. Continuing to remove edges of $\bar{T}$ shared with the exterior face in this manner guarantees that a single connected graph results.

Let P' be the polygon that results after all holes are cut in the above manner. Then P' has $n + 2h$ vertices, since two vertices are introduced per cut, but because cuts do not create new triangles, it still has t triangles. Applying Theorem 1.1 to P' yields coverage by $\lfloor (n + 2h)/3 \rfloor = \lceil t/3 \rceil$ guards.

The proof for orthogonal polygons is exactly the same, except that Theorem 2.2 is invoked to obtain the result. □

Although this easily obtained theorem has a pleasing form when expressed in terms of t and q, it appears to be weak: no one has found examples of polygons that require this many guards. In fact, it is difficult to find an example that requires more than $\lfloor n/3 \rfloor$ guards independent of the number of holes. But we show in the next section that there are such polygons.

5.2. GENERAL POLYGONS WITH HOLES

Sidarto discovered the one-hole polygon shown in Fig. 5.2a. It has $n = 8$ vertices, $h = 1$ hole, and requires three guards. Note that $3 > \lfloor 8/3 \rfloor$. Shermer discovered the polygons in Figs. 5.2b and 5.2c, which also have

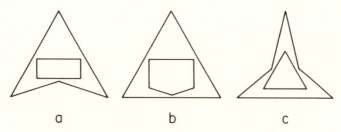

Fig. 5.2. One-hole polygons of 8 vertices that require 3 guards.

eight vertices and require three guards. These one-hole examples can be extended to establish $\lfloor(n + 1)/3\rfloor$ necessity for one hole: Figs. 5.3a and 5.3b show two examples for $n = 11$, due, respectively, to Shermer and Delcher.[2] Finally, the examples can be extended to more than one hole: Fig. 5.4 shows Shermer's method of stitching together copies of the basic one-hole example. The polygon shown has $n = 24$ vertices, $h = 3$ holes, and requires nine guards. This example establishes $\lfloor(n + h)/3\rfloor$ necessity for h holes. We will not attempt to prove that the claimed number of guards is necessary in the examples just mentioned, as it should be obvious from the figures. The following theorem summarizes the implications of these examples.

THEOREM 5.2 [Shermer 1982]. $\lfloor(n + h)/3\rfloor$ guards are sometimes necessary for a polygon of n vertices and h holes.

Note that Fig. 5.4 also establishes that $\lfloor 3n/8 \rfloor$ guards are sometimes necessary if we express the result solely as a function of n.

The gap between the necessity of $\lfloor(n + h)/3\rfloor$ and the sufficiency of $\lfloor(n + 2h)/3\rfloor$ has proved very difficult to close. Since the gap widens as h increases, it is not as insignificant as it might first appear. The strongest result available is that $\lfloor(n + h)/3\rfloor$ guards suffice for $h = 1$, a theorem proved independently by Aggarwal and Shermer (Shermer 1984). We will follow Shermer's proof technique here.

Fig. 5.3. One-hole polygons of 11 vertices that require 4 guards.

---

2. I assigned this as a homework problem in my computational geometry class. Julian Sidarto and Thomas Shermer, and Arthur Delcher, were students in that class in 1982 and 1985, respectively.

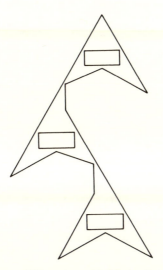

Fig. 5.4. A polygon of 24 vertices with 3 holes that requires 9 guards.

5.2.1. Reduced Triangulations

Before outlining the proof, we first perform a reduction that eliminates irrelevancies. The dual of a triangulation of a polygon with one hole has one cycle surrounding the hole, with (perhaps) several trees attached to the cycle. The next lemma shows that we can clip all the trees down to at most one node. Define a *reduced triangulation* as one such that every subgraph of the triangulation dual G that may be disconnected from G by the removal of a single arc, has exactly one node. Note that this definition is independent of the number of holes in the polygon from which the triangulation derives. We restrict the next lemma to one-hole polygons although it does extend to the general case.

LEMMA 5.3. If $\lfloor (n+1)/3 \rfloor$ combinatorial guards suffice to dominate every reduced triangulation of a polygon of n vertices and one hole, then $\lfloor (n+1)/3 \rfloor$ guards suffice to dominate every triangulation of n vertices and one hole.

Proof. The proof is by induction on the number of trees of more than one node attached to cycles of the triangulation dual G. The basis is established by the antecedent of the lemma: $\lfloor (n+1)/3 \rfloor$ guards suffice for a reduced triangulation, which by definition has no attached trees of more than one node. For the general step, assume $\lfloor (n+1)/3 \rfloor$ guards suffice for any triangulation with $s' < s$ trees of at least two nodes, and let G be a non-reduced triangulation with s such trees. Let T be one of these trees, detachable from G by the removal of one arc r. The situation is as illustrated in Fig. 5.5. Let a and b be the endpoints of the diagonal whose dual is r. Let m be the number of vertices in the polygon Q composed of the triangles of T, *not including a and b*. We show that all but at most the root

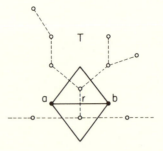

Fig. 5.5. A tree T attached at diagonal ab to a cycle, which extends to the left and right.

triangle of T can be covered "efficiently," that is, with one guard per three vertices. The proof proceeds in three cases, depending on the value of m mod 3. The easiest cases are considered first.

Case 0 $(m = 3k)$.   The polygon Q has $m + 2$ vertices, and it may therefore be covered by $\lfloor (m + 2)/3 \rfloor = k$ guards by Theorem 1.1. Let $P - Q$ be the polygon remaining after removal of Q—that is, the deletion of all vertices in T except a and b, and all incident edges. Since $P - Q$ has $s - 1$ attached trees of one node or more, the induction hypothesis guarantees coverage with $\lfloor (n - m + 1)/3 \rfloor$ guards. Thus P may be covered with

$$\lfloor (n - m + 1)/3 \rfloor + k = \lfloor [(n - m + 1) + m]/3 \rfloor = \lfloor (n + 1)/3 \rfloor.$$

guards.

Case 2 $(m = 3k + 2)$.   The strategy used in Case 0 will lead to $k + 1$ guards here, which is insufficient for our purposes, so another approach must be taken. Augment Q to Q' by adding the triangle on the other side of ab, whose apex is x. Q' is a polygon of $m + 3 = 3k + 5$ vertices and may therefore be covered with $\lfloor (3k + 5)/3 \rfloor = k + 1$ guards by Theorem 1.1. Fisk's proof of that theorem (Section 1.2.1) assigns one vertex of triangle abx a guard. If x is assigned a guard, it may be moved to a or b while maintaining complete coverage of Q'. Thus we may assume that a or b is assigned a guard. Suppose without loss of generality that a is assigned a guard. Let P' be the result of removing all of Q', all triangles incident on a, and splitting vertex x into two vertices. See Figs. 5.6a and 5.6b. P' has $n - m - 1 + 1$ vertices, since it is missing the m vertices of Q and vertex a,

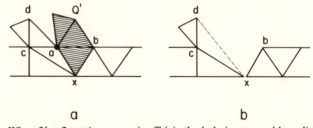

a   b

Fig. 5.6. When $3k + 2$ vertices comprise T (a), the hole is removed by splitting x (b).

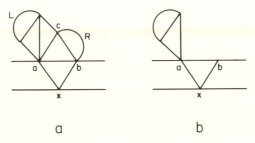

Fig. 5.7. When $3k + 1$ vertices comprise T (a), one case is handled by covering R and abc together, and L separately (b).

but gains a vertex from the split of x. Splitting x removes the hole, but P' is not necessarily a polygon, as pieces may be attached at vertices only. But now connect each vertex of P' that was adjacent to a in P, to x. In Fig. 5.6b, vertex d is so connected. These connections are not always geometrically possible, but for this case we are only concerned with the combinatorial structure of the graph. The reconnections do not increase the number of vertices, but they restore P' to be a triangulation graph of a polygon without holes. There is now no need to use the induction hypothesis; rather apply Theorem 1.1 to P', resulting in coverage by

$$\lfloor (n - m)/3 \rfloor = \lfloor [(n - 3(k + 1)) + 1]/3 \rfloor = \lfloor (n + 1)/3 \rfloor - (k + 1)$$

guards. Together with the $k + 1$ guards used to cover Q', the lemma is established in this case.

Case 1 ($m = 3k + 1$). Let the triangle forming the root of T be abc. Let l be the number of vertices in the left subtree L, not including a and c, and let r be the number of vertices in the right subtree R, not including b and c. Thus $m = l + r + 1$; see Fig. 5.7a. We consider two subcases dependent on the values of l and r mod 3.

Subcase 1a ($l = 3k_1$ and $r = 3k_2$; $m = 3(k_1 + k_2) + 1$). As in Case 0, cover L and R with k_1 and k_2 guards. By the induction hypothesis, $P - L - R$ can be covered with

$$\lfloor [n - (l + r) + 1]/3 \rfloor = \left\lfloor [n - 3(k_1 + k_2) + 1]/3 \right\rfloor = \lfloor (n + 1)/3 \rfloor - (k_1 + k_2)$$

guards, establishing the theorem. This is the only case in which T cannot be entirely removed, but is instead reduced to a single triangle abc.

Subcase 1b ($l = 3k_1 + 1$ and $r = 3k_2 + 2$; $m = 3(k_1 + k_2 + 1) + 1$). Let R' be the polygon obtained by adding abc to R. R' has $3k_2 + 5$ vertices. Cover R' with $k_2 + 1$ guards by Theorem 1.1. Fisk's coloring procedure guarantees that one vertex of abc is assigned a guard. If either a or b (say a) is guarded, then proceed exactly as in Case 2: delete R' and a, and split x. The calculations are just as in Case 2, establishing the lemma. If on the other hand c is guarded, then delete R' and all triangles of L incident on c, as in

Fig. 5.7b. This leaves at most $l + 1 = 3k_1 + 2$ vertices either disconnected from P or attached at a. Addition of graph edges if necessary restores this piece to a triangulation graph of a polygon L' without increasing the number of vertices. Cover L' with k_1 guards by Theorem 1.1. Now the remainder of P has $n - m$ vertices and $s - 1$ attached trees. By the induction hypothesis it may be covered with

$$\lfloor (n - m + 1)/3 \rfloor = \lfloor [n - 3(k_1 + k_2 + 1)]/3 \rfloor = \lfloor n/3 \rfloor - (k_1 + k_2 + 1)$$

guards. Together with the $k_2 + 1$ guards used to cover R', and the k_1 guards used for L', complete coverage has been achieved with fewer than $\lfloor (n + 1)/3 \rfloor$ guards.

All cases have now been covered, and the lemma established. □

The idea of reconnecting "broken" pieces into a polygon triangulation graph is from Shermer (1985). Note that this technique was used only when induction was unnecessary, or was applied only to an attached tree. This is crucial, as the geometry of the reduced triangulation is important in the proof of Theorem 5.3 below, and cannot be warped by curved reconnections that need to be straightened in the manner used in Lemma 3.1.

5.2.2. Tough Triangulations

We may now proceed with Shermer's proof of $\lfloor (n + 1)/3 \rfloor$ sufficiency for a polygon with one hole. The first step of the proof reveals why the problem is hard: there exist triangulations of polygons with h holes that require $\lfloor (n + 2h)/3 \rfloor$ *combinatorial* guards for domination. Thus the problem cannot be reduced to pure combinatorics by an arbitrary triangulation. Before proving this we introduce some notation.[3] Lemma 5.3 permits us to restrict attention to reduced triangulations. Let T be a reduced triangulation of a polygon with one hole. Then T consists of a single cycle of triangles, each with perhaps one attached triangle that is not part of the cycle. A cycle triangle is *based* on the inner boundary if it has exactly one vertex, its apex, on the outer boundary of the polygon, and based on the outer boundary if just its apex is on the inner boundary. Note that the base edge of a cycle triangle based on the inner boundary may not itself be on the inner boundary because of a tree attached to the base; this is why the definition is phrased in terms of the apex. Label a cycle triangle "1" if it has no attached non-cycle triangle, and "2" if it does. Then T is represented as a string of characters over the alphabet {"1", "2", "/"}, formed by concatenating all the labels of the cycle triangles, and inserting a "/" between labels λ_1 and λ_2 if the λ_1 triangle is based on the inner boundary and the λ_2 triangle is based on the outer boundary, or vice versa. Thus each "/" records a switch in basing. This string of characters will be called the *string* associated with T.

   Figure 5.8 shows an example. Starting at the indicated lowest triangle and

---

3. The notation is due to Shermer (1984), but slightly modified here.

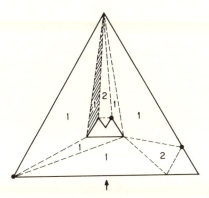

Fig. 5.8. A triangulation of 10 vertices with string 121/121/1/1/ that requires 4 guards: the 3 shown (dots) do not cover the shaded triangle.

proceeding counterclockwise, we obtain the string 121/121/1/1/. Note that the sum of the integers in the string is equal to the total number of triangles in T, and because $t = n$ when $h = 1$ by Lemma 5.2, this is the same as the number of vertices of the polygon. We will employ standard regular expression notation to condense the strings: " $+$ " for "or," s^k for k repetitions of string s, and s^* for zero or more repetitions of s. Thus the above string is equivalent to $(121/)^2(1/)^2$ and is an instance of $(1(21)^*/)^4$. We consider two strings equivalent if one is a cyclic shift of the other, or a cyclic shift of the reverse of another. Finally note that the strings make no distinction between the inner and outer boundaries, and in fact this distinction is irrelevant for combinatorial guards.

A complete characterization of those triangulations that require $\lfloor (n + 2h)/3 \rfloor$ combinatorial guards for $h = 1$ is provided by the following theorem (Shermer 1984).

THEOREM 5.3 [Shermer 1984]. A reduced triangulation T of a polygon with one hole requires $\lfloor (n + 2)/3 \rfloor$ combinatorial guards for complete domination iff the string for T has the form $(1(21)^*/)^{6k-2}$.

We will call a string that is an instance of $(1(21)^*/)^{6k-2}$ *tough*. Figure 5.8 satisfies the theorem: $n = 10$ and it requires $\lfloor 12/3 \rfloor = 4$ combinatorial guards; an attempted cover with three guards is shown in the figure. Figure 5.9 shows a polygon with the string $(121/)^{10}$; here $n = 40$ and $\lfloor 42/3 \rfloor = 14$ guards are required. Even triangulations whose strings are tough but do not correspond to any non-degenerate polygon require $\lfloor (n + 2)/3 \rfloor$ combinatorial guards. Figure 5.10 shows the smallest possible instance, $(1/)^4$, where $n = 4$ and $g = \lfloor 6/2 \rfloor = 2$. Figure 5.8 is the smallest instance realizable as a polygon. All these examples are from Shermer (1984).

Proof of Theorem 5.3. We first prove that a triangulation graph T with a tough string requires $\lfloor (n + 2)/3 \rfloor$ combinatorial guards. The proof is by induction, in two parts. First it is shown that the claim holds for strings of

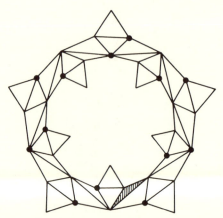

Fig. 5.9. A triangulation of 40 vertices with string $(121/)^{10}$ that requires 14 guards: the 13 shown (dots) do not cover the shaded triangle.

the form $(1/)^{6k-2}$. Then it is shown that each addition of a (21) section requires another guard.

Triangulations of the form $(1/)^{6k-2}$ have a particularly simple structure, illustrated for $k = 2$ in Fig. 5.11. Each vertex is adjacent to exactly three triangles. Thus $g = \lceil t/3 \rceil$ guards are necessary. But since $t = n = 6k - 2$, $g = \lceil (6k - 2)/3 \rceil = 2k = \lfloor (n + 2)/3 \rfloor$, establishing the first claim.

Now assume that all triangulations T of n vertices with tough strings require $g = \lfloor (n + 2)/3 \rfloor$ guards, and consider adding three vertices to such a T by insertion of a (21) section S after a "1" triangle and before a "/" switch. Clearly any triangulation of $n + 3$ vertices that is an instance of the tough form $(1(21)^*/)^{6k-2}$ can be obtained by such an insertion. Assume, in contradiction to our goal, that the insertion does not increase the number of guards required beyond g. We claim then that T could have been covered by $g - 1$ guards. S must be covered in one of the three ways illustrated in Figs. 5.12a, 5.12b, or 5.12c. If S is covered as in Fig. 5.12a, then removal of the section and the guard results in domination of T by $g - 1$ guards. If S is covered as in Fig. 5.12b, then deleting S merges two guards, again resulting in coverage by $g - 1$ guards. Finally, if S is covered as in Fig. 5.12c, then removal of S leaves two guards, one of which (the bottom one in the figure) is superfluous because every triangle to which it is adjacent is already covered. So again T can be dominated by $g - 1$ guards. This contradicts the assumption that g are necessary, establishing that the form $(1(21)^*/)^{6k-2}$ always requires $\lfloor (n + 2)/3 \rfloor$ combinatorial guards.

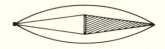

Fig. 5.10. A triangulation of 4 vertices with string $(1/)^4$ that requires 2 guards: the 1 shown (dot) does not cover the shaded triangle.

Fig. 5.11. A triangulation of 10 vertices with string $(1/)^{10}$ that requires 4 guards: the 3 shown (dots) do not cover the shaded triangle.

Now we prove the theorem in the other direction, in the contrapositive form: if a triangulation T does *not* have a tough string, then fewer than $\lfloor (n+2)/3 \rfloor$ combinatorial guards suffice for domination. Each 1 in a tough string must be followed by $(2+/)$, and each 2 by 1. Thus, any non-tough triangulation must contain a fragment of the form 11, 22, or 2/. Each of these cases is treated separately.

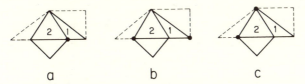

Fig. 5.12. Three ways to guard a (21) section.

Case 1 (11). Let ab be the diagonal shared between the two "1" triangles, with b an apex of both, as shown in Fig. 5.13a. Place a guard at b, delete all covered triangles, and add in extra edges as needed to restore to a polygon with no holes, as shown in Fig. 5.13b. The result is a triangulation of a polygon of no more than $n-2$ vertices, and so T may be dominated with $1 + \lfloor (n-2)/3 \rfloor = \lfloor (n+1)/3 \rfloor$ guards.

Case 2 (22). Again let ab be the shared diagonal, with a incident to all four triangles, as shown in Fig. 5.14a. Place a guard at a, delete the four adjacent triangles, and split node b into two nodes, as shown in Fig. 5.14b. The result is a polygon of $n-2$ vertices, so again T can be dominated with $1 + \lfloor (n-2)/3 \rfloor = \lfloor (n+1)/3 \rfloor$ guards.

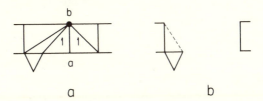

Fig. 5.13. Guarding a 11 fragment (a) removes the hole (b).

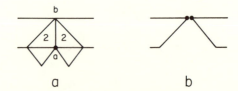

Fig. 5.14. Guarding a 22 fragment (a) removes the hole after splitting a vertex (b).

Case 3 (2/). Here we must consider several subcases, depending on the triangles adjacent to the 2/ fragment.

Case 3a (2/1). See Fig. 5.15a. Place a guard at *a* and delete adjacent triangles. The result is a polygon of $n - 2$ vertices, and we proceed as in Case 1.

Case 3b (2/2). Again we consider subcases.

Subcase (2/21). See Fig. 5.15b. Place a guard at *a* as in Case 3a.

Subcase (2/22). This was already handled in Case 2.

Subcase (2/2/1). This was already handled in Case 3a.

Subcase (2/2/2). See Fig. 5.15c. Place a guard at *a*, delete all adjacent triangles, and split vertex *b*. Now proceed as in Case 2.

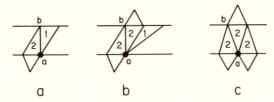

Fig. 5.15. The three cases for the fragment 2/ are all handled by guarding vertex *a*.

We have thus shown that $\lfloor (n + 1)/3 \rfloor$ combinatorial guards suffice whenever one of the fragments 11, 22, or 2/ are present in *T*'s string, establishing the theorem. □

5.2.3. Convex Pairs and Triplets

The second step of Shermer's proof of Theorem 5.3 is to further characterize those one-hole polygon triangulations that might require $\lfloor (n + 2)/3 \rfloor$ guards, this time involving the geometry of the triangulation and using geometric guards. In particular, if a tough triangulation contains either a "c-pair" or a "c-triplet," then $\lfloor (n + 1)/3 \rfloor$ guards suffice. The third and final step is to show that every tough triangulation must contain one of these two structures.

A *c-pair* is a pair of adjacent cycle triangles that together form a convex quadrilateral.

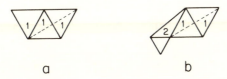

Fig. 5.16. Flipping a 1/1 c-pair leads to 11/1 (a) or 2/1/1 (b).

LEMMA 5.4. A polygon with a tough triangulation containing a c-pair may be covered with $\lfloor (n+1)/3 \rfloor$ vertex guards.

Proof. The strategy is to flip the diagonal of the c-pair, changing the structure of the triangulation to non-tough. Since the triangulation has the string $(1(21)^*/)^{6k-2}$, the c-pair has either the form 1/1 or 21 (or equivalently 12). Each case is considered separately.

Case 1 (1/1). Flip the diagonal of the c-pair. Since the quadrilateral is convex, this is possible. The resulting triangulation is not tough, as can be seen in Fig. 5.16. If the triangle preceding the c-pair is of type 1, then the fragment 1/(1/1) is changed to 11/1 (Fig. 5.16a). If the preceding triangle is of type 2, then the fragment 2(1/1) is changed to 2/1/1. Neither of these new fragments are substrings of any tough string. By Theorem 5.3, then, $\lfloor (n+1)/3 \rfloor$ guards suffice.

Case 2 (21). Again flip the diagonal. The resulting triangulation, shown in Fig. 5.17, is not reduced. But this is just Case 2 of the proof of Lemma 5.3. Place a guard at a, delete all adjacent triangles, split vertex c in two, and restore to a polygon triangulation by adding diagonals as necessary. Three vertices are deleted, and one added. Since the result is a polygon, coverage by $1 + \lfloor (n-2)/2 \rfloor = \lfloor (n+1)/3 \rfloor$ guards has been achieved. ◻

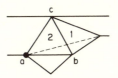

Fig. 5.17. Flipping a 21 c-pair leads to the case considered in Fig. 5.6.

A *c-triplet* is a triple (A, B, C) of consecutive cycle triangles such that first, B is of string type 1, and second, the union of the three triangles may be partitioned into two convex pieces.

LEMMA 5.5. A polygon with a tough triangulation containing a c-triplet may be covered with $\lfloor (n+1)/3 \rfloor$ vertex guards.

Proof. Let a be the vertex common to the c-triplet triangles A, B, and C, as shown in Fig. 5.18a. Delete B and split vertex a. The result is a polygon of no holes with $n+1$ vertices, which may therefore be covered with $\lfloor (n+1)/3 \rfloor$ vertex guards by Theorem 1.1. In particular, perform the

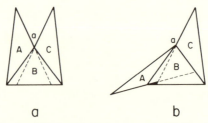

a   b

Fig. 5.18. A c-triplet is covered if *A* and *C* are covered (a), but *B* is not covered if the triangles do not form a c-triplet.

coverage with Fisk's coloring procedure; then both *A* and *C* must have a guard in one of their corners. Now put back *B*. Because the three triangles form a c-triplet, *B* is also covered by the guards covering *A* and *C*. □

Note that if the triangles did not form a c-triplet, as in Fig. 5.18b, *B* would not necessarily be covered. Similarly, if *B* were of string type 2, the triangle attached to *B* would not necessarily be covered.

We finally come to the last step of the proof. For a triangle t_i, define the open cone delimited by the two edges of t_i passing through the apex as $\alpha(i)$, and define the similar region off the right base vertex as $\beta(i)$; see Fig. 5.19.

LEMMA 5.6. Any tough triangulation of a polygon contains either a c-pair or a c-triplet.

Proof. The proof is by contradiction. Assume a tough triangulation contains no c-pair or c-triplet. Then we will show that it cannot close into a cycle, and so is not the triangulation of a polygon with one hole.

Identify two adjacent cycle triangles of the form 1/1; such a fragment must exist because the general form is $(1(21)^*/)^{6k-2}$. We will identify triangles by subscripts on their type. The selected 1/1 fragment is labeled $1_0/1_1$. We expand this string to the right in all possible ways compatible with the general tough form, and show that a particular geometric structure always results. Let a string *S* end at the right with 1_i, and let v_i be the vertex at the tip of the ear 1_i. Then define an embedding of *S* to be *nesting* if v_i is

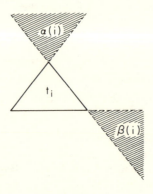

Fig. 5.19. The apex cone α and base cone β for a triangle.

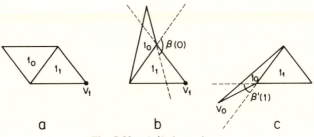

Fig. 5.20. $1_0/1_1$ is nesting.

in the base cone $\beta(i-1)$ of the triangle adjacent to 1_i. We now show that $1_0/1_1$ is nesting.

The general form of this fragment is as shown in Fig. 5.20a. In order to avoid a c-pair, either the configuration shown in Fig. 5.20b or 5.20c must hold. In Fig. 5.20b, $v_1 \in \beta(0)$, and so the nesting definition is satisfied. Figure 5.20c is just Fig. 5.20b reflected in a horizontal line, and we assume without loss of generality that 5.20b obtains.

The string $1_0/1_1$ may be extended only with $/1$ or 21 while remaining compatible with the tough form. We consider each case separately.

Case 1 $(1_0/1_1/1_2)$. The general form is shown in Fig. 5.21a. In order to avoid a c-pair in $1_1/1_2$, either $v_2 \in \alpha(1)$ or $v_2 \in \beta(1)$. The former choice (Fig. 5.21b) leads to a c-triplet, and the latter choice (Fig. 5.21c) is a nesting configuration.

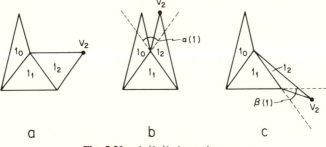

Fig. 5.21. $1_0/1_1/1_2$ is nesting.

Case 2 $(1_0/1_1/2_21_3)$. As in Case 1, we must have $v_2 \in \beta(1)$. To avoid a c-pair in 2_21_3, we must have $v_3 \in \beta(2)$, as illustrated in Fig. 5.22. Again the configuration is nesting.

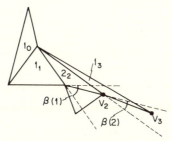

Fig. 5.22. $1_0/1_1/2_21_3$ is nesting.

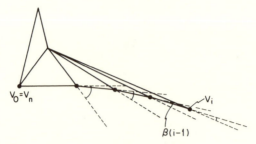

Fig. 5.23. Repeated nesting prevents v_n from coinciding with v_0.

Both Case 1 and 2 may be extended only with /1 or with 21. Extension of Case 1 results in the same two cases again, although the possibility that $v_3 \in \alpha(2)$ is blocked by 1_0, so this choice does not have to be ruled out by showing that it leads to a c-triple. Similarly extension of Case 2 brings us back to the same two cases. We conclude that every embedding of the string compatible with the tough form is nesting.

But now the contradiction is immediate. The repeated nesting forces $v_i \in \beta(i-1)$, and since these base cones are clearly nested inside one another (see Fig. 5.23), the embedding cannot wrap back around to permit $v_n = v_0$. $\square$

THEOREM 5.4 [Aggarwal, Shermer 1984]. $\lfloor (n+1)/3 \rfloor$ vertex guards suffice to cover any n vertex polygon with one hole.

Proof. Lemma 5.3 established that if the theorem holds for reduced triangulations, then it holds for all triangulations. So we restrict our attention to reduced triangulations. Theorem 5.3 shows that if the reduced triangulation is not tough, then $\lfloor (n+1)/3 \rfloor$ vertex guards suffice. So we need only consider tough triangulations. Lemmas 5.4 and 5.5 show that if a tough triangulation contains a c-pair or a c-triplet, then $\lfloor (n+1)/3 \rfloor$ guards suffice. And Lemma 5.6 shows that every tough triangulation contains one of these structures, so there are no further possibilities. $\square$

It does not seem easy to extend this proof to more than one hole. Nevertheless, there is considerable evidence for the following conjecture.

CONJECTURE 5.1 $\lfloor (n+h)/3 \rfloor$ vertex guards are sufficient to cover any polygon of n vertices and h holes.

5.3. ORTHOGONAL POLYGONS WITH HOLES

The status of the art gallery problem for orthogonal polygons is similar to that for general polygons in that it is unsolved in its most general form. There are, however, four interesting differences: the number of guards does not seem to be dependent on h, there is a simple proof of the one-hole theorem, there is a two-hole theorem, and vertex guards do not suffice for more than one hole.

Recall that the quadrilateralization theorem (2.1) holds for orthogonal polygons with holes. However, the coloring argument used to obtain $\lfloor n/4 \rfloor$ sufficiency does not work if there are cycles in the dual of the quadrilateralization. Nevertheless, no examples of orthogonal polygons with holes are known to require more than $\lfloor n/4 \rfloor$ guards. This leads to the following conjecture.

CONJECTURE 5.2. $\lfloor n/4 \rfloor$ point guards suffice to cover any orthogonal polygon of n vertices, independent of the number of holes.

The gap between this conjecture and the best general result, $\lfloor (n + 2h)/4 \rfloor$ (Theorem 5.1), is substantial.

Aggarwal established the truth of the conjecture for $h = 1$ and $h = 2$. His proof for one hole is long and complicated (Aggarwal 1984). The two-hole theorem is by no means a simple extension of the one-hole theorem; further complications arise.[4] Recently Shermer found a simple proof of the one-hole theorem. This is the only proof we will present in this section.

His proof is "simple," however, only if we accept a non-trivial lemma proved by Aggarwal to the effect that only reduced quadrilateralizations need be studied. A *reduced quadrilateralization* is one for whose dual G the following conditions hold:

(1) Every subgraph that may be disconnected from G by the removal of a single arc of G has exactly one node, called a *leaf*;
(2) the quadrilaterals of no two such leaf nodes share a vertex.

For a polygon with one hole, the dual of a reduced quadrilateralization is a single cycle with attached leaf nodes satisfying condition (2). Note that the definition of a reduced quadrilateralization parallels that of a reduced triangulation used in the previous section, with the additional restriction of discarding neighboring non-cycle quadrilaterals.

Aggarwal established the following analog of Lemma 5.3.

LEMMA 5.7. If $\lfloor n/4 \rfloor$ guards suffice to dominate every reduced quadrilateralization of n vertices and one hole, then $\lfloor n/4 \rfloor$ guards suffice to cover every quadrilateralization of n vertices and one hole.

The proof of this lemma is at least as complex as that of Lemma 5.3, but it is very similar in spirit, and we will not detail it here (Aggarwal 1984, Prop. 3.10). This lemma permits us to concern ourselves solely with reduced quadrilateralizations.

We need a simple characterization of the cycle quadrilaterals of one-hole orthogonal polygons before proceeding. Each cycle quadrilateral has all four of its vertices on the boundary of the polygon. If a quadrilateral has

---

4. This proof is only sketched in Aggarwal (1984), but he has rather detailed notes.

two vertices on the exterior boundary and two on the hole boundary it is called *balanced*; otherwise it is called *skewed*.

LEMMA 5.8 Any quadrilateralization of an orthogonal polygon with one hole has an even number (at least four) of balanced quadrilaterals.

Proof. We first establish that the number of polygon edges bounding the cycle quadrilaterals towards the exterior is even. Of course this is trivial if all the quadrilateral edges are polygon edges, because an orthogonal polygon has an even number of edges. Let $e_1, \ldots, e_k$ be the cycle quadrilateral edges towards the exterior, and let n_i be the number of polygon edges in the portion of the polygon P_i bound by e_i that does not include the hole. If e_i is a polygon edge, then $n_i = 1$; otherwise n_i is odd, since P_i is quadrilateralizable and therefore has an even number of boundary edges including e_i. Since each n_i is odd, and $\sum_{i=1}^{k} n_i$, the total number of polygon edges, is even, the number of terms k must be even. This establishes the claim.

Since each balanced quadrilateral contributes 1 to k, and each skewed quadrilateral contributes 0 or 2 to k, the number of balanced quadrilaterals must be even. To establish that there must be at least four balanced quadrilaterals, note that the four extreme edges of the hole (top, bottom, left, right), cannot be part of a skewed quadrilateral. □

We may now proceed with Shermer's proof of the one-hole theorem.

THEOREM 5.5 [Aggarwal 1984]. $\lfloor n/4 \rfloor$ vertex guards suffice to cover any n vertex orthogonal polygon with one hole.

Proof [Shermer 1985]. Let Q be a reduced quadrilateralization of an orthogonal polygon with one hole. Associate a graph H with Q as follows. The nodes of H correspond to the quadrilaterals of Q, and two nodes are connected by an arc iff their quadrilaterals share a *vertex*. An example is

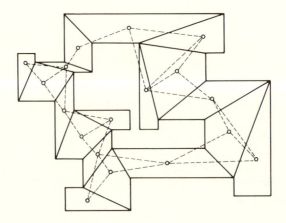

Fig. 5.24. Two nodes are adjacent in H if their quadrilaterals share a vertex.

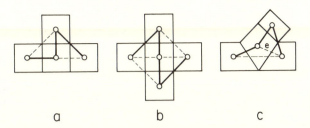

Fig. 5.25. Hamiltonian paths through balanced (a and b) and skewed (c) cycle quadrilaterals.

shown in Fig. 5.24. We claim that H is Hamiltonian, that is, it contains a cycle that touches each node exactly once.

First it is easy to see that the quadrilaterals that form a cycle in the dual of Q form a cycle in H as well, since quadrilaterals that share a diagonal share vertices. We now "stitch" the leaf nodes into this cycle. Let A, B, and C be three consecutive cycle quadrilaterals. If B is balanced it may have either one or two attached leaf quadrilaterals (Figs. 5.25a and 5.25b); if B is skewed, it may have one attached leaf quadrilateral (Fig. 5.25c). In all three cases it is possible to form a Hamiltonian path from A to C including B and any attached leaf nodes, as illustrated in the figures. Concatenation of these Hamiltonian paths for all cycle quadrilaterals playing the role of B can be seen to result in a Hamiltonian cycle γ for H by the following argument.

A leaf attached to a skew quadrilateral may be brought into the cycle in only one way, as shown in Fig. 5.25c. To reduce the graph to situations where choice remains, contract the edge e shown in Fig. 5.25c for every such skew quadrilateral, and delete the attached leaf node. Perform this contraction of e even if the skew quadrilateral has no attached leaf node. After contraction (or "squashing") of e, every edge of H incident to either endpoint of e is made incident to one node that "represents" both endpoints. Applying this transformation to the complicated section of H shown in Fig. 5.26a, for example, reduces it to the simpler fragment shown in Fig. 5.26b. After contraction of all such skew quadrilaterals, the resulting graph H' is a mixture of the two cases in Figs. 5.25a and 5.25b. Because no two leaf quadrilaterals share a common vertex by definition of a reduced quadrilateralization, and because the contraction process does not destroy this property, H' is a simple pasting together of the patterns in Figs. 5.25a and 5.25b. Note that the Hamiltonian path in those figures always use the edge(s) between a balanced cycle quadrilateral and its attached leaf node(s) (the vertical edges in Fig. 5.25). Contracting these edges produces a further reduced graph H'' which is always a simple cycle; see Fig. 5.26c. Now start with the obvious Hamiltonian cycle for H'', and "reverse" the transformations above. From H'' to H' there are choices available, but it is clear that a Hamiltonian cycle can always be achieved: because every leaf node is adjacent to three consecutive cycle nodes, an exit in the required direction is always available to a path traveling the vertical edge from cycle node to

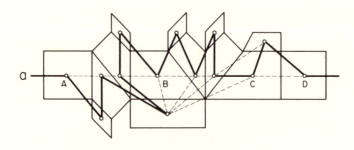

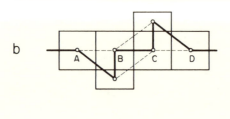

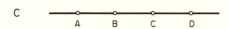

Fig. 5.26. A section of H with a Hamiltonian path (a), after contraction of skewed quadrilaterals (b), and after contraction of vertical edges (c).

leaf node. Reversal from H' to H is straightforward, as there is no choice. The result is the claimed Hamiltonian cycle γ of H.

Let q be the number of quadrilaterals in Q. Recall that by Lemma 5.2, $q = n/2$. If q is even, then every other edge of γ forms a perfect matching in H: a set of edges that is incident on each node exactly once. Each edge of the matching corresponds to a vertex of the polygon. Placing guards at the vertices associated with the edges of the matching covers the two quadrilaterals whose nodes are endpoints of the edge. Thus this guard placement covers the entire polygon with $q/2 = n/4 = \lfloor n/4 \rfloor$ guards.

Now suppose that q is odd. If the number of cycle quadrilaterals is even, then there must be at least one leaf quadrilateral. If the number of cycle quadrilaterals is odd, then by Lemma 5.8 there must be at least one skewed cycle quadrilateral. Both of these cases guarantee the existence of three quadrilaterals consecutive in γ that can be covered by one vertex guard. Place a guard at this vertex and delete the three nodes from γ, forming γ'. γ' has an even number of nodes and forms a Hamiltonian path. Again every other edge of γ' represents a perfect matching, and placing guards at the corresponding vertices results in complete coverage. The number of guards used is $1 + (q-3)/2 = (q-1)/2 = (n-2)/4 = \lfloor n/4 \rfloor$. □

As mentioned earlier, Aggarwal has also proven that $\lfloor n/4 \rfloor$ guards suffice

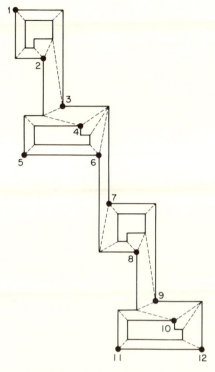

Fig. 5.27. A four-hole polygon of 44 vertices that requires 12 vertex guards.

to cover any orthogonal polygon with two holes. The most interesting aspect of the two-hole theorem is that $\lfloor n/4 \rfloor$ vertex guards do *not* suffice for polygons of two or more holes: Fig. 5.27 shows a four-hole polygon with $n = 44$ that require 12 vertex guards, 3 surrounding each hole.[5] However, $10 < \lfloor 44/4 \rfloor$ guards suffice if they are not restricted to vertices: movement of guards 2 and 8 horizontally to the right to the polygon boundary permits the elimination of guards 3 and 9. Extension of this example to multiple holes has led Aggarwal and Shermer to make the following conjectures (respectively).

CONJECTURE 5.3. $\lfloor 3n/11 \rfloor$ vertex guards are sufficient to cover any orthogonal polygon with any number of holes.

CONJECTURE 5.4. $\lfloor (n + h)/4 \rfloor$ vertex guards are sufficient to cover any orthogonal polygon with any number of holes.

---

5. Aggarwal (1984, p. 137), as modified by Shermer.

6

EXTERIOR VISIBILITY

6.1. INTRODUCTION

Derick Wood and Joseph Malkelvitch independently posed two interesting variants of the original Art Gallery Problem, which Wood dubbed *The Fortress Problem* and *The Prison Yard Problem*. The first asks for the number of guards needed to see the exterior of a polygon, and the second asks for the number needed to see both the exterior and the interior. The first has been satisfactorily solved, but the second remains tantalizingly open.

6.2. FORTRESS PROBLEM

How many vertex guards are needed to see the exterior of a polygon of n vertices? An exterior point y is seen by a guard at vertex z iff the segment zy does not intersect the interior of the polygon.

6.2.1. General Polygons

A convex n-gon establishes that $\lceil n/2 \rceil$ guards are occasionally necessary: a guard is needed on every other vertex. See Fig. 6.1. One might conjecture that in fact placing guards on every other vertex is always sufficient, even for non-convex polygons, but Fig. 6.2 (an example due to Shermer) demonstrates that this simple strategy will not work: placing guards on either the odd or the even indexed vertices leaves a portion of the exterior uncovered. It is, however, not difficult to establish the sufficiency of $\lceil n/2 \rceil$ using a 3-coloring of an exterior triangulation.

THEOREM 6.1 [O'Rourke and Wood 1983]. $\lceil n/2 \rceil$ vertex guards are necessary and sufficient to see the exterior of a polygon of n vertices.

Proof. Triangulate the portion of the plane that is inside of the convex hull but exterior to the polygon. Call the resulting graph of n nodes G''; see Fig.

146

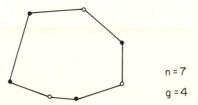

n = 7
g = 4

Fig. 6.1. A convex polygon requires $\lceil n/2 \rceil$ vertex guards (solid dots) to cover the exterior.

6.3a. Add an additional node v_∞ to G'' outside the hull and make it adjacent to every node on the hull; call this graph of $n+1$ nodes G' (Fig. 6.3b). Finally, choose some hull vertex x and split it into two vertices x' and x'', apportioning the previous connections from x between x' and x'' so that the graph remains planar, and adding a new arc so that v_∞ is adjacent to both x' and x''. Call the resulting graph of $n+2$ nodes G (Fig. 6.3c).

We claim that this graph is a triangulation graph of a polygon. This can be seen by "opening up" the convex hull at $x' - x''$ and moving v_∞ far enough away to permit all its connections to be straight lines. Since G is a triangulation graph, it can be 3-colored. The least frequently used color, say red, occurs no more than $\lfloor (n+2)/3 \rfloor$ times. If v_∞ is not colored red, then

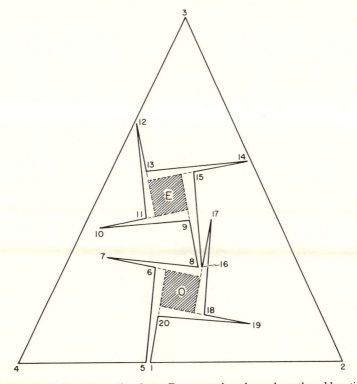

Fig. 6.2. Guards on the even vertices leave E uncovered, and guards on the odd vertices leave O uncovered.

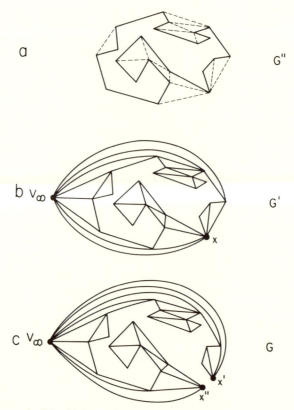

Fig. 6.3. The graph G in (c) is produced from a triangulation of the hull pockets (a) by connecting all hull vertices to v_∞ (b) and splitting some hull vertex x.

placing guards at the red nodes covers the exterior of the original polygon with $\lfloor (n+2)/3 \rfloor \leq \lceil n/2 \rceil$ vertex guards.

If, however, v_∞ is colored red, this strategy will not work, since no guard may be placed at v_∞ as it is not a vertex of the polygon. In this case, place guards with the second least frequently used color. Suppose the number of occurrences of the three colors are $a \leq b \leq c$, with $a + b + c = n + 2$. Since $a \geq 1$, $b + c \leq n + 1$. Thus $b \leq \lfloor (n+1)/2 \rfloor = \lceil n/2 \rceil$.

Finally, in either case, every triangle incident to v_∞ is dominated, and since v_∞ is not guarded, every other hull vertex must be guarded. These guards clearly cover the exterior outside the hull. The exterior inside the hull is covered by the usual 3-coloring argument.   □

6.2.2. Orthogonal Polygons

Although more guards are needed to cover the exterior than the interior of an arbitrary polygon ($\lceil n/2 \rceil$ versus $\lfloor n/3 \rfloor$), with orthogonal polygons the numbers required differ only slightly: $\lceil n/4 \rceil + 1$ for the exterior versus $\lfloor n/4 \rfloor$ for the interior.

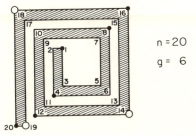

Fig. 6.4. An orthogonal spiral requires $\lceil n/4 \rceil + 1$ vertex guards (solid) to cover the exterior.

THEOREM 6.2 [Aggarwal 1983]. $\lceil n/4 \rceil + 1$ vertex guards are necessary and sufficient to see the exterior of an orthogonal polygon of n vertices.

Proof. Necessity follows from the spiral of $n = 4m$ vertices shown in Fig. 6.4. Starting from the interior of the spiral, it is clear that the vertices labeled 1, 4, 8, 12, 16, ..., $4(m-3)$ are an optimal choice for guard locations; a second optimal choice is 7, 11, 15, ..., $4m-1$. At the outside arm there is some choice where to place the last few guards. The first sequence can continue in one of two ways: either ..., $4(m-2)$, $4(m-1)$, $4m$ (the solid circles in Fig. 6.4), or ..., $4(m-2)$, $4(m-2)+2$, $4(m-1)+2$, $4m-1$ (the empty circles in the figure). In either case $m+1$ guards are used. Similar reasoning shows that $m+1$ guards are required for other choices of guard locations. If the spiral is extended by two more vertices, $n = 4m+2$, then $m+2$ guards are required. In all cases, $\lceil n/4 \rceil + 1$ guards are required.

The sufficiency proof follows almost directly from the L-shaped partition discussed in Sections 2.5 and 2.6. Given an n vertex orthogonal polygon P, remove the horizontal edge e with largest y-coordinate (or any one with maximum height if there are several), extend the two adjacent vertical edges upward and enclose the entire polygon with a bounding rectangle as illustrated in Fig. 6.5. The interior of this new $n+4$ vertex polygon P'

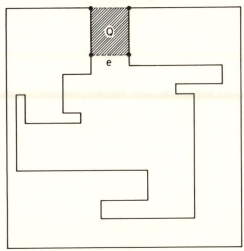

Fig. 6.5. The exterior of an orthogonal polygon may be converted into the interior of another by deleting the highest edge e and enclosing within a rectangle.

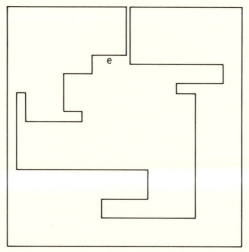

Fig. 6.6. An alternative enclosing strategy, used when n is divisible by 4.

coincides with the immediately surrounding exterior of P, except for the rectangle Q shaded in the figure, which is exterior to both.

The crucial observation is that the guard placement procedure described in Section 2.6 locates guards *only* on reflex vertices. Since the six new vertices of P' are all convex, guards covering the interior of P' will all be located on vertices of P. It should be clear that coverage of the immediate exterior of P by vertex guards implies coverage of the entire exterior: each side of the smallest rectangle enclosing P must have a guard on it, and these guards cover the infinite plane outside the rectangle. By Theorem 2.5, the interior of P' can be covered with $\lfloor (n+4)/4 \rfloor$ such guards. The region Q will need its own guard, yielding a total of $\lfloor n/4 \rfloor + 2$ guards. When $n \equiv 2 \pmod 4$, this formula is identical to $\lceil n/4 \rceil + 1$. Note that the guard placement must cover the entire infinite plane, as the bounding rectangle can be chosen to be arbitrarily large.

If $n \equiv 0 \pmod 4$, we have the freedom to augment P' by two vertices without increasing the number of guards, because of the presence of the floor function in Theorem 2.5. Therefore, modify P' to have $n+6$ vertices as shown in Fig. 6.6. Note that now the interior of P' and the immediate exterior of P exactly coincide: Q has been removed. P' can be covered with $\lfloor (n+6)/4 \rfloor = \lfloor n/4 \rfloor + 1$, which coincides with $\lceil n/4 \rceil + 1$ since $n \equiv 0 \pmod 4$. $\quad\square$

6.2.3. Guards in the Plane

The surprising asymmetry between Theorems 1.1 and 6.1, which respectively state that $\lfloor n/3 \rfloor$ guards suffice to cover the interior of a polygon but $\lceil n/2 \rceil$ may be needed to cover the exterior, can be removed by a loosening of restrictions on the guard placements. We will show in this section that

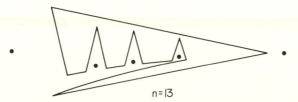

Fig. 6.7. $\lceil n/3 \rceil$ point guards are necessary to cover the exterior of a polygon.

$\lceil n/3 \rceil$ guards are necessary and sufficient to cover the exterior of a polygon if the guards are not restricted to vertices of the polygon, but may be located anywhere in the plane exterior to the polygon or on the polygon boundary. Such guards are called *point guards* to contrast with the vertex guards used in the previous section. This theorem restores a pleasing symmetry between interior and exterior coverage: $\lfloor n/3 \rfloor$ versus $\lceil n/3 \rceil$; even the floor and ceiling operators interchange naturally.

Necessity of $\lceil n/3 \rceil$ guards is established by turning the comb example of Fig. 1.2 "inside-out." Figure 6.7 shows a 13-vertex example that requires $5 = \lceil 13/3 \rceil$ guards. The general construction with k comb prongs has $n = 3k + 4$ vertices are requires $k + 2 = \lceil n/3 \rceil$ guards. Necessity for the other two possible values of $n \bmod 3$ are obtained by adding one or two extraneous vertices to this example.

Sufficiency of $\lceil (n + 1)/3 \rceil$ guards is easily established.

LEMMA 6.1. $\lceil (n + 1)/3 \rceil$ point guards suffice to cover the exterior of an n vertex polygon P.

Proof. Rotate P so that vertex a is uniquely highest and b uniquely lowest, and add two vertices λ and ρ below the lowest vertex of P, and far enough away to both see a. See Fig. 6.8. Triangulate the interior of the convex hull exterior to the polygon, and add diagonals from λ and ρ to every hull vertex visible to them. Finally split vertex a in two. The result is a triangulated

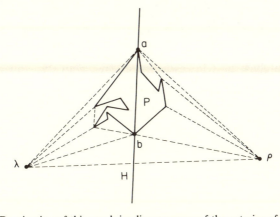

Fig. 6.8. Domination of this graph implies coverage of the exterior of the polygon.

polygon of $n + 3$ vertices. Cover this polygon with $\lfloor (n+3)/3 \rfloor = \lceil (n+1)/3 \rceil$ guards by Theorem 1.1. We now argue that these guards cover the entire exterior.

Clearly the portion interior to the hull is covered. Now consider the left half-plane H determined by a line through a and b. If a guard is assigned to λ, then it covers all of H exterior to the hull. If λ has no guard, then since every hull edge in the left chain between a and b forms a triangle with λ, at least one endpoint of each hull edge must have a guard. But then these guards cover the exterior in H. Applying the same argument to the right half-plane establishes the lemma. $\square$

One of the longest proofs in the first draft of this book was devoted to removing "a third of a guard" from this lemma. The proof followed the same general approach as that used in Lemma 6.1, but difficulties arise because combinatorial dominance of arbitrary exterior triangulations of the type just considered cannot suffice to establish the theorem, as shown in Fig. 6.9. Here $n = 6$, so $\lceil n/3 \rceil = 2$, but $\lceil (n+1)/3 \rceil = 3$. The triangle abc requires one guard in any combinatorial domination. But then two further guards will be required regardless of how the exterior is triangulated. The figure shows that indeed only two point guards are necessary, one at each of λ and ρ, but these guards represent a combinatorial dominance only if the exterior is retriangulated. Our proof involved a long cascade of cases, and an abandonment of combinatorics for geometry at a critical junction (Aggarwal 1984). Fortunately, this theorem has gone the way of Chvátal's theorem and the Kahn, Klawe, Kleitman theorem in that a proof far simpler than the original has been found. Recently Shermer discovered a concise coloring argument, which we present below.

THEOREM 6.3 [Aggarwal and O'Rourke 1984]. $\lceil n/3 \rceil$ point guards are sometimes necessary and always sufficient to cover the exterior of a polygon P of $n > 3$ vertices.

Proof [Shermer 1986]. Necessity has already been established. If P is convex, then two guards placed sufficiently far away on opposite sides of P suffice to cover the exterior. Since $n > 3$, $2 \le \lceil n/3 \rceil$.

Suppose then that P has at least one pocket—that is, an exterior polygon interior to the hull and bound by a hull edge. Rotate P so that a and b are uniquely the highest and lowest vertices, respectively, and add two new

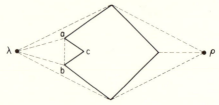

Fig. 6.9. A graph that requires 3 combinatorial guards for dominance, but only 2 point guards are needed for coverage of the exterior.

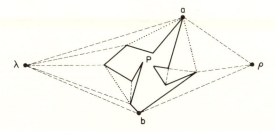

Fig. 6.10. If the number of hull vertices is even, this graph is 3-colorable.

vertices λ and ρ on opposite sides of P and sufficiently distant so that they both can see both a and b. Triangulate the pockets of the hull, and connect λ and ρ to all visible hull vertices, as shown in Fig. 6.10. The strategy is as follows. Since $\lceil n/3 \rceil = \lfloor (n+2)/3 \rfloor$, if we could show that the constructed triangulation graph G were 3-colorable, placing guards with the least frequently used color would establish the theorem via the same argument for exterior coverage used in Lemma 6.1. But G is not always 3-colorable: the graph in Fig. 6.9 requires four colors. Shermer's idea is to modify the graph so that it is always 3-colorable.

Let h be the number of hull vertices. Two cases will be considered: h even and h odd.

Case (h even). G is always 3-colorable in this case, regardless of the choice of λ and ρ. To see this, color the hull vertices alternately with colors 1 and 2. Then λ and ρ may be colored 3. Each pocket lid (shown dotted in Fig. 6.10) is an edge of the polygon forming the pocket. With the constraint that the lid is colored $(1, 2)$, a pocket polygon may be 3-colored as in Section 1.3.1. The result is a 3-coloring of G, implying domination with $\lfloor (n+2)/3 \rfloor$ guards. By the argument in the proof of Lemma 6.1, these guards cover the entire exterior.

Case (h odd). The above approach will not work, as the hull cannot be 2-colored. Let yz be a pocket lid, and let x be the apex of the triangle in the pocket supported by yx. Now orient P and choose ρ so that

(1) ρ can see x,
(2) $x\rho$ is not parallel to any polygon edge, and
(3) ρ is distant enough to see an "antipodal" pair of vertices a and b, vertices that admit parallel lines of support.

Condition (2) is imposed so that a and b are ensured to become uniquely highest and lowest as before. Clearly it is always possible to choose such a ρ. Place λ on the opposite side of P as in the previous case. See Fig. 6.11. The quadrilateral ρyxz is convex by construction. Delete diagonal yz from G, and add diagonal ρx. (This is the necessary retriangulation mentioned earlier.) If we now consider x part of the hull, we have increased the number of hull vertices to be even. Now proceed as in the previous case. Color the cycle of hull vertices and x colors 1 and 2 in alternation, color λ

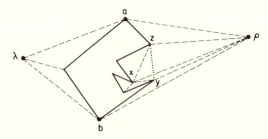

Fig. 6.11. If the number of hull vertices is odd, one vertex x within the hull is connected to ρ to make a 3-colorable graph.

and ρ color 3, and 3-color all pocket polygons. Dominate G with $\lfloor (n + 2)/3 \rfloor$ guards. The argument for exterior coverage used in the proof of Lemma 6.1 must be modified slightly, since it may be that neither endpoint of the hull edge yz is assigned a guard. But in that case, x will be assigned a guard, and the complete exterior is still covered.   □

Note that the proof uses at most two guards in the plane strictly exterior to the polygon; the remainder are located at vertices.

6.3. PRISON YARD PROBLEM

How many vertex guards are needed to simultaneously see the exterior and interior of a polygon P of n vertices? An interior point x is seen by a guard at vertex z if the segment zx does not intersect the exterior of P, and an exterior point y is seen by z if zy does not intersect the interior of P. It should be emphasized that the guards are restricted to vertices; the problem is quite a bit different (and easier) if the guards are permitted to be located arbitrarily far away from the polygon. Permitting the guards to be anywhere on the boundary of the polygon does not seem to affect the problem's complexity, so we will only consider vertex guards.

6.3.1. General Polygons

The worst case known is the same as that for the fortress problem: a convex n-gon (Fig. 6.1). This establishes that $\lceil n/2 \rceil$ guards are occasionally necessary. The only sufficiency result so far obtained is rather weak and inelegant:

THEOREM 6.4 [O'Rourke 1983]. For a multiply-connected polygon of n vertices, r of which are reflex, and h of which are on the convex hull of the polygon,

$$\min\left(\lceil n/2 \rceil + r,\ \lfloor (n + \lceil h/2 \rceil)/2 \rfloor,\ \lfloor 2n/3 \rfloor\right)$$

vertex guards are sufficient to see both the interior and exterior. Note that,

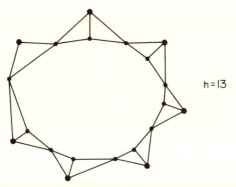

Fig. 6.12. Addition of $\lceil h/2 \rceil$ nodes exterior to the hull leads to $n/2 + h/4$ guards (modulo floors and ceilings).

ignoring ceilings and floors, the above formula may be written in the more revealing form

$$n/2 + \min\,(r,\, h/4,\, n/6)$$

Proof.   Each of the three formulas is derived by a separate method.

(1) $\lceil n/2 \rceil + r$

Use Theorem 6.1 to cover the exterior with $\lceil n/2 \rceil$ guards, and Theorem 1.5 to cover the interior when $r \geq 1$. If $r = 0$, the polygon is convex and $\lceil n/2 \rceil$ clearly suffice.

(2) $\lfloor (n + \lceil h/2 \rceil)/2 \rfloor$

Triangulate the interior of the convex hull, including both the interior of the polygon and the exterior within the hull. Add $\lceil h/2 \rceil$ new vertices outside the hull, each (except for perhaps one) adjacent to three hull vertices, as shown in Fig. 6.12. The resulting graph is planar and so may be 4-colored. Place guards at nodes colored with the two least frequently used colors. Together these colors cannot be used more than half of the total number of vertices—that is, not more than $\lfloor (n + \lceil h/2 \rceil)/2 \rfloor$. Since every triangle has three differently colored vertices, at least one guard is in the corner of each triangle. If any of the outside-hull vertices are assigned guards, place the guard on the middle of its three adjacent hull vertices, or either one if only adjacent to two. The inside of the hull is covered because it is partitioned into triangles; the exterior of the hull is covered because every hull edge has a guard on at least one endpoint.

(3) $\lfloor 2n/3 \rfloor$

Triangulate the interior of the hull as above. Add a single new vertex v_∞ outside the hull, and connect it to every hull vertex (Fig. 6.13). The resulting graph is planar and can be 4-colored. Place guards on the two least frequently used colors not matching the color assigned to v_∞. Suppose the

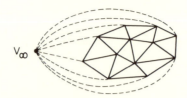

Fig. 6.13. Connecting every hull vertex to v_∞ leads to $\lfloor 2n/3 \rfloor$ guards.

number of nodes colored i is c_i, so that

$$c_1 \leq c_2 \leq c_3 \leq c_4, \tag{1}$$

$$c_1 + c_2 + c_3 + c_4 = n + 1. \tag{2}$$

If v_∞ is colored 1, 2, 3, or 4, the two colors used for guards occur $(c_2 + c_3)$, $(c_1 + c_3)$, $(c_1 + c_2)$, and $(c_1 + c_2)$ times, respectively. Clearly the first case is the worst because of the inequality (1). In this case, since $c_1 \geq 1$, Equation (2) becomes

$$c_2 + c_3 + c_4 \leq n$$

and Equation (1) implies that $c_2 + c_3 \leq \lfloor 2n/3 \rfloor$.

Now the argument is the same as above: every triangle has at least one guard at a vertex, and the exterior triangles are likewise covered without using a guard at v_∞. $\square$

If the guards are not restricted to lie on the boundary of the polygon, then it is easy to establish $\lfloor n/2 \rfloor + 1$ sufficiency: triangulate the interior of the hull, and add two vertices sufficiently far outside the hull to connect every hull vertex by a straight line (as in Fig. 6.10, but with interior triangulation as well); 4-color the resulting graph and place guards on the two least frequently used colors.

It seems, however, that this freedom to place guards outside of the polygon is not needed:

CONJECTURE 6.1. $\lceil n/2 \rceil$ vertex guards are sufficient to see the interior and exterior of a polygon of n vertices.

Proving or disproving this conjecture is one of the most interesting open problems in this field.

Before proceeding to orthogonal polygons, it will be instructive to prove $\lfloor 2n/3 \rfloor$ sufficiency by a different method. Cover the exterior with $\lceil n/2 \rceil$ guards according to Theorem 6.1. Now triangulate the interior of the polygon, and remove all vertices assigned a guard and their incident edges. The resulting graph may be disconnected (as in Fig. 6.14), but it will have a total of no more than $n - \lceil n/2 \rceil = \lfloor n/2 \rfloor$ nodes. Further delete any vertices or edges of this graph that are not part of any triangle; these clearly are covered from all sides by guards. Now apply the interior visibility argument: 3-color and place guards at the least frequently used color. Note that although the components are not necessarily triangulation graphs of simple

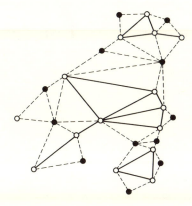

Fig. 6.14. The dashed edges are incident on a guarded vertex (solid dots).

polygons, they are nevertheless 3-colorable, as each is a subgraph of such a graph. This requires at most an additional $\lfloor n_i/3 \rfloor$ guards for each connected component of n_i nodes; note that $n_i \geq 3$. Thus the total number of guards required is $\lceil n/2 \rceil + \lfloor \lfloor n/2 \rfloor /3 \rfloor$. This formula equals $\lfloor 2n/3 \rfloor$, except when $n \equiv 1 \pmod 6$, in which case it equals $\lfloor 2n/3 \rfloor + 1$. A similar argument will be used in the next section.

6.3.2. Orthogonal Polygons

Clearly the separate interior and exterior visibility results for orthogonal polygons (Theorems 2.2 and 6.2) may be combined to yield $\lfloor n/4 \rfloor + \lceil n/4 \rceil + 1 \leq \lceil n/2 \rceil + 1$ sufficiency for vertex guards. This straightforward combination of interior and exterior results may be improved slightly by following the above sketch of the alternate $\lfloor 2n/3 \rfloor$ proof. Interestingly, the proof employs both methods known for achieving the interior orthogonal result.

THEOREM 6.5 [O'Rourke 1983]. $\lfloor 7n/16 \rfloor + 5$ vertex guards are sufficient to see both the interior and exterior of a simple orthogonal polygon.

Proof.   Cover the exterior with $\lceil n/4 \rceil + 1$ guards according to Theorem 6.2. Now partition the interior into convex quadrilaterals as guaranteed by Theorem 2.1. Discard every edge that has a guard at one of its endpoints. This may disconnect the graph, but the total number of vertices is no more than $n - (\lceil n/4 \rceil + 1)$; see Fig. 6.15. Further delete all vertices and edges that are not part of any quadrilateral; this is justified since guards cover all sides of such edges and around all such vertices. Four-color the pieces (as was done in the proof of Theorem 2.2) and place guards on the least frequently used color. Each piece of n_i nodes will need no more than $\lfloor n_i/4 \rfloor$ guards; note that $n_i \geq 4$. The total number of guards used is

$$\lceil n/4 \rceil + 1 + \left\lfloor \frac{n - \lceil n/4 \rceil - 1}{4} \right\rfloor.$$

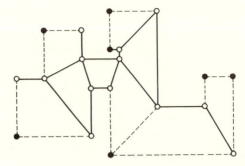

Fig. 6.15. The dashed edges are adjacent to a guard as in Fig. 6.14.

This expression is no larger than $\lfloor 7n/16 \rfloor + 5$; the constant 5 can be reduced for certain values of n mod 16. $\quad\Box$

This result appears to be nearly as weak as the $\lfloor 2n/3 \rfloor$ result for arbitrary polygons.

6.4. ALGORITHMS

Because the partitioning theorems in this chapter employ techniques from previous chapters, such as triangulation, 3-coloring, and L-shape partitioning, few new algorithmic questions are raised. The only new technique used is 4-coloring of a planar graph. Unfortunately, Appel and Haken's proof leads to a rather complex $O(n^2)$ algorithm (Appel and Haken 1977; Frederickson 1984). Using this algorithm with algorithms discussed in previous chapters, we arrive at the worst-case time complexities shown in Table 6.1. Here $O(T)$ is the time complexity for triangulation; the current best result is $T = n \log \log n$.

Table 6.1

Problem	Techniques	Guards	Time
Fortress			
general	triangulation, 3-coloring	$\lceil n/2 \rceil$	$O(T)$
orthogonal	L-shaped partition	$\lceil n/4 \rceil + 1$	$O(T)$
Prison Yard			
general	exterior	$\lceil n/2 \rceil + r$	$O(T)$
	triangulation, 4-coloring	$\lfloor (n + \lceil h/2 \rceil)/2 \rfloor$	$O(n^2)$
	triangulation, 4-coloring	$\lfloor 2n/3 \rfloor$	$O(n^2)$
	exterior, triang., 3-coloring	$\lfloor 2n/3 \rfloor + 1$	$O(T)$
orthogonal	exterior, quadrilateralization,		
	4-coloring	$\lfloor 7n/16 \rfloor + 5$	$O(T)$

Although 4-coloring is a time consuming process, several linear algorithms are known for 5-coloring (Chiba *et al.* 1981; Frederickson 1984). Using one of these algorithms improves the speed from $O(n^2)$ to $O(T)$ in two instances in the table, but increased the number of guards: since guards must be placed with three out of the five colors to guarantee that every triangle receives a guard, the number of guards becomes $\lfloor 3(n + \lceil h/2 \rceil)/5 \rfloor$ and $\lfloor 3n/4 \rfloor$, respectively.

6.5. NEGATIVE RESULTS

Two natural approaches to solving the prison yard problem lead to conjectures which, if true, would either settle the problem or represent a significant advance. This section formulates these conjectures and presents counterexamples.

6.5.1. Triangulation

Triangulate the interior of an n-vertex polygon (including the interior of any holes) and the exterior inside the hull. Now extend rays to infinity from each hull vertex.

*Conjecture. Each triangle and each unbounded region of the above described figure can be dominated by $\lceil n/2 \rceil$ combinatorial vertex guards.

If this conjecture were true, then the prison yard problem would be solved for polygons with holes. Figure 6.16 is, however, a counterexample. There is just one Hamiltonian cycle of the triangulation: the convex hull. Thus this figure can only arise from a convex decagon, which can be easily covered

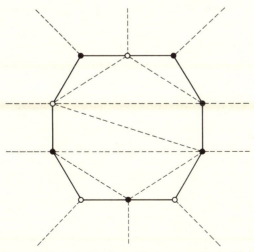

Fig. 6.16. A 10-node graph that requires 6 combinatorial guards (solid dots) for domination.

with five guards. But since there exists a triangulation of this decagon (as shown) that cannot be dominated by five guards, one cannot hope to prove $\lceil n/2 \rceil$ sufficiency starting with an arbitrary triangulation.

6.5.2. Convex Partitioning

Another method of reducing the problem to combinatorics is to form a convex partitioning of the plane from the n-vertex polygon. Such partitions of the interior of the polygon were considered by Chazelle (Chazelle 1980) and discussed in Section 1.4. At each vertex of the polygon, extend a ray that bisects the angle at the vertex outward if the vertex is convex and inward if it is reflex. The ray is extended to its first intersection with a polygon edge on another ray. The bisection procedure may be applied to the vertices in any order. Chazelle proved (for interior partitionings) that the resulting graph can be made cubic (each node has degree 3) by slightly varying the ray angles to avoid "coincidences." The same result holds for the interior and exterior partitioning. An example is shown in Fig. 6.17.

LEMMA 6.5. Each n-vertex polygon (with or without holes) induces a cubic convex partitioning of the plane into $n + 1$ regions.

Proof. That the partition can be chosen so that its graph is cubic follows from Chazelle's method (Chazelle 1980). That the number of regions is $n + 1$ is established by the following argument. Initially there are $h + 2$ regions: the exterior of the polygon, its interior, and the interior of each of the h holes. The first ray towards the exterior of the polygon does not increase the number of regions; similarly the first ray from each of the h holes towards the exterior of the holes cannot increase the number of

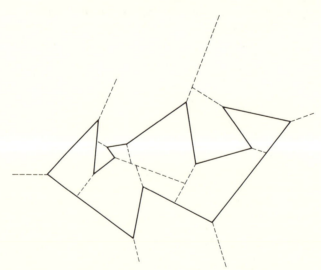

Fig. 6.17. A convex partitioning of the plane induced by a polygon; here $n = 14$ and 15 regions result.

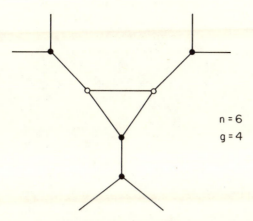

Fig. 6.18. A convex partitioning of 6 vertices that requires 4 combinatorial guards (solid dots) for domination.

regions. Each of these $h + 1$ cuts can be thought of as reducing the multiply-connectedness by 1 without increasing the number of regions. Each of the remaining $n - (h + 1)$ cuts increments the number of regions by 1. So the total number of regions is $(h + 2) + [n - (h + 1)] = n + 1$. $\square$

Now each vertex of the original polygon sits at the junction of precisely three convex regions. A guard placed at a vertex covers all three regions entirely, since they are convex. So the task is to select $\lceil n/2 \rceil$ vertices, each covering three regions, such that all $n + 1$ convex regions are covered by at least one vertex. This scheme leads to the following conjecture.

*Conjecture. Any convex partitioning of the plane into $n' = n + 1$ regions can be dominated with $\lfloor n'/2 \rfloor = \lceil n/2 \rceil$ vertex guards.

This conjecture is both stronger and weaker than what is needed to prove $\lceil n/2 \rceil$ sufficiency for the prison yard problem. It is stronger in that its claim is for *all* convex partitions, but those arising from the angle bisection technique represent only a subclass (for instance, an n-vertex polygon will generate a partition with no more than $2n$ edges). It is weaker in that only the polygon vertices are candidates for guard location: ray-ray intersections may lay arbitrarily far outside of the polygon. Nevertheless, the conjecture would represent an advance if true, and would be interesting in its own right. Figure 6.18 shows a simple counterexample, however. There are $n = 6$ vertices and $2n = 12$ edges, but $g = 4 > \lceil n/2 \rceil = 3$ guards are necessary. This figure was derived from its non-Hamiltonian dual graph, which can be seen to have no perfect matching after three regions are covered by one guard, by Tutte's theorem (Tutte 1947; Harary 1969).[1] The partitioning in the

---

1. A *matching* is a collection of edges that share no nodes. A *perfect matching* is one that matches every node. Tutte's theorem states that a graph G has a perfect matching iff it has an even number of nodes and there is no set S of nodes such that the number of odd components of $G - S$ exceeds $|S|$. If there is an S such that the number of components (even or odd) of $G - S$ exceeds $|S|$, then G is non-Hamiltonian.

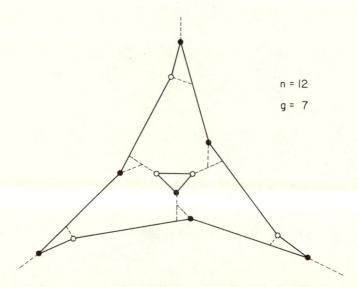

Fig. 6.19. A convex partitioning of 12 vertices that requires 7 combinatorial guards (solid dots) for domination.

figure could never arise from the bisection process, however, as that process always produces regions with at least three bounding edges each. This suggests tightening the conjecture to convex partitions whose dual graphs have degree at least 3. Again, however, a counterexample can be derived from a non-Hamiltonian dual that has no perfect matching after deletion of three nodes with one guard, as shown in Fig. 6.19. This figure has $n = 12$ vertices, $n' = n + 1 = 13$ regions, and $21 < 2n$ total edges. It requires $g = 7 > \lceil n/2 \rceil = 6$ guards. In addition, this partitioning *can* arise from the bisection process: from a polygon with one hole, as shown in the figure.

This last figure definitely establishes that this attempted reduction to combinatorics cannot prove $\lceil n/2 \rceil$ sufficiency for multiply-connected polygons; it remains possible that the conjecture holds for convex partitions arising from polygons with no holes.

6.5.3. Monotone Polygons

We will end this pessimistic section on a positive note by showing that convex partitions lead to a proof of the prison yard conjecture for the special case of monotone polygons.

THEOREM 6.6 [O'Rourke 1984]. $\lceil n/2 \rceil$ guards are occasionally necessary and always sufficient to see the interior and exterior of a monotone polygon of n vertices.

Proof. Assume that the polygon is monotone with respect to the y axis. It will be no loss of generality to assume that the vertices extreme in the y direction are unique; call the highest a and the lowest b. Partition the plane

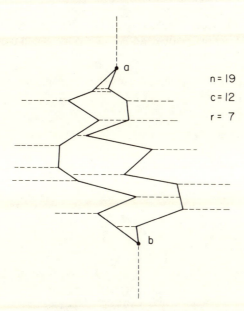

n = 19
c = 12
r = 7

Fig. 6.20. A convex partitioning of the plane induced by a monotone polygon with 12 convex and 7 reflex vertices.

into convex regions as follows. Draw vertical rays from b and a towards the exterior of the polygon, and draw horizontal rays from each convex vertex, again towards the exterior. Finally, draw horizontal segments from each reflex vertex towards the interior of the polygon to the polygon's opposite chain. See Fig. 6.20.

Note that the exterior regions form a ring around the polygon, with each pair of adjacent exterior regions sharing a convex vertex. Thus, if there are c convex vertices, the exterior regions can be covered with $\lceil c/2 \rceil$ guards, one on every other convex vertex. We will use the convention that a is assigned a guard; clearly we have that flexibility. The interior regions form a vertical stack, with each pair of adjacent regions sharing a reflex vertex. If there are r reflex vertices, then there are at most $r + 1$ interior regions; this maximum is achieved when no two reflex vertices have the same y-coordinate. Because a guard is placed at a, the top interior region is already covered, leaving r to be covered. These can be covered with $\lceil r/2 \rceil$ guards, one on every other reflex vertex (sorted by their y-coordinate, not their position in the polygon's boundary).

Now $n = c + r$, and we have just established that all regions can be covered with $\lceil c/2 \rceil + \lceil r/2 \rceil$ guards. If at least one of c or r is even, then this formula accords with $\lceil n/2 \rceil$, and we are finished. If both are odd, however, the two ceilings yield one more guard than $\lceil n/2 \rceil$. But, since c is odd, b must be assigned a guard either clockwise from a or counterclockwise from a, choosing every other one. Therefore, we can assume that b is assigned a guard when c is odd. Now the bottom interior region is covered, and only

$r - 1$ contiguous interior regions need to be covered. Since $\lceil c/2 \rceil +$ $\lceil (r-1)/2 \rceil = \lceil n/2 \rceil$ when both c and r are odd, we have established the lemma. □

Several miscellaneous problems involving exterior visibility will be considered in Chapter 10.

7

VISIBILITY GRAPHS

7.1. INTRODUCTION

It is my belief that some of the fundamental unsolved problems involving visibility in computational geometry will not be solved until the combinatorial structure of visibility is more fully understood. Perhaps the purest condensation of this structure is a *visibility graph*. The nodes of a visibility graph correspond to geometric components, such as vertices or edges, and two nodes are connected by an arc of the graph if the components can "see" one another, perhaps under some restricted form of visibility. The canonical example is the vertex visibility graph of a polygon: its nodes correspond to the vertices of a polygon, and its arcs to lines of visibility between vertices in the interior or along the boundary of the polygon. No characterization of these graphs is available, and in fact almost no general properties are known. ElGindy has pioneered their investigation in his thesis (ElGindy 1985). He obtained a specialized result by restricting the class of graphs to maximal outerplanar graphs. This result is presented in Section 7.2. Although this result is very restricted, it is the most general obtained to date.

Section 7.3 explores a different type of visibility graph: the nodes correspond to edges of an orthogonal polygon, and two nodes are connected by an arc if their edges can see one another along a line orthogonal to the edges. These graphs are especially simple for polygons in "general position": then there are always precisely two components, both of which are trees. A partial characterization of tree pairs is presented in Section 7.3.

Finally, in Section 7.4, visibility graphs for a set of disconnected vertical line segments are studied. Here a node is associated with each segment, and arcs correspond to horizontal visibility. In this case a very pleasing characterization theorem has been obtained by Wismath (1985), and independently by Tamassia and Tollis (1985). We present Wismath's proof.

The investigation of visibility graphs is in its infancy, and new results can be expected not only for the graphs discussed in this chapter, but also for other types of visibility graphs.

7.2. VERTEX VISIBILITY GRAPHS

As just mentioned, two nodes are adjacent in the vertex visibility graph (or just "visibility graph" when no confusion is possible) of a polygon if and only if the line segment determined by the associated vertices is at no point exterior to the polygon. Thus the connections represent lines of sight between vertices. For a polygon of n vertices, the vertex visibility graph can have as many as $\binom{n}{2}$ arcs, when the polygon is convex and the graph is the complete graph K_n (Fig. 7.1a), or as few as $2n - 3$ arcs, when the polygon has $n - 3$ reflex vertices (Fig. 7.1b). Although visibility graphs seem "abundant,"[1] not every graph of e edges with $2n - 3 \leq e \leq n(n - 1)/2$ is a visibility graph. Consider the $n = 5$ node graph G shown in Fig. 7.2a with $e = 8 > 2n - 3$ edges. We present now an *ad hoc* argument showing that it is not the visibility graph of any polygon.

The vertex v_1 is adjacent to all other vertices. This implies that the polygon is a *fan*: a star polygon with v_1 in the kernel. It is clear that the arcs corresponding to the boundary edges of the polygon form a Hamiltonian cycle of the graph, since the definition of visibility permits the endpoints of each polygon boundary edge to see one another. There are four distinct Hamiltonian cycles in G, as illustrated in Fig. 7.2b; but due to the symmetry of G, all four lead to the same structure of internal visibility lines. So we can restrict our attention to Fig. 7.2a. Because v_2 can see v_5, v_1 cannot be reflex. Thus (v_1, v_2, v_5) forms an ear of the polygon. Because v_3 and v_4 can see v_1, v_2 and v_5 must be convex, as illustrated in Fig. 7.2c. Vertex v_4 must be reflex to block v_3's line of sight to v_5. But this implies that v_2 can see v_4, an arc not in G. This establishes that G is not a visibility graph of a polygon.

One of the few general properties of visibility graphs that can be stated is the obvious one used in the preceding paragraph: a visibility graph must contain at least one Hamiltonian cycle, corresponding to the boundary of the polygon. Unfortunately, the problem of deciding whether an arbitrary graph contains a Hamiltonian cycle is NP-complete (Garey and Johnson

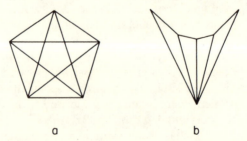

a   b

Fig. 7.1. Visibility graphs can have as many as $n(n - 1)/2$ edges (a) or as few as $2n - 3$ (b).

---

1. How abundant is not known. It is not even known if the number of visibility graphs is $\Omega(n^2)$.

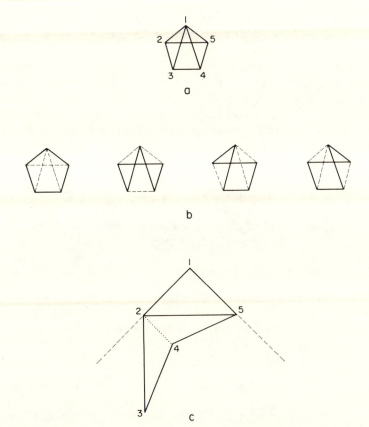

Fig. 7.2. A graph that is not a visibility graph (a), its Hamiltonian cycles (b), and an attempted embedding (c).

1979). It is an interesting open question to see if the problem of finding a Hamiltonian cycle in a visibility graph remains intractable.

Given this uncertainty surrounding the complexity of finding a Hamiltonian cycle, ElGindy and Avis posed the problem of determining whether a given graph can be embedded in the plane as a visibility graph with a *given* Hamiltonian cycle forming the boundary of the polygon. Equivalently, we can assume the vertices of the given graph are labeled $1, \ldots, n$ such that the path $(1, \ldots, n)$ forms a Hamiltonian cycle. We call the problem of determining (if possible) an embedding for such a labeled graph the visibility graph *reconstruction* problem. Even in this (apparently) easier form, the problem remains unsolved. However, ElGindy obtained an interesting result by further specialization.

7.2.1. Maximal Outerplanar Graphs

Maximal outerplanar graphs are an important subclass of planar graphs with many applications. A graph is *outerplanar* if it can be embedded in the plane so that all of its nodes lie on the exterior face. In our setting this exterior face is the boundary of the polygon. A *maximal outerplanar graph* (or *mop*) is an outerplanar graph such that the addition of a single arc results in a graph that is not outerplanar. ElGindy showed that every mop is a visibility graph, and provided an algorithm for constructing a representative embedding (ElGindy 1985).

We will only consider mops of at least three nodes. The arcs on the exterior face will be called *exterior arcs*; all others are *interior arcs*. We will first state a few properties of mops.

LEMMA 7.1.   A graph is a mop if it is a triangulation graph of a polygon.

Proof. Let G be a triangulation graph of a polygon. G is clearly outerplanar. No internal diagonals may be added without crossing other diagonals, and any external diagonal necessarily hides a vertex from the exterior face. Thus G is maximal, and a mop. This establishes the lemma in one direction.

Let G be a mop. We establish that:

(1)   There is exactly one vertex adjacent to both endpoints of each exterior edge.
(2)   There are exactly two vertices adjacent to both endpoints of each interior edge.
(3) G has no cutpoints.

Together these three conditions imply that G is a triangulation graph of a polygon.

Let e be an exterior edge of G, and suppose in contradiction to (1), vertices x and y are both adjacent to both endpoints of e. In an embedding of G, x and y must lie in the same half-plane determined by e, otherwise e would not be exterior. But then either G is non-planar (Fig. 7.3a), or one of x or y is interior (Fig. 7.3b) so G is not outerplanar. In either case, we reach a contradiction, establishing (1).

Let e be an interior edge of G. By the same argument as above, there can be at most one vertex in each of the two half-planes determined by e

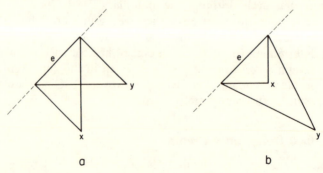

Fig. 7.3.   The endpoints of an exterior edge e can both be adjacent to only one vertex.

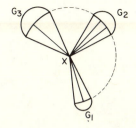

Fig. 7.4. If x is a cutpoint, then arcs (dashed) may be added to G.

adjacent to both endpoints, and there must be one in each since e is interior. This establishes (2).

Let x be a cutpoint[2] of G, and let $G_1, \ldots, G_k$, $k \geq 2$, be the components of $G - x$. Then if G is embedded with G_i angularly adjacent to G_{i+1} about x, an arc may be added between G_i and G_{i+1} for $i = 1, \ldots, k - 1$ without making x internal; see Fig. 7.4. Thus G is not maximally outerplanar, establishing (3) by contradiction.

Finally, (1) and (2) show that G is composed entirely of triangles, and (3) shows that the boundary is a polygon. □

Now that the class of mops has been revealed to be the familiar class of polygon triangulation graphs, the next property we need is obvious.

LEMMA 7.2. A mop G has a unique Hamiltonian cycle.

Proof. The exterior edges of G correspond to the boundary of the polygon, and clearly form a Hamiltonian cycle. Since each interior edge cuts the polygon in two pieces, the inclusion of an interior edge in a Hamiltonian cycle would force the path into one piece or the other without possibility of return. Thus the exterior edge Hamiltonian cycle is unique. □

It is easy to find the unique Hamiltonian cycle in linear time from any standard representation of G (Beyer *et al.* 1979). Thus for mops the usually difficult problem of identifying a Hamiltonian cycle becomes easy.

We may now state ElGindy's result.

THEOREM 7.1 [ElGindy 1985]. Every mop G is a vertex visibility graph of a monotone polygon.

Following ElGindy, we will establish this theorem by presenting an embedding algorithm and proving its correctness. First we will present a small example to illustrate the main ideas.

Consider the mop G of seven nodes shown in Fig. 7.5a. We first embed the triangle $(1, 2, 6)$ with $(1, 2)$ horizontal. We then embed 7 horizontally between 1 and 6 and above the $(2, 6)$ line, and embed 4 between 6 and 2

---

2. A cutpoint x of a graph G is a node whose removal (deletion of x and all incident edges) disconnects the graph. The remainder of G is denoted by $G - x$.

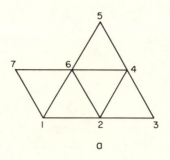

a

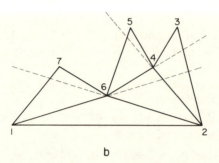

b

Fig. 7.5. A mop (a) and an embedding as a visibility graph (b).

and above the $(1, 6)$ line; see Fig. 7.5b. Finally, 5 is embedded between 6 and 4 and above the $(2, 4)$ line, and 3 is embedded between 4 and 2 and above the $(6, 4)$ line. The result is a polygon monotone with respect to the horizontal with G as its visibility graph.

The algorithm can be phrased as a recursive procedure for embedding a triangle. Its three inputs are B, a bottom bounding line segment, and l and r, the left and right embedded vertices forming the base of the triangle. The procedure marks each vertex it embeds; initially all vertices are unmarked.

procedure *triangle*(B, l, r)
   $m \leftarrow$ a point ε above the midpoint of B.
   if there exists an unmarked vertex v adjacent to both l and r **then**
      Erase (l, r) [unless $(l, r) = (1, 2)$].
      Embed v at m and mark v.
      Draw (l, v) and (v, r).
      Update adjacency lists.
      $B \leftarrow (v, r)$ extended between l and v.
      triangle(B, l, v).
      $B \leftarrow (l, v)$ extended between v and r.
      triangle(B, v, r).

The procedure is called initially with $l = 1$, $r = 2$, and $B = (1, 2)$. We now argue for its correctness.

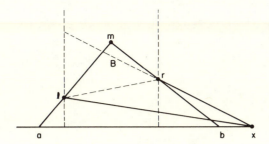

Fig. 7.6. The trapezoid *abrl* must be empty of vertices.

Consider a particular invocation of *triangle*(B, l, r). Assume as an induction hypothesis that the algorithm has performed correctly so far. Then (l, r) represents an exterior edge of the polygon embedded so far, and so both are adjacent to exactly one vertex x. B is determined by xr. Let a and b be the intersection points of (m, l) and (m, r) with the polygon boundary when extended, as illustrated in Fig. 7.6. Then the trapezoid (a, b, r, l) must be empty of embedded vertices: x is outside since m is above B, and any other veretx inside would see both l and r, contradicting the uniqueness of x. Thus m is only visible to l and r, correctly embedding the visibility edges of the given graph.

Although we have not detailed the data structure manipulations in the algorithm, it is not difficult to implement the algorithm to achieve $O(n)$ time complexity.

7.2.2. Convex Fans

ElGindy also studied a special class of polygons he called "convex fans." A *fan* is a star polygon whose kernal includes a vertex of the polygon. A *convex fan* is a fan whose kernel includes a convex vertex. An example is shown in Fig. 7.7. The problem of reconstructing a representative polygon that achieves a given vertex visibility graph of a convex fan seems far easier than the general problem. ElGindy conjectured a characterization (ElGindy 1985), but reconstruction remains elusive. In fact, it is not even clear how to reconstruct an *orthogonal convex fan* from its visiblity graph, despite the highly constrained staircase structure of such polygons (see Fig. 7.8). At this writing I only can see how to reconstruct orthogonal convex fans of uniform step height, a *very* special case.

Finally, it should be mentioned that Ghosh has recently established necessary conditions for a graph to be a vertex visibility graph, and conjectures that his conditions are also sufficient (Ghosh 1986). One of his conditions is that every "ordered" cycle (one whose labels are in sorted order) in the graph of at least four nodes, must have a chord. This explains why the graph of Fig. 7.2a is not a visibility graph: the 4-cycle $(2, 3, 4, 5)$ has no chord. A proof of his conjecture (his other conditions are not easy to state succinctly) seems difficult.

Fig. 7.7. A convex fan.

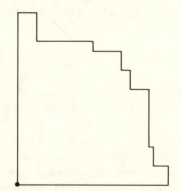

Fig. 7.8. An orthogonal convex fan.

7.3.   EDGE VISIBILITY TREES IN ORTHOGONAL POLYGONS[3]

Considerable simplification of the visibility graph problem results by restricting the polygon and the visibility relation to the orthogonal world. Define an *orthogonal edge visibility graph* (or just a visibility graph) G for an orthogonal polygon P as follows. G contains a node for each edge of P, and two nodes associated with horizontal [vertical] edges e_i and e_j are

---

3. The research reported in this section is the result of collaboration with Heather Booth.

connected by an undirected arc in G iff they can see one another along a vertical [horizontal] line—that is, iff there exists a vertical [horizontal] line segment interior to P with endpoints on e_i and e_j and which does not otherwise intersect the boundary of P. We will restrict our attention to polygons in *general position*: those such that no two vertices can be connected by an internal horizontal or vertical line segment that does not intersect P's boundary. Throughout this section we will use "polygon" to mean "orthogonal polygon in general position."

We will show in the next subsection that the visibility graph of an orthogonal polygon consists of two disjoint trees. Together these trees always have exactly $n - 2$ edges for a polygon of n vertices; this is in marked contrast with the wide variability possible with vertex visibility graphs. We will say that a tree is *realizable* if there is a polygon that has the tree as one of the two components of its visibility graph. A *labeling* of a tree of n nodes is a bijection between the nodes and the set of integers $\{0, 1, \ldots, n - 1\}$. A labeling of a tree is realizable if there is a polygon that realizes the tree, and such that the polygon edges may be numbered $0, 1, \ldots, n - 1$ in a counterclockwise traversal of the boundary to agree with the labeling. Finally, we say that two trees can *mesh* if they are jointly realizable by the same polygon.

In this section we characterize which single trees are realizable and which of their labelings are realizable. Meshable labelings of tree pairs are also characterized, and two algorithms for constructing a realization of two labeled trees are provided. Finally, we provide a partial characterization of when two (unlabeled) trees can mesh. Extending this to a complete characterization is the major open question raised by this investigation.

The next subsection establishes the basic properties of visibility trees, and presents an algorithm for constructing a realization. Section 7.3.2 proves the characterization theorems for labeled trees. Section 7.3.3 studies unlabeled trees, and concludes with a characterization of "universal" trees.

7.3.1. Realization of Visibility Trees

Without the general position assumption, the visibility graph could have many disconnected components, as shown in Fig. 7.9. For polygons in general position, however, the visibility graph has just two components, the horizontal and vertical trees:

LEMMA 7.3.   The orthogonal edge visibility graph G of a polygon P of n edges in general position consists of two disconnected trees, T_H and T_V, each of $n/2$ nodes.

Proof.   By our definition of visibility, horizontal edges cannot see vertical edges. Thus there must be at least two components. We now show that the horizontal edges form a single tree, which we call the vertical tree T_V for the polygon; note that "vertical" here refers to the direction of visibility, not to the orientation of the edges.

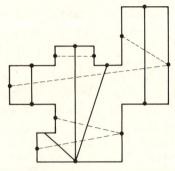

Fig. 7.9. A disconnected edge visibility graph for a polygon not in general position.

We first show that the nodes corresponding to any two horizontal edges e_i and e_j of P are connected by a path in G. Let x_i and x_j be points in the interior of P vertically visible to e_i and e_j, respectively. Because the interior of P is connected, there is a simple path π within P connecting x_j to x_j. Let a_x and b_x be the horizontal edges above and below a point x of π. There is an arc between the nodes in G corresponding to a_x and b_x. Now imagine x moving from x_i to x_j along π. Because of the general position assumption, at most one of a_x or b_x changes at any point x. Thus for any transition point x, there are arcs in G between the nodes corresponding to the edges just before x to those corresponding to the edges at x. Thus the collection of nodes associated with a_x and b_x for all x on π forms a connected graph. See Fig. 7.10. Thus the vertical visibility component of G is connected.

It only remains to show that this component of G has no cycles. But it is clear that if it did, then P would have a hole, contradicting the assumption that P is a polygon without holes.   □

We now make a brief exploration of realizability, a concept which will be studied further in the following subsections.

LEMMA 7.4.   Every tree is realizable.

Proof.   Given a tree T, choose any node as root, and assign it level 0. Assign to each other node a a level equal to the number of arcs in T from the root to a. First construct a "staircase" polygon as shown in Fig. 7.11a that realizes T as its vertical visibility tree to level 1. Then add staircases to

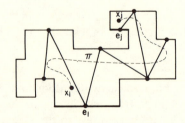

Fig. 7.10.   The vertical visibility component of a polygon in general position is connected.

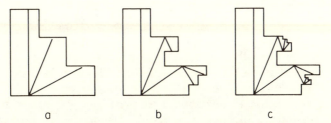

Fig. 7.11. The refinement process generates a polygon to realize any tree.

the steps to include level 2 nodes (Fig. 7.11b). This process can clearly be extended indefinitely, at each stage capturing the nodes at one level lower (Fig. 7.11c). The resulting polygon realizes T as its vertical visibility tree. □

This simple result naturally leads to the next question:

LEMMA 7.5. Not every pair of trees are jointly realizable.

Proof. The tree shown in Fig. 7.12 cannot mesh with itself, providing the smallest example of a pair of trees that can not be simultaneously realized by one polygon. We defer a proof of this to Lemma 7.14 in Section 7.3.3. □

Before investigating the properties of visibility trees further, we describe algorithms to compute the visibility trees for a given polygon, and to construct a realization for a labeled tree pair.

Computation of, say, the horizontal visibility tree can be accomplished easily in $O(n \log n)$ time with a plane sweep. The vertical edges of the polygon are sorted by their upper end point. A sweep line H is then passed over the polygon from top to bottom, stopping at each vertex. A data structure S holds all the vertical edges pierced by H, organized into a dictionary. Vertical edges pierced by H alternately bound the interior of P and the exterior of P. When two vertical edges become newly adjacent in S, then if they bound the interior of P, an arc is connected between their corresponding nodes. Insertion and deletion of vertical edges into S can be performed in $O(\log n)$ time with appropriate implementation. The result is that the entire visibility tree can be constructed with a single pass in $O(n \log n)$.

However, the Tarjan–Van Wyk triangulation algorithm constructs a trapezoidization in $O(n \log \log n)$ time (Section 1.3.2), and this trapezoidization contains all the information necessary to construct a visibility tree. This yields the following lemma.

Fig. 7.12. The smallest tree that cannot mesh with itself, $S_2(3)$.

LEMMA 7.6. The visibility trees of a given polygon can be constructed in $O(n \log \log n)$ time.

Algorithms for the other direction, constructing a polygon that realizes two given labeled trees, are more interesting. Here we will briefly sketch one algorithm, and later (Theorem 7.2) provide another.

It will be convenient to introduce here a concept equivalent to labeling but which dispenses with the integer labels. Define a *circle embedding* of a tree (or just an *embedding*) as a layout of the tree within a circle in the plane such that each arc is mapped to a chord of the circle, and all nodes of the tree are mapped to lie on the circle. The circle corresponds to the boundary of the polygon "inflated" to a circle, and an embedding is topologically equivalent to a layout of the visibility trees within the polygon itself. Figure 7.13 shows an example. Any embedding of a tree of *n* nodes corresponds to *n* counterclockwise labelings of the tree, corresponding to the *n* choices for the location of the 0 label. A labeling of a tree maps to a unique embedding, and often labels will be drawn around the circle. Embeddings ignore the irrelevant distinction between labelings that result from the circular shifts around the circle.

Now consider all the arcs incident to some particular node, say node 0 in Fig. 7.13. The portion of the polygon that realizes the subtree from 0 to its immediate descendants is a "histogram" (Section 2.3) or "Manhattan skyline" (Wood and Yap 1985) polygon, consisting of bottom edge 0 and top edges 12, 14, 18, and 24 in that order counterclockwise. In fact, this polygon is the orthogonal *edge visibility* polygon (Avis and Toussaint 1981b) for edge 0, enclosing all the points visible to edge 0 by an internal vertical line segment. We would now like to identify which vertical edges of the

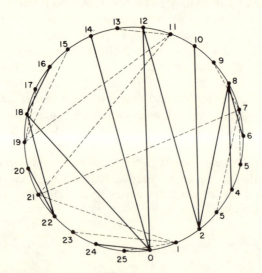

Fig. 7.13. A circle embedding of a visibility graph. The solid lines represent vertical visibility arcs, and the dashed horizontal arcs.

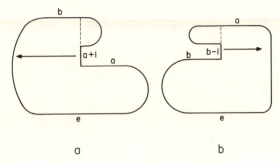

Fig. 7.14. If e sees a and b and no edge between, then either $a + 1$ (a) or $b - 1$ (b) is the determining vertical edge.

original polygon determine the vertical edges of this edge visibility polygon. Once these are identified, we know their left-to-right sorting.

Let e be a bottom edge whose node has degree greater than one, and let a and b be two edges visible from e, with the edges occurring in counterclockwise order e, a, b, and with no edges between a and b also visible to e. Then the vertical edge of e's edge visibility polygon between a and b is either determined by $a + 1 \pmod{n}$ or $b - 1 \pmod{n}$, as illustrated in Figs. 7.14a and 7.14b, respectively. Which case obtains can be decided by checking whether node $a + 1 \pmod{n}$ is connected by an arc to any node in the range from b counterclockwise to e. Thus in Fig. 7.13, let $e = 0$, $a = 14$, and $b = 18$. Since $a + 1 = 15$ connects to 19, $a + 1$ is the determining vertical edge; for $a = 18$ and $b = 24$, $b - 1 = 23$ is the determining edge. Continuing in this manner, we can conclude from edge 0's edge visibility polygon that $25 < 23 < 15 < 13 < 1$, where $i < j$ means that x-coordinate of edge i is less than that of edge j.

Combining this information for every horizontal edge's edge visibility polygon, we can construct a partial order for the vertical edges. Similarly, a partial order for the horizontal edges can be constructed by examining the edge visibility polygons for the vertical edges. The results for the example of Fig. 7.13 are:

Vertical edges:

$$21 < 19 < 23 < 15 < 13 < 1 < 11 < 9 < 3 < 5 < 7$$
$$25 < \quad\quad < 17$$
$$0 \quad 1 \quad 2 \quad 3 \quad 4 \quad 5 \quad 6 \quad 7 \quad 8 \quad 9 \quad 10$$

Horizontal edges:

$$0 < 24 < 22 < 2 < 10 < 20 < 14 < 16 < 18$$
$$6 < 4 < \quad\quad < 8 \quad\quad < 12$$
$$0 \quad 1 \quad 2 \quad 3 \quad 4 \quad 5 \quad 6 \quad 7 \quad 8$$

Below each partial order are listed integers that will be used as the x-coordinate for the odd vertical edges, and the y-coordinate for the even

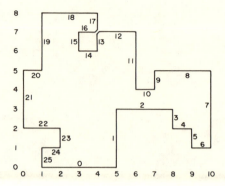

Fig. 7.15. A reconstructed polygon that realizes the graph in Fig. 7.13.

horizontal edges. The construction of a polygon that realizes these partial orders is now straightforward: the vertex between an adjacent horizontal and vertical edge is given an x-coordinate by the vertical edge and a y-coordinate by the horizontal edge, using the indices listed below the partial orders shown above. Thus the vertex between edges 0 and 1 lies at $(5, 0)$, between 1 and 2 at $(5, 3)$, and so on. The polygon generated from this process is illustrated in Fig. 7.15, and indeed it realizes the visibility graph in Fig. 7.13. This polygon may self-overlap (the one in Fig. 7.15 does at $(4, 7)$), but these overlaps may be removed easily by adjusting edge lengths.

LEMMA 7.7. A joint realization of two given labeled trees can be constructed in $O(n)$ time.

Proof Sketch. Each edge visibility polygon produces a chain of orderings. Each vertical edge may appear in at most four visibility polygons of horizontal edges, and similarly for each horizontal edge. Thus the total number of elements of these chains is no more than $4n$. It is easy to merge these chains in linear time (a claim we will not support here), resulting in $O(n)$ time to compute the partial orders. The remainder of the construction also takes just linear time. Details will not be presented.   □

7.3.2. Realization of Labeled Trees

In this section we characterize when one tree or a pair of labeled trees are realizable. Note that Lemmas 7.4 and 7.5 address the equivalent questions for unlabeled trees. The answers we provide in this section are more complicated.

We first study embeddings of one tree. Call two nodes of an embedded tree *2-adjacent* if they are adjacent on the circle if the other tree is ignored; note that 2-adjacent nodes receive labels i and $i + 2 \pmod{n}$ in a labeling. Define the *distance* between two 2-adjacent nodes as the number of arcs in the path in the tree between them. Let d_i be the distance between node i

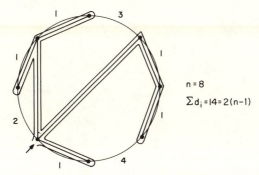

$$n = 8$$
$$\sum d_i = 14 = 2(n-1)$$

Fig. 7.16. The sum of the distances between adjacent nodes is equivalent to a double traversal of the tree.

and its counterclockwise neighbor. Our first characterization theorem is that an embedding of a tree is realizable iff (1) the chords are non-crossing, and (2) for all i, $d_i \leq 3$. We now present a series of lemmas leading to the proof of this theorem.

LEMMA 7.8. $\sum d_i = 2(n - 1)$, for any non-crossing embedding of a tree of n nodes, where the sum is taken over all nodes i of the tree.

Proof. Figure 7.16 shows that summing up the distances between all 2-adjacent nodes is equivalent to traversing the tree twice. Since a tree of n nodes has $n - 1$ edges, the sum of the distances is $2(n - 1)$. □

LEMMA 7.9. Let n_k be the number of 2-adjacent node pairs to one side of a chord of a non-crossing embedding, that are separated by distance k in the tree (the endpoints of the chord are included). Then $\sum_{k=1}^{\infty} (2 - k)n_k = 1$.

Proof. Remove the portion of the tree to the other side of the distinguished chord, and let the resulting tree have n nodes. Then $\sum n_k + 1 = n$, since this sum counts the total number of nodes. Also we have $\sum k n_k + 1 = \sum d_i$, since both sides of the equation represent the total sum of distances. Applying Lemma 7.8 yields $\sum d_i = 2(n - 1)$. Substituting these relationships into the claimed equation proves the lemma:

$$\sum (2 - k)n_k = 2 \sum n_k - \sum k n_k$$
$$= 2(n - 1) - [2(n - 1) - 1]$$
$$= 1 \quad \square$$

Lemmas 7.8 and 7.9 both hold for arbitrary circular embeddings. We now focus on realizable embeddings.

LEMMA 7.10. In a realizable embedding, the distance d_i between each pair of 2-adjacent nodes satisfies $d_i \leq 3$. Moreover, the two angles in a realizing polygon between two 2-adjacent nodes are determined by d_i as

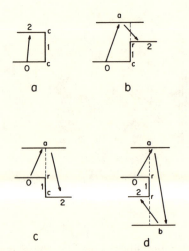

Fig. 7.17. Four possible angle sequences at two vertices: cc, cr, rc, and rr.

follows, where c and r mean convex and reflex angles, respectively:

$$d_i = 1: \quad cc$$
$$d_i = 2: \quad rc \text{ or } cr$$
$$d_i = 3: \quad rr$$

Proof. Let an arbitrary horizontal edge of a polygon, which we take to be a bottom edge without loss of generality, be labeled 0, and label the remaining edges with increasing index counterclockwise. The right endpoint of 0 is either a convex or a reflex vertex. If this endpoint is convex, then distinguish two further cases, depending on whether the upper endpoint of 1 is convex or reflex. The former case is illustrated in Fig. 7.17a, and justifies the claimed correspondence between $d_i = 1$ and cc. In the latter case (Fig. 7.17b), there must be an edge a above 1, leading to $d_i = 2$ and angles cr.

If the right endpoint of 0 is reflex, we again have two cases depending on whether the lower endpoint of 1 is convex or reflex. In the former case (Fig. 7.17c), there is again an edge a above 1, and $d_i = 2$ with angles rc. In the latter case (Fig. 7.17d), there must be an edge a above 1 and an edge b below, leading to $d_i = 3$ with angles rr.

As there are no further possibilities, the lemma is established. $\square$

Let C and R be the number of convex and reflex angles in a polygon. Then it follows from Lemma 2.12 that $C - R = 4$. We can derive this relationship from Lemmas 7.9 and 7.10 as follows. By Lemma 7.10, $d_i \le 3$, so the equation in Lemma 7.9 becomes $n_1 - n_3 = 1$. The correspondence between values of d_i and the included convex and reflex angles in Lemma 7.10 shows that the excess of C over R is determined by $2n_1$ and the excess of R over C by $2n_3$. Choosing any arc of an embedded tree and applying

Lemma 7.9 to each side shows that C exceeds R by $2(n_1 - n_3) = 2$ on each side. Therefore, $C - R = 4$ for the entire polygon.

This argument shows that if an embedding satisfies $d_i \leq 3$, then a polygon with the appropriate number of convex and reflex angles exists, since it is known that all angle sequences that satisfy $C - R = 4$ are achievable (Culberson and Rawlins 1985). It is only a short step further to show that a polygon exists that realizes the embedding:

THEOREM 7.2 [Booth and O'Rourke 1985]. An embedding of a tree is realizable iff

(1) No two chords cross: the embedding is planar; and
(2) For all nodes i, $d_i \leq 3$.

Proof. Assume that polygon P realizes an embedding of T as its vertical visibility tree. Lemma 7.10 establishes that (2) holds for the embedding. Suppose that (1) does not hold. Let arc ab be crossed by cd. Since ab is an arc, the corresponding horizontal edges a and b of P may be connected with a vertical line segment L. Since the edge c is distinct from a and b, it must be strictly to the right or left of L. If the arcs cross, then edge d must be on the other side of L. But then edges c and d cannot be connected by a vertical line, contradicting the inclusion of cd as an arc of the visibility tree. This establishes the easy direction of the theorem.

Assume that an embedding of T satisfies (1) and (2). We seek to construct a polygon P that realizes the embedding. The construction starts with a rectangle, and successively refines it, encompassing more and more of the given embedding. Choose any arc of the embedding as a starting point. The vertical visibility tree consisting of this single arc is realized by a rectangle.

For the general refinement step, assume that we have constructed a polygon P' that realizes an *interior subtree* T' of the embedding. An interior subtree T' is one such that all arcs not in T' are towards the outer boundary of the circle, in the sense that each arc of $T - T'$ has only arcs of $T - T'$ to one side, or equivalently, no arc of $T - T'$ has arcs of T' to both sides. For example, the edges $(0, 12)$, $(0, 14)$, and $(2, 12)$ in Fig. 7.13 form an interior subtree of the vertical visibility tree (solid lines). In the same figure, the edges $(0, 12)$ and $(0, 18)$ do not form an interior subtree, because the edge $(0, 14)$ has edges of the subtree to both sides. Choose an arbitrary *boundary* arc ab of T'—that is, one that has only arcs of $T - T'$ to one side S, or equivalently, no arcs of T' to one side. We now specify two nodes c and d within this sector S. All the nodes in S are connected by a path in T to either a or b without using arc ab. Because no two arcs cross (1), it must be the case that there are two 2-adjacent nodes c and d such that c is connected to a and d is connected to b. See Fig. 7.18. (It may be that $c = a$ and/or $d = b$.) By (2), the distance δ_{cd} between c and d is no more than 3. The refinement step has three cases depending on the value of δ_{cd}.

Case $\delta_{cd} = 1$. Here we must have $c = a$ and $d = b$, and no refinement is needed.

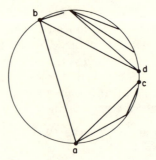

Fig. 7.18. The refinement of *ab* includes *c* and *d* in the next step.

Case $\delta_{cd} = 2$. Either $c = a$ or $d = b$ but not both; assume that $a = c$ without loss of generality. Then replace polygon P' with P as shown in Fig. 7.19a by replacing the indicated vertical edge by a step. (This introduces *cr* angles; *rc* angles could be introduced instead. Either leads to a realization. This incidentally shows that the realization need not be unique.) This new polygon realizes $T' \cup bd$, which is an internal subtree.

Case $\delta_{cd} = 3$. Both c and d are distinct from a and b. Replace polygon P' with P as shown in Fig. 7.19b by introducing a tab into the indicated vertical edge. P now realizes $T' \cup ac \cup bd$, which is an internal subtree.

This completes the description of the refinement step. Starting from an arbitrary arc and a rectangle, repeating this refinement step until all arcs have been included results in a polygon that realizes the original embedding. ☐

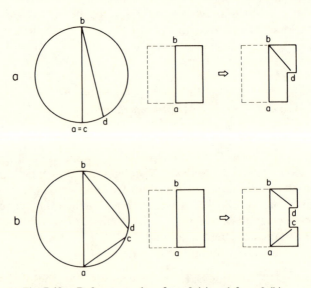

Fig. 7.19. Refinement when $\delta_{cd} = 2$ (a) and $\delta_{cd} = 3$ (b).

Note that conditions (1) and (2) of the theorem can both be phrased as constraints on labelings. For example, (2) can be phrased as: the distance in the tree between the nodes labeled i and $i + 2 \pmod n$ (where n is the total number of vertices in the polygon) is no more than 3.

We now turn to the problem of characterizing when a *pair* of labeled or embedded trees are *jointly* realizable. We start with some observations on insufficient characterizations. If both the horizontal and vertical trees in an embedding individually satisfy the conditions of Theorem 7.2, they are not necessarily jointly realized by the same polygon. It may be that the two unlabeled trees cannot mesh (Lemma 7.5), so there is no jointly realizable embedding. Or it may be that the particular embeddings do not consistently mesh the c/r patterns implied by Lemma 7.10. More surprisingly, it is possible for the embeddings to individually satisfy the conditions of Theorem 7.2, and to consistently mesh their implied c/r patterns, and still not be jointly realizable. Figure 7.20a shows an example. The next lemma shows why this embedding is not realizable. Define two nodes as *1-adjacent* if their labels differ by 1 $(\bmod n)$; thus 1-adjacent nodes correspond to consecutive edges of a polygon, and lie in different trees.

LEMMA 7.11. In a realizable embedding of two trees, all the regions on

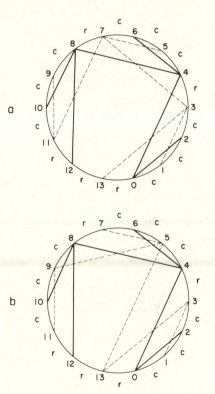

Fig. 7.20. Unrealizable embeddings: in (a), the 12-13 region is bound by 6 chords; in (b) 13 violates the projection constraint.

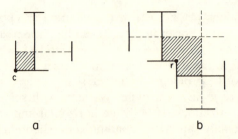

Fig. 7.21. Regions between adjacent edge nodes must be bound by 2(a) or 4(b) chords.

the outer boundary between two 1-adjacent nodes of the circle are bound by either two or four chords. Moreover, if such a region is bound by two chords, then the included angle in a realization is convex; if by four chords, the angle is reflex.

Proof. If an angle of a polygon is convex, then the visibility arcs to the two 1-adjacent edges cross, and the closest such arcs to the corner bound the corner by two chords; see Fig. 7.21a. If an angle is reflex, then the corner is bound by four alternating horizontal and vertical arcs, as shown in Fig. 7.21b. □

The region between nodes 12 and 13 of Fig. 7.20a is bound by six chords, and so violates Lemma 7.11. However, it is possible for an embedding to satisfy the conditions of Lemma 7.11 and *still* not be realizable. Figure 7.20b shows an example. The next lemma explains why.

LEMMA 7.12. In a realizable embedding of two trees, each consecutive triple of nodes *a, x, b* must satisfy the following *projection* constraints (where δ_{ab} is the distance between *a* and *b* in their tree):

$\delta_{ab} = 1.$ [no constraint]

$\delta_{ab} = 2.$ Let *acb* be the length 2 path in the tree from *a* to *b*. Then every arc incident to *x* must cross either *ac,* or *bc,* but not both. See Fig. 7.22a.

$\delta_{ab} = 3.$ Let *acdb* be the length 3 path in the tree from *a* to *b*. Then every arc incident to *x* must cross *cd*. See Fig. 7.22b.

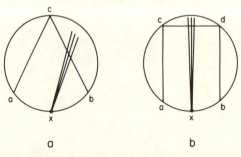

Fig. 7.22. The two projection constraints.

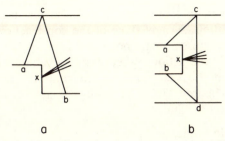

Fig. 7.23. Embeddings illustrating the two constraints of Fig. 7.22.

Proof. By Lemma 7.10, $\delta = 2$ corresponds to *cr* and *rc* angles, and $\delta = 3$ to *rr* angles. Figure 7.23a shows that x can only project across *bc* when the included angles are reflex and convex; if the step is reversed, then x can only project across *ac*. Figure 7.23b shows that x can only project across the middle of the three link path between *a* and *b*. □

Node 13 in Fig. 7.20b projects across both $(0, 4)$ and $(4, 8)$, violating the distance 3 case of the lemma.

Finally we show that these projection constraints are sufficient to characterize realizable embeddings.

THEOREM 7.3. [Booth and O'Rourke 1985]. An embedding of two trees T_V and T_H is realizable iff

(1) Each tree embedding satisfies the conditions of Theorem 7.2 (which characterized embeddings of single trees), and
(2) Every node of both trees satisfies the projection constraints of Lemma 7.12.

Proof. Assume there is a polygon that jointly realizes the embeddings. Then it individually realizes each embedding, so (1) follows from Theorem 7.2. Lemma 7.12 shows that (2) is satisfied. This completes the proof in the easy direction.

Assume that an embedding is given that satisfies conditions (1) and (2) of the theorem. We seek to construct a polygon P that realizes T_V and T_H as its vertical and horizontal visibility trees. The construction is by a refinement procedure very similar to that used in the proof of Theorem 7.2, although here we must refine both trees simultaneously. The refinement will be phrased in terms of T_V, with the refinement of T_H induced by that of T_V. Choose any arc of the embedding of T_V as the starting point. The induced subtree of T_H is also a single arc, and these two subtrees are realized by a rectangle.

For the general refinement step, we need to define refinement inducement. Let T'_V be an interior subtree of T_V, as defined in the proof of Theorem 7.2. The *induced subtree* T'_H is constructed by identifying ("lumping" together) all nodes of T_H that lie inside a sector bound by one boundary arc of T'_V. Thus when T'_V is a single arc, all nodes on either side of the arc are lumped into one, and T'_H is also just a single arc; this is the starting configuration. At any stage of the construction, each boundary arc of T'_V encompasses just a single node of T'_H.

We now specify the actions taken during a refinement step. An arbitrary boundary arc ab of T'_V is chosen for refinement. The nodes c and d of T_V are specified as in Theorem 7.2, and again the action taken depends on the distance δ_{cd} between c and d.

Case $\delta_{cd} = 1$. No refinement needed.

Case $\delta_{cd} = 2$. As in Theorem 7.2, assume $a = c$; let x be the node of T_H between a and d, and let y represent all the nodes of T_H between d and b. By (2) of the theorem statement, x must project across either ab or bd. In the former case, modify P' as shown in Fig. 7.24a, adjusting the relative lengths of the vertical edges x and y so that they are visible to the appropriate edges to the left of ab. In the latter case, modify as shown in Fig. 7.24b. Here the length of x is arbitrary, as it only sees y. In either case, the new polygon P jointly realizes $T'_V \cup bd$, which is an internal subtree, and the subtree of T_H induced by $T'_V \cup bd$.

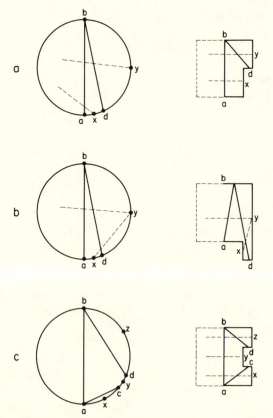

Fig. 7.24. Refinement when $\delta_{cd} = 2$ (a and b) and $\delta_{cd} = 3$ (c).

Case $\delta_{cd} = 3$. Let y be the node of T_H between c and d, and let x and z represent the nodes of T_H bound by the arcs ac and db respectively. Replace polygon P' with P as illustrated in Fig. 7.24c, adjusting the relative lengths of x, y, and z so that they are opposite the appropriate edges on the opposite side of ab. P jointly realizes $T'_V \cup ac \cup bd$ and the induced subgraph of T_H.

This completes the description of the refinement step. Applying this repeatedly constructs a polygon that jointly realizes the given embeddings of T_V and T_H. □

The technique used in the proof provides an alternative to the algorithm sketched in Section 7.3.1 for constructing a realization of two labeled trees. The procedure can be implemented straightforwardly in linear time, as long as the children of each node are sorted by label. But this can be accomplished in linear time with a radix sort. Thus the alternative algorithm also runs in $O(n)$ time. Details would take us too far afield and will not be presented.

7.3.3. Universal Trees

Although Theorem 7.3 completely answers the question of when two labeled trees can mesh, it does not help much in deciding whether two unlabeled trees can mesh. It only says that two trees can mesh if there exists a labeling that satisfies the conditions of the theorem. As there are an exponential number of possible tree labelings, it would be useful to characterize realizability directly in terms of structural features of the unlabeled trees. I have been unable to find such a characterization. I can, however, give a partial characterization, as follows. Define a *universal* (unlabeled) tree as one that can mesh with any other tree of the same number of nodes. Recall that Lemma 7.5 claimed that not all trees are universal. In this section we prove that a tree is universal iff it is a *caterpillar*, a tree that does not contain the graph shown in Fig. 7.12 as a subtree. The goal of this section is to prove this theorem.

One of the keys to the theorem is the study of trees similar to that shown in Fig. 7.12, which we call *2-stars*. A *2-star* $S_2(k)$ is a tree of k length 2 paths joined at one node, called the root of the 2-star. Thus $S_2(k)$ has $2k + 1$ nodes. The tree in Fig. 7.12 is $S_2(3)$.

LEMMA 7.13. Any tree T that meshes with $S_2(k)$ must have an embedding in which at most one pair of 2-adjacent nodes a and b are separated by a distance of 3. Moreover, if there is such a pair, then a jointly realizable embedding must locate the root of $S_2(k)$ between a and b.

Proof. The constraints of Theorem 7.2 imply that there are only two essentially different realizable embeddings of $S_2(k)$: one in which all the level 2 nodes (where the root is level 0) are immediately counterclockwise of their level 1 parents (Fig. 7.25a), and one in which a portion of the level

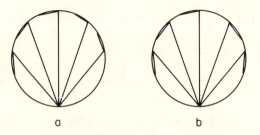

Fig. 7.25. Embeddings of $S_2(k)$.

2 nodes are clockwise and the remaining counterclockwise of their level 1 parents (Fig. 7.25b). Any other arrangement leads to nodes being separated by a distance greater than 3, violating (2) of the theorem. Applying Lemma 7.10, we obtain the following sequence of convex and reflex angles for the two embeddings, where standard regular expression notation is used:

(a) $cc\ (cc\ rr)^{k-1}\ cc\ (cr + rc)$
(b) $(cr + rc)(rr\ cc)^i(cr + rc)(cc\ rr)^j\ cc\ (cr + rc)$, where $i + j = k - 2$.

Both sequences start at the root and proceed counterclockwise. For example, in Fig. 7.25b, $i = 1$, $j = 2$, and $k = 5$.

Now any embedding of T that is jointly realizable with $S_2(k)$ must consistently mesh its angle sequence implied by Lemma 7.10 with either (a) or (b). It is clear that any sequence that meshes with (a) contains no instance of rr, and that a sequence that meshes with (b) can contain at most one instance of rr, obtained by choosing the rc alternative counterclockwise of the root in (b), and choosing the cr alternative at the end of (b), just clockwise of the root. In this case, the root of $S_2(k)$ lies between two reflex vertices. ☐

LEMMA 7.14. $S_2(k)$ cannot mesh with any tree T that contains $S_2(3)$ as a subtree.

Proof.   Figure 7.26 shows three distinct ways that the $S_2(3)$ subtree of T may be embedded. A fourth embedding may be obtained by replacing the right half of Fig. 7.26c (right of rc) with the right half of Fig. 7.26a, but we

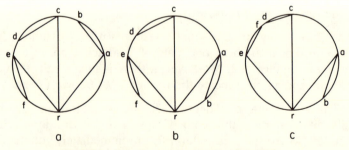

Fig. 7.26.   The three ways of embedding $S_2(3)$.

will see that both cases are handled identically. All other possible embeddings are reflections of these. (Note that since in general $S_2(3)$ will be a proper subtree of T, nodes d and f in Fig. 7.26c may satisfy $\delta_{df} \leq 3$ due to intervening arcs.) By Lemmas 7.9 and 7.10, we know that $n_1 - n_3 = 1$, where n_k are the number of pairs of nodes to one side of any arc that are separated by distance k. Recall that by Lemma 7.10, n_1 counts the number of included cc angles, and n_3 the number of rr angles.

In Fig. 7.26a, there must be two instances of rr angles to the left of arc ra, since ab, ef, and cd each contribute at least 1 to n_1, which forces $n_3 \geq 2$. Lemma 7.13 now shows that $S_2(k)$ cannot mesh with this embedding, since at most one pair of nodes can be separated by distance 3.

In Fig. 7.26c, there must be at least two instances of rr angles to the left of arc rc, since cd, ef, and re each contribute at least one to n_1. This eliminates this and the fourth embedding not drawn as embeddings that can mesh with $S_2(k)$.

Figure 7.26b represents a potential mesh, since there can be just one instance of rr angles, to the left of arc rc and ra. In fact, it is clear that this one instance must lie between d and e. By Lemma 7.13, if $S_2(k)$ is to mesh with this embedding, the root must be fall between these two reflex vertices, and so lies between d and e. In Lemma 7.12 we proved that a node between two 2-adjacent nodes separated by distance 3 must project through the middle link. A similar statement may be proved for any node between two perhaps non-2-adjacent nodes separated by distance 3; the proof is similar to that of Lemma 7.12 and will not be detailed. In this particular situation, it says that the root of $S_2(k)$ cannot project across re or cd, but may either stay within $ercd$ or project across rc. But this means that it is impossible for $S_2(k)$ both to reach nodes between e and f, and between f and r. This establishes that $S_2(k)$ cannot mesh with T. $\square$

This lemma finally provides the proof for Lemma 7.5. The lemma establishes that a tree that contains $S_2(3)$ as a subtree is not universal, because there is at least one tree with which it cannot mesh. Trees that do not contain $S_2(3)$ are known as *caterpillars*, and have the general appearance shown in Fig. 7.27a. They may be characterized as trees with the property that removal of all leaf nodes (and their incident arcs) results in a simple path.

THEOREM 7.4 [O'Rourke 1985]. A tree is universal iff it is a caterpillar.

Proof. Lemma 7.14 establishes that every universal tree is a caterpillar. We now show that every caterpillar can mesh with every other tree with the same number of nodes, and so is universal. The proof is constructive: given an arbitrary caterpillar and any other tree with the same number of nodes, we construct a polygon that jointly realizes them. The proof is somewhat complicated, so we will present an overview first.

Define an *hourglass* polygon that realizes a vertical visibility tree T as follows. Let e be a distinguished edge of T, and assign a level to all nodes of

a

b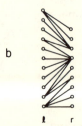

Fig. 7.27. A caterpillar (a) and its arrangement in two vertical columns (b).

T as their minimum distance from an endpoint of e. The polygon is defined by a series of refinements, as was done in Lemma 7.4. At the level 0 step, the polygon is a rectangle, and realizes just e. Next inward and outward staircases replace the vertical sides of the rectangle to include all level 1 nodes of T, as shown in Fig. 7.28, giving the polygon its characteristic shape. Staircases are added to each step to include level 2 nodes (just as in Fig. 7.11), and so on. Hourglass polygons have the property that they easily realize certain caterpillars.

Arrange the nodes of a caterpillar C along two vertical lines, as shown in Fig. 7.27b. Let l and r with $l \geq r$ be the number of nodes on the left and right lines, respectively. Clearly each C has a unique (l, r) pair. We claim that if T contains an edge e such that the remaining nodes of T can be embedded to either side of e, with $l - 1$ nodes to the left and $r - 1$ to the right, then C and T can be jointly realized by an hourglass polygon. To see this, first construct an hourglass polygon realizing the described embedding of T. Next, adjust the lengths of the vertical edges to achieve C as the horizontal tree, as illustrated in Fig. 7.28. Clearly this can always be done if the hourglass polygon has l vertical edges on the left and r on the right, which it must by our assumptions. When an hourglass polygon realizes C and T in this way, we say the two trees can *balance*.

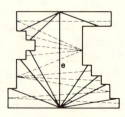

Fig. 7.28. An hourglass polygon realizes a caterpillar as its horizontal tree; here the vertical tree is refined only to level 1.

We can now sketch the proof. Given C and T, if they can balance, then the balancing hourglass polygon establishes the theorem. If they cannot balance, then we will show that we can arrange to balance a subtree C' of C and a subtree T' of T with an hourglass polygon, and gather the remaining nodes $C - C'$ and $T - T'$ in an isolated region. The process is repeated, with the "leftover" diminishing at each step. The final result is a series of hourglass polygons, horizontally displaced and connected top to bottom, which together jointly realizes C and T. We now proceed with the details.

Let the given C have the (l, r) pair l_1 and r_1, with $l_1 + r_1 = n$ and $l_1 \geq r_1$, and let $l_1 - r_1 = \delta \geq 0$. Choose an arbitrary node b_1 of T as the "base." Choose an arc e_1 of T incident to b_1 such that the remaining nodes of T may be arranged on either side of e_1, with L_1 nodes to the left and R_1 to the right (so $L_1 + R_1 + 2 = n$), such that the quantity

$$\beta_1 = |(L_1 - R_1) - \delta_1|$$

is minimal among all arcs e_1 incident to b_1 and all arrangements of nodes. That is, L_1 and R_1 are as close to l_1 and r_1 as is possible for the choice of b_1; β_1 is a measure of "imbalance" between C and T. Consider now two cases: $\beta_1 = 0$ and $\beta_1 > 0$.

Case $\beta_1 = 0$.   Then

$$L_1 - R_1 = \delta_1 = l_1 - r_1.$$

Substituting $R_1 = n - 2 - L_1$, and $r_1 = n - l_1$, yields

$$L_1 = l_1 - 1$$
$$R_1 = r_1 - 1$$

There are precisely the conditions for exact balance, so the hourglass polygon jointly realizes C and T, establishing the theorem.

Case $\beta_1 > 0$.   Let t_1 be the top node at the other end of e_1. Call whichever side (right or left) has an excess (or equal amount) of T nodes over C nodes the *high side*. We first prove that t_1 must have descendants to the high side. Suppose that left is the high side, and that t_1 has no descendants to that side. Then b_1 must have descendants to the left, otherwise $L_1 = 0$, and since $L_1 \geq l_1$, $l_1 = 0$, which is impossible. Then by choosing any edge e_1' incident to b_1 and contributing to L_1 as a new partition edge as illustrated in Fig. 7.29, L_1 can be decremented by 1 and R_1 can be incremented by 1. This decreases $L_1 - R_1$ by 2. Since $\beta_1 = |(L_1 - R_1) - \delta_1|$ is minimal, and since

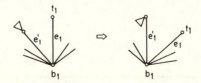

Fig. 7.29. Shifting one node from L_1 to R_1 when t_1 has no left descendants.

$(L_1 - R_1) > \delta_1 > 0$ in the case under consideration (left side high and $l_1 > r_1$), it can only be the case that $\beta_1 = 1$ and the change by 2 changes the signed term from $+1$ to -1. But we now show that β_1 can never equal 1. Suppose

$$(L_1 - R_1) - \delta_1 = 1.$$

Substituting $\delta_1 = l_1 - r_1$, $R_1 = n - 2 - L_1$, and $r_1 = n - l_1$ yields

$$L_1 - l_1 = -\tfrac{1}{2},$$

which is impossible as the difference must be an integer. The argument is similar if the right is the high side. Therefore, t_1 has descendants to the high side.

Let Δ_1 be the minimal number of nodes in a subtree descendant of t_1 to the high side. We prove that $\Delta_1 \geq \beta_1$. For suppose $\Delta_1 < \beta_1$. Assume first that left is the high side, so that $L_1 \geq l_1$ and $R_1 < r_1$. Then flipping Δ_1 nodes from L_1 to R_1 changes them to

$$L_1' = L_1 - \Delta_1$$
$$R_1' = R_1 + \Delta_1.$$

These imply a β_1' of

$$\beta_1' = |(L_1' - R_1') - \delta_1|.$$

Since $(L_1 - R_1) > \delta_1$ in this case, we have $\beta_1 = (L_1 - R_1) - \delta_1$. Substituting for L_1', R_1', and δ_1 yields

$$\beta_1' = |-2\Delta_1 + \beta_1|,$$

which is less than β_1 under the assumption $\Delta_1 < \beta_1$, contradicting the assumed minimality of β_1. If on the other hand right is the high side, then flipping Δ_1 from right to left, and noting that now $-\beta_1 = (L_1 - R_1) - \delta_1$, leads to

$$\beta_1' = |2\Delta_1 - \beta_1|,$$

again a contradiction for the same reason.

This establishes that $\Delta_1 \geq \beta_1$.

Now the plan is to remove Δ_1 nodes from the high side, balance the remainder with an hourglass polygon, and start another hourglass polygon off to the side for the Δ_1 nodes. If Δ_1 nodes are removed from the high side, then calling the new quantities to either side of e_1 L_1' and R_1', it must be that both $L_1' < l_1$ and $R_1' < r_1$, since Δ_1 is more than enough to reduce the excess to a deficit on the high side. (Note that it may be that one of $L_1' = 0$ or $R_1' = 0$ holds.) Call T minus these Δ_1 nodes T_1.

We now specify an appropriate spot to "slide" the Δ_1 nodes into a second hourglass. Consider again the layout of C between two vertical lines, as illustrated in Fig. 7.30. Define a *diagonal* of C to be either the lowest or the highest arc in the layout, or one whose endpoints are both of degree more than 1. Let a diagonal d have d_L and d_R nodes of C below it on the left and

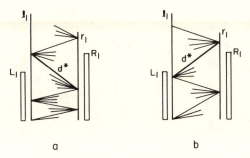

Fig. 7.30. The diagonal d^* is the lowest diagonal that may be used to "slide" nodes into the next hourglass.

right lines of the layout respectively. Define diagonal d^* to be the lowest diagonal such that either $L_1' < d_L^*$ and $d_R^* < R_1'$ (Fig. 7.30a), or $L_1' > d_L^*$ and $d_R^* > R_1'$ (Fig. 7.30b); d^* always exists.

If $d_L^* > L_1'$, then the slide will be to the left; if $d_R^* > R_1'$, then the slide will be to the right. Assume the latter case without loss of generality. Form an hourglass polygon with $L_1' + 1$ and $R_1' + 1$ nodes on the left and right that realizes T_1. Let $l_2 = l_1 - L_1' - 1 > 0$ and $r_2 = r_1 - R_1' - 1 > 0$. Adjust the lengths of the vertical edges of the hourglass polygon so that (a) it realizes C as far up the layout as possible (call this subtree C_1), and (b) the remaining l_2 and r_2 nodes can be laid out at the top right. This is illustrated in Fig. 7.31. Nodes above d_L^* but below $L_1' + 1$ must be realized in the hourglass polygon H_1; nodes below d_R^* but above $R_1' + 1$ must be slid to the right.

The hourglass polygon H_1 now realizes T_1 and C_1. It should be clear that the remaining Δ_1 nodes of T, and l_2 and r_2 of C, bring us back to the exact same situation as we faced at the start. The base node b_2 for the vertical tree is fixed; an edge e_2 is chosen to minimize β_2. If β_2 is zero, then the polygon can be completed with an hourglass. If $\beta_2 > 0$, then the extra nodes are slid off the top to either the right or left as appropriate, and the process repeated.

Let Δ_i be the number of nodes slid off from T at the ith step of this procedure. Clearly $\Delta_i > \Delta_{i+1}$, since Δ_{i+1} is chosen from among the Δ_i

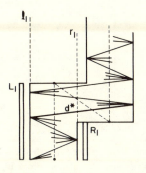

Fig. 7.31. A "slide" to the right.

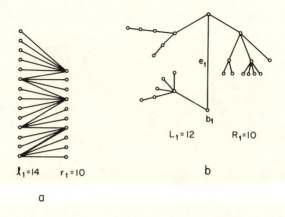

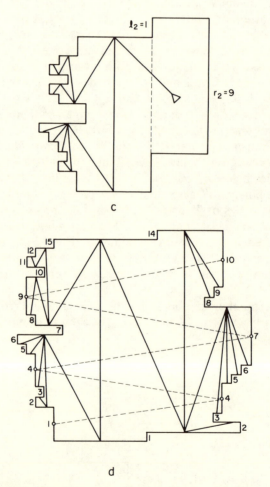

Fig. 7.32. An example of meshing a caterpillar (a) with a tree (b). The first hourglass polygon is shown in (c), and the final polygon realizing both trees in (d). Only the diagonals of the caterpillar are shown in (d).

nodes, and Δ_{i+1} cannot include the endpoints of e_i. Thus the sequence of Δ's is strictly decreasing. Also we proved that $\Delta_i \geq \beta_i$, so the sequence of β imbalances are bounded by a strictly decreasing sequence. Thus we must eventually reach a step j, where $\beta_j = 0$, and the polygon can be completed with a balanced hourglass. This completes the construction. $\square$

Figure 7.32 illustrates the result of the construction procedure of the theorem in a particular case. C is shown in Fig. 7.32a; it has $l_1 = 14$ and $r_1 = 10$, so $\delta_1 = l_1 - r_1 = 4$. The tree T to be meshed is shown in Fig. 7.32b, with e_1 and b_1 distinguished. It is easy to check that the minimal β_1 is achieved as illustrated, with $L_1 = 12$ and $R_1 = 10$. Thus $\beta_1 = |(L_1 - R_1) - \delta_1| = 2$. Right is the high side, since $R_1 \geq r_1$. There is no choice for Δ_1: we must slide off all of R_1. Thus $\Delta_1 = 10$. After removal of Δ_1, we have $L_1' = 12$ and $R_1' = 0$. The diagonal d^* is the lowest edge in Fig. 7.32a whose endpoints both have degree greater than 1. The construction of the first hourglass polygon is shown in Fig. 7.32c; the caterpillar is not drawn in this figure. For the second polygon, $l_2 = l_1 - L_1' - 1 = 1$ and $r_2 = r_1 - R_1' - 1 = 9$ nodes remain. Thus $\delta_2 = 8$. Now it is easy to arrange the nodes in T such that balance is achieved: $L_2 = 0$ and $R_2 = 8$. These imply that $\beta_2 = 0$: exact balance. The final polygon is shown in Fig. 7.32d.

7.3.4. Discussion

The major question left unresolved is: given two unlabeled trees, determine whether or not they can mesh, and if so, construct a realization. If either of the given trees is a caterpillar, Theorem 7.4 provides the answer. But the ratio of the number of caterpillars on n nodes to the number of free trees on n nodes goes to zero as n goes to infinity, so caterpillars are relatively infrequent. If both trees are not caterpillars, we can only answer this question by trying all possible labelings and applying Theorem 7.3. A characterization in terms of the structure of the two trees would be desirable.

7.4. BAR VISIBILITY GRAPHS

Perhaps the most satisfying result obtained to date in the area of visibility graphs is the characterization theorem of "bar visibility graphs" obtained by Wismath (1985), and independently by Tamassia and Tollis (1985). In a *bar visibility graph* (or just a *bar graph*), the nodes represent vertical line segments, and two nodes are connected by an arc iff their two vertical bars A and B can see each other horizontally and non-degenerately. More precisely, there must exist a non-zero height rectangle bounded by A and B to the right and left that does not intersect any other bar. This notion of visibility is sometimes called ε-visibility (Tamassia and Tollis 1986), since the bars must be able to see one another over a beam of visibility of

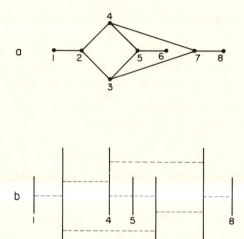

Fig. 7.33. The smallest bar unrepresentable graph (a) and an attempted realization.

thickness $\varepsilon > 0$. Note that this non-degenerate visibility was used in the previous section, but there it was enforced by requiring the polygon to be in general position.

Bar visibility graphs differ from orthogonal polygon visibility trees in two respects: the bars do not have to connect into a polygon, and they have two "sides." These two changes considerably widen the class of graphs that are *bar representable*—that is, those for which there is a collection of bars that realize the visibility graph. First it is clear that every bar graph is planar. Embed the nodes of the graph at, say, the lower endpoint of each bar. Since none of the visibility rectangles intersect, the arcs of the graph may be embedded along the length of these rectangles and down the sides of the bars without crossovers. But not every planar graph is bar representable. Figure 7.33a shows a graph *G*, and Fig. 7.33b shows an attempted realization that fails to embed a bar for node 6. After presentation of the characterization theorem, we will see that this is the smallest bar unrepresentable planar graph. We will follow Wismath's presentation throughout (Wismath 1985).

Our first positive result, halfway to the characterization theorem, is that every biconnected planar graph (defined below) is bar representable. To prove this result we must first introduce "*st*-numbering." An *st-numbering* of a graph *G* of *n* nodes is a 1-1 function λ that maps each node to a distinct number in $\{1, 2, \ldots, n\}$, with $\lambda(s) = 1$ and $\lambda(t) = n$, where *s* and *t* are two distinguished nodes, such that for every node *y* different from *s* and *t*, there are nodes *x* and *z* adjacent to *y* such that $\lambda(x) < \lambda(y) < \lambda(z)$. The two distinguished nodes *s* and *t* can be thought of as source and termination points of a "PERT" digraph, where each edge is oriented to point from lower to higher labels. We now quote two results on *st*-numbering as lemmas (Lempel *et al.* 1967; Even and Tarjan 1970).

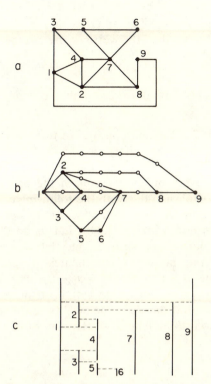

Fig. 7.34. An *st*-numbered graph (a), and embedding into strips (b) of nodes (solid dots) and pseudo-nodes (open circles), and a realization (c).

LEMMA 7.15 [Lempel, Even, and Cederbaum 1966]. For every edge *st* of a biconnected graph *G*, there is an *st*-numbering of *G*.

LEMMA 7.16 [Even and Tarjan 1976]. Given an edge *st* of a biconnected graph, an *st*-numbering can be found in $O(n)$ time.

A *biconnected graph* is one that contains no *cut point,* no node whose removal disconnects the graph; in other words, there are at least two disjoint paths between any two distinct nodes.[4] It is easy to construct connected planar graphs which are not biconnected, and which are not *st*-numerable. Therefore, attention will be restricted to biconnected graphs. Wismath's first result is the following.

LEMMA 7.17. Every planar biconnected graph *G* is bar representable.

Proof. By Lemma 7.15, *G* is *st*-numerable for any edge *st*. Fix an edge *st* and an *st*-numeration. The proof is by construction of a layout of bars, based on this *st*-numbering, that realizes *G*. We will illustrate the proof with the graph *G* shown in Fig. 7.34a with the indicated *st*-numbering.

---

4. "Nonseparable" is a synonym for "biconnected," and "articulation point" is a synonym for "cut point."

Start with a planar embedding of G as in Fig. 7.34a, and deform G, maintaining planarity, so that the vertices are arranged in vertical strips $S_1, S_2, \ldots$, such that

(1) $s \in S_1$.
(2) For all $v \neq s$, $v \in S_i$ iff all lower numbered nodes adjacent to v are in strips $S_1, \ldots, S_{i-1}$.

This is shown in Fig. 7.34b (solid nodes). No two vertices in the same strip are adjacent. Thus they can safely be mapped to bars with the same x-coordinate, since they cannot see one another. All that remains is adjustment of the lengths and placements of the bars to match the graph edges. Wismath accomplished this with the following clever scheme.

Introduce a "pseudo-node" on each edge that passes completely through a strip; see the open nodes in Fig. 7.34b. Let v_{ij} be the jth node (real or pseudo) from the bottom in strip i, and let x_{ij}, a_{ij}, and b_{ij} be the x-coordinate, top, and bottom y-coordinates, respectively, of the bar associated with node v_{ij}, and let $L_{ij} = a_{ij} - b_{ij}$. For $v_{11} = s$, let $x_{11} = 0$, $a_{11} = 1$, $b_{11} = 0$, so $L_{11} = 1$. Define the length of the bar for v_{ij} to be long enough to encompass all its incident "beams" from the left, each of which is a proportional fraction of the lengths of the bars from which they emanate:

$$L_{ij} = \sum_k \frac{L_{i-1,k}}{deg_f(v_{i-1,k})},$$

where $deg_f(v)$ is the forward degree of v—that is, the number of neighbors to its right. The bars are placed at the same x-coordinate within each section, stacked end to end vertically:

$$b_{i1} = b_{11} = 0,$$
$$a_{ij} = b_{ij} + L_{ij},$$
$$b_{ij} = a_{i,j-1}.$$

Applying this procedure to Fig. 7.34b produces the layout shown in Fig. 7.34c. For example, the length of the only bar for a real node (7) in S_5 is $L_{51} = L_{41} + (1/2)L_{31} + L_{32} + (1/3)L_{23}$. Finally, the bars representing the introduced pseudo-nodes are removed. Clearly the resulting layout realizes G. $\square$

It is easy to implement the construction in this proof with a linear algorithm using Lemma 7.16.

The class of bar representable graphs is wider than established by this lemma. This class can be described by loosening the definition of *st*-numerability, as follows. Let λ be a 1-1 labeling function from the nodes to $\{1, 2, \ldots, n\}$. Define a λ-*max* to be a node that has no higher labeled neighbor, and similarly define a λ-*min*. An *st*-numbering has one λ-min and λ-max, at s and t, respectively. Define a graph G to be *st**-numerable if there is a λ function and a planar embedding of G such that all λ-max and all λ-min nodes are on the exterior face, and they are separable into a λ-max group and a λ-min group, separable in the sense that it is possible to introduce two new vertices v_- and v_+ in the exterior face such that v_- connects to each λ-min node and v_+ to each λ-max node, while preserving planarity. This definition is admittedly ungainly, but it will be rephrased shortly. First we show that it precisely captures the bar representable graphs.

THEOREM 7.5.   A biconnected graph G is bar representable iff G is st^*-numerable.

Proof.   Suppose G is st^*-numerable. Then embed G as guaranteed by the definition of st^*-numerability. If there is more than one λ-max node, add a new vertex v_+ in the exterior face and connect it to all λ-max nodes. Similarly add v_- connected to all λ-min nodes if there is more than one. Call the resulting graph G'. Now assign $\lambda(v_-) = 0$ and $\lambda(v_+) = n + 1$. Then it is clear that each node except v_- and v_+ has a smaller and larger labeled neighbor. Thus G' is st-numerable. Since G was assumed to be biconnected, and since v_+ and v_- (if present) have degree at least two, G' is also biconnected. Lemma 7.17 then guarantees that G' is bar representable. Removing the bars associated with the v_- and v_+ nodes results in a realization for G.

Suppose G is bar representable, realized by a particular layout of bars. Convert the layout into *normal form* by translating the bars to the vertical lines $x = 1, 2, \ldots$, and moving each one as far to the left as is possible. Now number the bars 1 to n, from left to right, top to bottom. We claim that this is a st^*-numbering of the associated graph G. Consider any interior node v of G, one not on the boundary of the exterior face. Then it must have a neighbor to its left and its right. But since the left neighbors have lower and the right neighbors higher labels, v is neither a λ-min nor a λ-max node. The λ-min and λ-max nodes are separable, since all the λ-max nodes occur for bars at tops of the columns, and λ-min nodes at the bottoms, and these bars are on the exterior face. $\square$

We now show that this theorem can be reformulated to replace st^*-numbering with more direct graph-theoretic features.

THEOREM 7.6 [Wismath, Tomassia and Tollis 1985]. G is bar representable iff there is a planar embedding of G with all cutpoints on the exterior face.

Proof.   Suppose G is bar representable. Then by Theorem 7.5, it is st^*-numerable, which by definition implies there is a planar embedding realizing the st^*-numeration. Suppose, in contradiction to the theorem, that there is a cutpoint x not on the exterior face of this embedding. Since x is a cutpoint, its removal disconnects G into two or more components. Because x is not on the exterior face, one of these components, say B, must be interior to a circuit C containing x; see Fig. 7.35. Now let b_+ be the node of

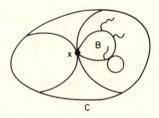

Fig. 7.35.   The component B must contain a λ-min or λ-max.

B that has the largest label among all the nodes of B, and let b_- be the node that achieves the smallest. Then x is the only connection between B and $G - B$, and since $\lambda(x)$ cannot be both larger than $\lambda(b_+)$ and smaller than $\lambda(b_-)$, either b_+ is a λ-max or b_- is a λ-min. This violates the definition of st^*-numbering, establishing the "if" direction of the theorem.

Suppose there is a planar embedding of G with all cutpoints on the exterior face. Then we can construct an st^*-numbering by using the st-numbering algorithm of Even and Tarjan (Lemma 7.16) to number the "blocks" of G depth-first. A *block* of a graph is a maximal biconnected component. Treat their algorithm as a procedure $ST(s, t, B, i)$ that st-numbers block B starting with $\lambda(s) = i$, where st is an edge of B. Each call to ST marks the block that it numbers. Then an algorithm for st^*-numbering from cutpoint s with $\lambda(s) = i$ is $ST^*(s, i)$ below.

$ST^*(s, i)$
   for all unmarked blocks B_i containing a cutpoint x **do**
      Choose unmarked t adjacent to x on the exterior face of B_i.
      $ST(x, t, B_i, i)$.
      $i \leftarrow i + |B_i| - 1$.
      for all cutpoints x_j in B_i **do**
         $ST^*(x_j, i)$.

Note that only the first cutpoint passed to ST^* becomes a λ-min; all the other cutpoints become λ-maxima. Therefore the λ-min and λ-max nodes are trivially separable. They are all on the exterior face because the cutpoints are. Thus a valid st^*-numbering is produced. Theorem 7.5 then implies that G is bar representable, concluding the proof of the theorem. $\square$

We obtain the final form of the characterization with a simple observation.

COROLLARY. Let G^+ be the graph obtained from G by connecting every cut point to a new vertex. Then G is bar representable iff G^+ is planar.

Since cutpoints of a graph can be identified in linear time by a depth-first search (Aho *et al.* 1974), and planarity may be tested in linear time with the Hopcroft–Tarjan algorithm (Hopcroft and Tarjan 1974), this yields a

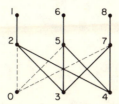

Fig. 7.36. The graph in Fig. 7.33a contains $K_{3,3}$ when augmented.

linear-time algorithm for recognizing bar representability. A simple modification of the layout procedure used in the proof of Theorem 7.5 establishes that a realization can be constructed in linear time.

We may finally see why the graph G in Fig. 7.33a is not bar representable. Add a node 0 connected to the three cutpoints 2, 5, and 7. Then the graph may be redrawn as in Fig. 7.36, revealing that $K_{3,3}$ is a subgraph. By Kuratowski's theorem, then, G is non-planar. It is also easy to see that this is the smallest bar unrepresentable graph.

8

VISIBILITY ALGORITHMS

8.1. INTRODUCTION

The notion of visibility leads to a number of algorithm questions independent of those motivated by art gallery problems. Although the structure of visibility graphs was investigated in the previous chapter, for example, we have yet to discuss the algorithmic construction of such graphs. Nor have we shown how to compute the portion of a polygon visible from an internal point. These and related questions will be addressed in this chapter.

The most fundamental problem is that just mentioned: given a point x in a polygon P, compute $V(x)$, the portion of P visible from x. $V(x)$ is called the *point visibility polygon* for x; it may be imagined as the region illuminated by a light bulb at x. It will be shown in the next section that $V(x)$ can be constructed in $O(n)$ time. Permitting holes in the polygon leads to $\Omega(n \log n)$ complexity (Section 8.5.1). In three dimensions, computation of $V(x)$ is the heavily studied "hidden surface removal" problem, which has recently been shown to have $\Theta(n^2)$ complexity (McKenna 1987).

Recall the definition of a kernel from Chapter 4: the *kernel* of a polygon P is the set of all points that can see the entire interior of P. Polygons with a non-null kernel are called *stars*.[1] Lee and Preparata showed that the kernel of a polygon can be computed in $O(n)$ time, which incidentally yields an algorithm for detecting whether a polygon is a star in linear time (Lee and Preparata 1979). We will not present their algorithm, but will use the idea of a kernel to introduce edge visibility.

Avis and Toussaint introduced and studied three different notions of edge visibility, extending the point visibility concept (Avis and Toussaint 1981b). Let P be a polygon and e an edge of P.

(1) P is *completely visible* from e if e is covered by the kernel of P: thus every point of P is visible to every point of e.
(2) P is *strongly visible* from e if e intersects the kernel of P: thus there is at least one point of e that can see all of P.

---

1. Such polygons are often called "star-shaped."

(3) *P* is *weakly visible* from *e* if every point of *P* is visible to some point of *P*.

Note that in the case of weak visibility, *e* does not have to intersect the kernel, and in fact *P* does not have to be a star to be weakly visible from an edge. An equivalent formulation is that a polygon is weakly visible from *e* if it would be entirely illuminated by a fluorescent light bulb whose extent matched *e*.

Avis and Toussaint addressed the question of detecting whether a polygon is visible from a given edge. This question is solved by Lee and Preparata's kernel algorithm for both complete and strong visibility, but not for weak visibility. They presented an $O(n)$ algorithm for detecting if *P* is weakly visible from *e* in Avis and Toussaint (1981b). We will not present their algorithm, but will make use of their definitions and theorems. The concept of weak visibility has proven to be the most fruitful of the three definitions, and henceforth the unqualified term "edge visibility" will refer to weak visibility.

A problem raised but not solved in Avis and Toussaint (1981b) is that of computing the edge visibility polygon $V(e)$ from an edge *e* of a polygon *P*: the portion of *P* illuminated by a light along *e*. For six years the fastest algorithms required $O(n \log n)$ time, but no lower bound larger than the trivial $\Omega(n)$ was known. Just recently an $O(n \log \log n)$ algorithm has been found, based on the Tarjan-Van Wyk triangulation algorithm (Section 1.3.2). We present an $O(n \log n)$ algorithm in Section 8.3, and sketch the new algorithm in Section 8.7. In Section 8.6 we will show that permitting holes in the polygon leads to a surprising jump in complexity to $\Omega(n^4)$.

A number of related visibility questions are surveyed in Section 8.7.

Finally, a remark on the style of algorithm presentation. Visibility algorithms tend to be complicated, involving, for example, delicate stack manipulations. It is not my intent to present these algorithms in the detail necessary for implementation; for that the reader is referred to the original papers. Rather I will attempt to convey the main ideas behind each algorithm while staying one step above the precise data structure manipulations.

8.2. POINT VISIBILITY POLYGON

The first linear algorithm for constructing the visibility polygon from a point inside a polygon was obtained by ElGindy and Avis in 1980 (ElGindy and Avis 1981). Prior to this, several supra-linear linear algorithms were published, and at least one suggested linear algorithm was shown not to work. ElGindy and Avis's algorithm requires three stacks, and is quite complicated. Later Lee proposed another linear algorithm that requires only one stack (Lee 1983). Most recently, Joe and Simpson have simplified the organization of Lee's algorithm (Joe and Simpson 1985), and it is their presentation that we follow here.

In order to achieve linear time, the vertices of the polygon cannot be sorted into a convenient organization, but rather must be processed in the order in which they appear on the boundary of the polygon. This order is inconvenient in that portions of the boundary not yet visited may obscure the otherwise visible portions of the boundary already visited. Thus the algorithm must be prepared to modify or abandon the structures it has constructed at any time.

Lee's algorithm accomplishes this with a single stack of vertices $S = s_0, s_1, \ldots, s_t$, where s_t is top of the stack. Let x be the point in the polygon from which visibility is being computed. Then the stack constitutes the vertices of $V(x)$ encountered so far *assuming the remaining portion of the boundary will not interfere*. Of course this assumption is in general not true, and as interference is detected, the stack is modified appropriately.

Let the vertices of the polygon be $v_0, v_1, \ldots, v_n = v_0$ in counterclockwise order. Place x at the origin and rotate and renumber so that v_0 is to the right of x on the horizontal line through x. For each vertex v_i of P, define its *angle about x $\alpha(v_i)$* to be the polar angle of v_i with respect to x, including any "winding" about x. This may be defined formally as:

(1) $\alpha(v_0) = 0$,
(2) $\alpha(v_i) = \alpha(v_{i-1}) + \sigma \cdot angle(v_{i-1}xv_i)$,

where $\sigma = +1$ if $xv_{i-1}v_i$ is a left turn, $\sigma = -1$ if a right turn, and $\sigma = 0$ if no turn. Thus if $\alpha(v_i) > 2\pi$, the boundary has "wound around" x from v_0 to v_i. It is clear that only vertices v with $0 \leq \alpha(v) \leq 2\pi$ are candidates for visibility from x.

The algorithm consists of three procedures: *Push, Pop,* and *Wait. Push* adds a new visible vertex to the top of the stack. *Pop* deletes one or more vertices from the stack when interference is detected. And *Wait* traverses a portion of the boundary known to be invisible, waiting for it to emerge back "into the light." With each call to *Wait* is associated a *window W*, which is a subsegment of the ray from x through s_t, one end of which is always s_t, and a direction (clockwise or counterclockwise) of passage. *Wait* traverses the boundary until it passes through W in the specified direction.

Each procedure is now described in more detail. Let $v_i v_{i+1}$ be the current edge being processed, and let the stack be $s_0, \ldots, s_t$.

Push

When this procedure is entered, $\alpha(v_{i+1}) \geq \alpha(s_t)$ and $\alpha(v_{i+1}) \geq \alpha(v_i)$. Two cases are distinguished, depending on the relation of $\alpha(v_{i+1})$ with 2π.

Case a ($\alpha(v_{i+1}) \leq 2\pi$).   This is the "normal" case. v_{i+1} is pushed onto the stack, and i is incremented. The next action is determined by the new edge $v_i v_{i+1}$, as follows (note that now $s_t = v_i$). If $i = n$, the algorithm is finished. If $\alpha(v_{i+1}) \geq \alpha(v_i)$, then *Push* is called again. If $\alpha(v_i) > \alpha(v_{i+1})$, then if the boundary makes a left turn at v_i, $v_i v_{i+1}$ obscures the stack (Fig. 8.1a) and *Pop* is called; and if the turn at v_i is a right turn, then the stack obscures v_{i+1} (Fig. 8.1b), and *Wait* is called with $W = s_t \infty$.

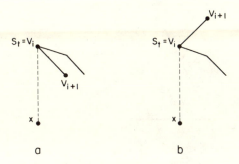

Fig. 8.1. If v_{i+1} obscures (a), *Pop* is called; if v_{i+1} is hidden (b), *Wait* is called.

Case b ($\alpha(v_{i+1}) > 2\pi$). Then the intersection of the ray xv_0 (which is at angle $0 \equiv 2\pi$) with v_iv_{i+1} is pushed on the stack, and *Wait* is called with $W = v_0s_t$.

Pop

The vertices of the stack are popped back to s_j, where s_j is the first stack vertex such that either

(a) $\alpha(s_{j+1}) \geq \alpha(v_{i+1}) > \alpha(s_j)$ (Fig. 8.2a), or
(b) $\alpha(s_{j+1}) = \alpha(s_j) \geq \alpha(v_{i+1})$, and y (defined in Fig. 8.2b) lies between s_j and s_{j+1}.

Case a.   The stack top is set to point y in Fig. 8.2a, and i is incremented. The next action is determined by the new edge v_iv_{i+1}, similar to Case *a* of *Push*. If $i = n$, halt. If $\alpha(v_i) > \alpha(v_{i+1})$, then *Pop* is called again. If $\alpha(v_{i+1}) \geq \alpha(v_i)$, then if v_i is a right turn, call *Push*, and if a left turn, call *Wait* with $W = v_is_t$.

Case b.   Ignoring the degenerate case when s_j, v_{i+1}, and s_{j+1} are collinear (see Joe and Simpson (1985)), *Wait* is called with $W = s_jy$, where y is as illustrated in Fig. 8.2b.

Wait

i is incremented until v_iv_{i+1} intersects W at point y from the correct direction. When that occurs, y is pushed on the stack, and either *Push* or

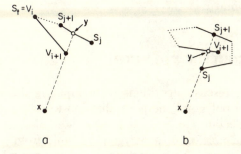

Fig. 8.2. Two *Pop* cases: v_{i+1} does (a) or does not (b) obscure s_{j+1}.

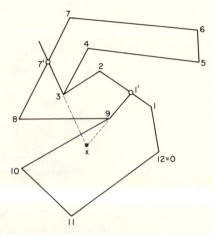

Fig. 8.3. A visibility polygon example: $V(x) = 0\ 1\ 1'\ 9\ 10\ 11$.

Pop is called depending on whether $\alpha(v_{i+1}) \geq \alpha(v_i)$ or vice versa, respectively.

A simple example is shown in Fig. 8.3. *Push* advances to 3, when $S = 0\ 1\ 2\ 3$. Since $\alpha(3) > \alpha(4)$ and 3 is a right turn, *Wait* is called with W as illustrated. *Wait* detects that 8 emerges through W, pushes $7'$ on the stack, and calls *Push*. The stack becomes $0\ 1\ 2\ 3\ 7'\ 8$ after 8 is pushed. Since $\alpha(8) > \alpha(9)$ and 8 is a left turn, *Pop* is called. All stack vertices down to 1 are deleted, and $1'$ and 9 are pushed to make the stack $0\ 1\ 1'\ 9$. Finally, *Push* advances until 0 is encountered again, when the stack is $0\ 1\ 1'\ 9\ 10\ 11$, which is indeed $V(x)$. This example does not invoke the more subtle aspects of the algorithm, but illustrates the main ideas.

A proof of correctness requires more detailed code, and the interested reader is referred to the original papers (ElGindy and Avis 1981; Lee 1983; Joe and Simpson 1985). It should be apparent that the algorithm requires only linear time: each vertex is scanned just once, at most two vertices are pushed on the stack at each iteration, and popped vertices are never pushed again. Thus the time complexity is $O(n)$. Finally we note that the same basic algorithm can be used to construct the portion of the boundary of P seen from an exterior point x.

8.3. EDGE VISIBILITY POLYGON

In this section we discuss algorithms for computing the visibility polygon from an edge of a polygon. The generalization to polygons with holes will be considered in Section 8.6.

Let $V(e)$ be the portion of a polygon P visible from $e = (a, b)$. Of the three notions of edge visibility introduced in (Avis and Toussaint 1981b), only one, weak visibility leads to an interesting algorithm problem for constructing $V(e)$. It is easy to see that the region *completely* visible from e is just the intersection of $V(a)$ and $V(b)$. These point visibility polygons can be constructed in $O(n)$ time as showed in the previous section, and their intersection can be constructed easily in $O(n)$ time.[2] There is no unique region *strongly* visible from e; rather there are many regions strongly visible from an edge. But the construction of the region *weakly* visible from e, which we henceforth call $V(e)$, is a fascinating algorithm question that does not seem reducible to or from any other problem.

There have been three remarkably diverse algorithms published to date for constructing $V(e)$ in $O(n \log n)$ worst-case time complexity. And as this book was under revision, an $O(n \log \log n)$ algorithm was announced by Guibas *et al.* (1986). Their method will be sketched in Section 8.7. Here we will first outline each of the three published algorithms briefly before presenting a new fourth algorithm.

Independently and approximately simultaneously, ElGindy (1985), and Lee and Lin (1986a), proposed $O(n \log n)$ algorithms for computing $V(e)$. The two algorithms are completely different, and both are rather complicated. Lee and Lin's algorithm performs two scans of the polygon boundary in opposite directions, computing for each vertex the extreme points of e that can see it. The data gathered in the passes are then merged to form $V(e)$. Their algorithm maintains a separate stack for each vertex of the polygon. The reason for the $O(n \log n)$ complexity is that occasionally a binary search must be performed on a stack to search for a vertex with a particular property.

ElGindy's algorithm first decomposes the polygon into monotone pieces, using the $O(n \log n)$ algorithm of Lee and Preparata (see Section 1.3.2), and applies an edge visibility algorithm to each piece. Curiously he shows that a natural algorithm that achieves linear time for monotone polygons leads to a quadratic algorithm if applied to the monotone pieces. He uses an algorithm that requires $O(n \log n)$ even on monotone polygons, but which is better suited to merging the individual monotone results: it leads to an $O(n \log n)$ algorithm for computing $V(e)$ in a simple polygon.

A third algorithm was recently presented by Chazelle and Guibas (1985), and it is as different from the first two as they are from each other. The main novelty is that the calculations are carried out in a dual space using the "two-sided plane" introduced in Guibas *et al.* (1983). A convex partition of the rays comprising $V(e)$ in the dual space is constructed in $O(n \log n)$ time using a divide-and-conquer algorithm based on Chazelle's polygon cutting theorem (Chazelle 1982). Once this partition is available, $V(e)$ can be constructed in linear time. This approach is very general and solves several other visibility questions, to which we will return in Section 8.7.

Finally we come to the new fourth algorithm. It is a traditional plane sweep, based on several ideas in Lee and Lin (1986a) and ElGindy (1985).

---

2. I thank Subhash Suri for discussions on this point.

Let the edge e from which visibility is being computed be oriented horizontally. We concentrate initially on computing $V(e)$ above e; the portion of $V(e)$ below e (if any) is easily found with the point visibility algorithm applied to the two endpoints of e. The first step of the algorithm is to sort the vertices of the polygon from lowest y-coordinate to highest. This immediately pegs the complexity at $\Omega(n \log n)$. A horizontal sweep line H will be moved from e upwards. Let H intersect edges $e_1, e_2, \ldots$ left to right at a particular height. These edges are maintained in a data structure E that permits $O(\log n)$ queries, insertions, and deletions in the standard manner (see for example, Section 1.3.2). Assume for simplicity of exposition that no edge of the polygon aside from e is horizontal, so that the edges may be unambiguously classified as *left* or *right* edges, implying that the exterior of the polygon is to the left or right respectively. Clearly e_1 is a left edge, and they alternate left/right in sequence.

Certain pairs of left and right edges in E will be distinguished as bounding "visibility windows." A *visibility window* W is an interval of H bound by the left edge e_a on the left and the right edge e_b on the right, such that e_a and e_b are adjacent in E, and some portion of the interval between on H, specifically the interval $x_a x_b$, is visible to e. See Fig. 8.4. x_a may lay on e_a, or it may be that e_a is left of x_a (as in Fig. 8.5); and similarly for x_b. In general there will be several visibility windows $W_1, W_2, \ldots$ active on H at any one time. Each visibility window will have further data structures associated with it, which we now detail.

With each point x on H visible to e we can associate two line segments $L(x)$ and $R(x)$ that connect x to the leftmost and rightmost points of e that can see x. Construction of these lines in $O(\log n)$ time for any x is the key to the algorithm. Let $c[L(x)]$ be the point of contact between $L(x)$ and the polygon; in case there are several, select the one closest to x. Define $c[R(x)]$ similarly. Each window can be partitioned into intervals wherein the points of contact remain unchanged as x varies over the interval. The locations x where $c[L(x)]$ changes determine the left critical lines $L_0, L_1, \ldots, L_l$, and similarly there are right critical lines $R_0, R_1, \ldots, R_r$ for each window. For any window, the contact points for these lines form a convex chain, as illustrated in Fig. 8.5. As in that figure, the left critical lines intersect H in the left-to-right order $L_l, \ldots, L_1, L_0$, and the right lines in the order $R_0, R_1, \ldots, R_r$, where smaller indicies connect to lower points on the contact chains. It will always be the case that R_0 connects to x_a and L_0 connects to x_b. Points of H to the left of R_0 and to the right of L_0 are not visible to e. For each window, the critical lines and their contact points are maintained in two data structures L and R that permit $L(x)$ and $R(x)$ to be

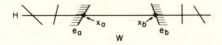

Fig. 8.4. A window W on the sweep line H; the shading represents the exterior of the polygon.

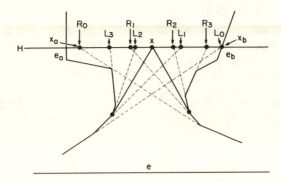

Fig. 8.5. The critical lines L_i and R_i, and the points of contact for x.

constructed in $O(\log n)$ time for any x in the window. As illustrated in Fig. 8.5, if x falls between L_i and L_{i+1}, then $c[L(x)] = c[L_i]$, and if x falls between R_i and R_{i+1}, then $c[R(x)] = c[R_i]$. Any standard dictionary data structure will suffice.

This completes the description of the data structures maintained as the sweep line advances. We now describe the actions taken as the line advances one step. Let H be the sweep line as it encounters the next vertex x. First x is located in the list of edges E in $O(\log n)$ time. If x is not interior to or on the boundary of any visibility window, the edges adjacent to x are inserted into and deleted from E in the standard manner in $O(\log n)$ time, and no further action is taken. If instead x lies in a window W, then three actions are taken: (1) visible segments in the window are output, (2) updates to the window due to the advance are made, and (3) updates to the window due to x are made. Each of these actions is described in detail below.

(1) Output of visible segments.

We will only describe the actions taken on the left boundary of the window; the right boundary is handled in the exact same manner. We first compute x_a, the leftmost visible point in W. The intersection of e_a, the left bounding edge of W, with H, y_a, is computed and located in the list of right critical edges R in $O(\log n)$ time. If y_a is visible, then $x_a = y_a$. Therefore, set x_a to be this point y_a if y_a is to the right or on R_0 (see Fig. 8.6); otherwise y_a is not visible and x_a is set to the intersection of R_0 with H. Let x'_a be the leftmost visible point of W when it was last updated, with

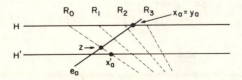

Fig. 8.6. The visible boundary segments $x'_a z$ and $z x_a$ are output.

the sweep line at H'. (This is not the immediately previous position of H in general, because each window is only updated when a vertex is encountered within it.) x'_a is the intersection of R_0 and H'. We now output the left boundary of the window from x'_a to x_a as visible. This boundary may consist of one or two segments:

(a) y_a is invisible, and so is strictly left of x_a. Then no portion of e_a between H' and H is visible, and both x'_a and x_a lie on R_0. Output one segment, $x'_a x_a$.

(b) y_a is visible, and so $x_a = y_a$ (Fig. 8.6). Then R_0 and e_a cross at a point z between H' and H; perhaps $z = x'_a$. Output two segments, $x'_a z$ and $z x_a$.

(2) Window updates due to advance.
Again we will only describe the updates related to the left bounding edge. Suppose $y_a = x_a$ is found to lie between R_i and R_{i+1}. The lines $R_0, R_1, \ldots, R_i$ are deleted from the data structure R. In Fig. 8.6, R_0, R_1, and R_2 are deleted. If any lines are deleted, then a new R_0 is created connecting x_a to $c[R_i]$. Similarly, x_a is located within L; if x lies between L_{j+1} and L_j, then $L_l, \ldots, L_{j+2}, L_{j+1}$ are deleted, and a new L_{j+1} is created (if any lines were deleted) connecting x_a to $c[L_j]$. If x_a is found to be to the right of L_0, or $R_0 = L_0$, then the window is closed.

(3) Window updates due to x.
We finally come to the processing that is dependent on the vertex x hit by H and its local neighborhood. Two cases are distinguished.

Case a ($x = y_a$ is the upper endpoint of e_a.). The edge distinguished as the left boundary of W must change. Let e' be the other edge incident to x. If e' is a left edge, then $e_a \leftarrow e'$; if e' is a right edge, then e_a is set to the first left edge to the left of x in E. Similar processing occurs when x is the upper endpoint of the right boundary.

Case b (The two edges e' and e'' adjacent to x to the left and right respectively both lie above H.). W splits into two windows W' bound by e_a and e', and W'' bound by e'' and e_b. Let x be located between R_i and R_{i+1}, and between L_{j+1} and L_j. The data structures R and L are split between the two windows, with W' receiving $R_0, \ldots, R_i$ and W'' receiving $R_{i+1}, \ldots, R_r$, and W' receiving $L_l, \ldots, L_{j+1}$ and W'' receiving $L_j, \ldots, L_0$. Note that this means that the top of the left convex chain and the bottom of the right convex chain become associated with W', and vice versa for W''. Finally, $L(x)$ and $R(x)$ are added to both W' and W''. For example, if x in Fig. 8.5 falls under Case b, then $i = 1$ and $j = 1$, and W' receives L_3, L_2, and $L(x)$, and R_0, R_1, and $R(x)$, and W'' receives $L(x), L_1$, and L_2, and $R(x), R_2$, and R_3.

This completes the description of the processing that occurs during each advance of H. The data structures are initialized with H collinear with e. E is initialized to contain every edge intersected by the initial position of H.

Let a and b be the left and right endpoints of e, and let e_a and e_b the edges in E closest to a and b respectively (a may be a lower endpoint of e_a, and similarly for b). Then there is one window initially, bound by e_a and e_b, which intersect H at x_a and x_b. Both L and R consist of two lines each: $L_0 = ax_b$, $L_1 = ax_a$; $R_0 = bx_a$, $R_1 = bx_b$.

A detailed proof of correctness would not be worthwhile in the absence of a more detailed description of the algorithm, which we have not provided. A few remarks about time complexity are in order, however. The sweep line advances exactly n times, once per vertex. At each advance, at most one window is updated. This is an important point, as it might seem natural to update all active windows with each advance. This, however, leads to a quadratic algorithm, and is not necessary: no visible segments can be lost by postponing window updating until a vertex is encountered within it. Each window update requires $O(\log n)$ time for data structure searches and updates, and constant processing to output the visible segments. Thus the total time complexity is $O(n \log n)$.

8.4. VISIBILITY GRAPH ALGORITHM

In this section we describe an $O(n^2)$ algorithm for constructing the visibility graph between the endpoints of a set of line segments. This is a very general problem, including, for example, construction of the visibility graph between vertices of a polygon with or without holes as special cases. Since so little is known about the structure of such graphs, however, the algorithm for line segments remains the fastest known algorithm for these special cases.

Perhaps the strongest motivation for the construction of visibility graphs is its application to the shortest-path problem. Lozano-Perez and Wesley showed that the shortest-path for a polygon amidst polygonal obstacles can be solved in $O(n^2)$ time using Dijkstra's shortest graph path algorithm applied to a certain visibility graph (Lozano-Perez and Wesley 1979). For several years the fastest algorithm known for constructing this visibility graph was $O(n^2 \log n)$; one such algorithm, for example, appeared in Lee's thesis (Lee 1978). Recently Welzl improved this to $O(n^2)$ (which is worst-case optimal) by exploiting an algorithm developed for constructing line arrangements.[3] This immediately gives an $O(n^2)$ algorithm for the shortest-path problem.

We will describe Welzl's algorithm here, taking time to explain the rudiments of the now considerable theory on line arrangements, which we will use again in Section 8.6.

Consider the set of three line segments shown in Fig. 8.7. The edges of the corresponding visibility graph G are drawn dashed in the figure. The

---

3. Several others discovered similar algorithms independently and slightly later; for example, Asano, Asano, Guibas, Hershberger, and Imai (1986).

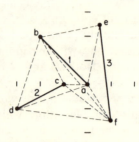

Fig. 8.7. A sample set of line segments. The origin is at a, and the unit hash marks on the (invisible) axes through a indicate the scale.

nodes of G are the endpoints of the line segments, and the arcs correspond to lines of visibility between endpoints. For the purposes of this section, we consider two points x and y visible to one another if the open segment (x, y) does not intersect any segment. This definition could be modified to permit "grazing contact" without altering the complexity of the algorithm. We first exhibit Lee's $O(n^2 \log n)$ algorithm for construction of G.[4]

The n endpoints determine $\binom{n}{2} = O(n^2)$ lines; in Fig. 8.7, $\binom{6}{2} = 15$ distinct slopes are determined. We will assume throughout the remainder of this section that all the slopes are distinct, as they are in this example. Sort these slopes from $-\infty$ to $+\infty$ in $O(n^2 \log n)$ time, and let $\alpha_1, \alpha_2, \ldots$ be the resulting sequence of sorted slopes. We will now show that G can be constructed from this list by an "angular sweep" in $O(n^2)$ additional time.

Let the line segments be labeled $s_1, s_2, \ldots$ in arbitrary order. For any direction α and any endpoint x, let $S_\alpha(x)$ be the segment first hit by a ray from x in direction α. If no segment is hit, define $S_\alpha(x) = s_0$, where s_0 is the "segment at infinity." For example, for $\alpha = 1$ (i.e., 45°), the endpoints in Fig. 8.7 have these values:

x	a	b	c	d	e	f
$S_\alpha(x)$	3	0	1	1	0	0

Let S_α be the function defined by $S_\alpha(x)$ for all x, that is, the vector shown in the previous table. The algorithm constructs $S_{\alpha_1}, S_{\alpha_2}, \ldots$ using the fact that each vector of this sequence differs very little from the one that precedes it.

In particular, suppose S_{α_i} has been constructed, and α_{i+1} is determined by the vertices a and b, with a of smaller X-coordinate than b. The algorithm advances to α_{i+1}, updating the vector and perhaps outputting an edge of the visibility graph. Let the ray from a through b hit $S_{\alpha_i}(a)$ at point c, and let $|xy|$ denote the distance between points x and y. Four cases are distinguished:

(a) a an b are endpoints of the same segment (Fig. 8.8a). Then $S_{\alpha_{i+1}} = S_{\alpha_i}$.

---

4. The presentation follows Welzl (1985).

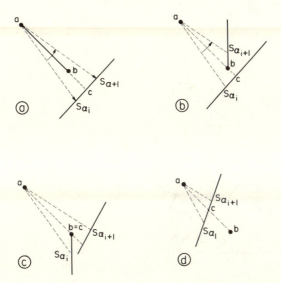

Fig. 8.8. Angular sweep transitions: the edge ab is output in (b) and (c) only.

   (b) $|ab| < |ac|$ (Fig. 8.8b).   Then $S_{\alpha_{i+1}} \leftarrow$ the segment containing b.
         Output edge ab.
   (c) $b = c$ (Fig. 8.8c).   Then $S_{\alpha_{i+1}}(a) \leftarrow S_{\alpha_i}(b)$. Output edge ab.
   (d) $|ab| > |ac|$ (Fig. 8.8d).   Then $S_{\alpha_{i+1}} = S_{\alpha_i}$.

It is clear that updating the vector requires only constant time per direction, as at most one element is altered, and its location can be accessed by pointers associated with each α_i. Thus a complete angular sweep takes $O(n^2)$ time, given an initial vector. This initial vector $S_{-\infty}$ can be constructed easily in $O(n \log n)$ time by a traditional plane sweep of a horizontal line. Thus G can be constructed in $O(n^2)$ given a sorting of the $O(n^2)$ directions. It remains an unsolved problem to obtain this sorting in better than $O(n^2 \log n)$ time, but Welzl showed that an *exact* sorting is not necessary: the angular sweep still works if the directions are only "topologically sorted" from the line arrangement. We now describe this clever idea.

The relevant line arrangement is dual to the set of endpoints. Let $p = (m, b)$ be a segment endpoint. Then the dual of p, T_p, is the line $y = mx + b$. Figure 8.9 shows the lines dual to the six endpoints of Fig. 8.7. The resulting structure is called an *arrangement of lines*. The lines dual to the two points $p_1 = (m_1, b_1)$ and $p_2 = (m_2, b_2)$, $y = m_1x + b_1$ and $y = m_2x + b_2$, intersect at

$$x' = \frac{b_2 - b_1}{m_1 - m_2} \quad \text{and} \quad y' = m_1 \left(\frac{b_2 - b_1}{m_1 - m_2} \right) + b_1.$$

The line determined by p_1 and p_2 has slope $\dfrac{b_2 - b_1}{m_2 - m_1}$ and intercept

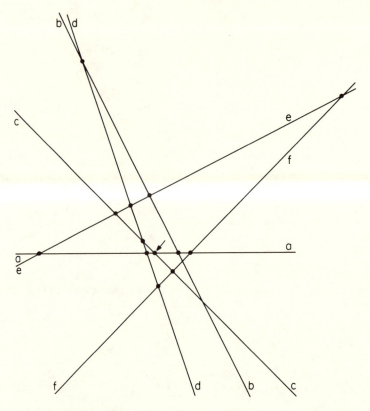

Fig. 8.9. The arrangement of lines dual to the vertices in Fig. 8.7. The arrow marks the origin of the coordinate system. The leftmost intersection (*ae*) has abscissa −5, and the rightmost (*ef*) has abscissa +8.

$-m_1\left(\dfrac{b_2 - b_1}{m_2 - m_1}\right) + b_1$. Thus the point of intersection (m, b) between T_{p_1} and T_{p_2} corresponds to the line $y = -mx + b$ passing through p_1 and p_2. If we imagine the line arrangement drawn in a space whose axes represent slope and intercept, then each intersection point in the arrangement corresponds to a direction determined by two endpoints, and the negative of the abscissa of an intersection point is the slope of the direction. Thus the *ef* intersection in Fig. 8.9 has abscissa 8, and the line determined by *e* and *f* in Fig. 8.7 has slope −8.

It should now be clear that a sorting of the intersection points in the arrangement from right to left corresponds directly to a sorting of the slopes determined by the endpoints, from smallest to largest. This is illustrated in Fig. 8.10, where all the distinct slopes derived from the point set of Fig. 8.7 are shown labeled with the points that determine them. Comparing with Fig. 8.9, we see that the order is preciely the right-to-left order of the intersection points in the arrangement.

It has been shown that the complete structure of a line arrangement of *n*

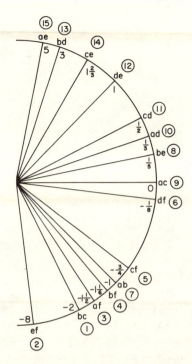

Fig. 8.10. The slopes of the intersection points in Fig. 8.9, labeled by the two lines meeting at that point, and by the slope. The circled numbers represent a topological sort.

lines that is, the incidence relations between all the vertices, edges, and faces determined by the lines, can be constructed in $O(n^2)$ time (Edelsbrunner *et al.* 1986; Chazelle, Guibas, and Lee 1985). This is a fundamental result which we will use but not prove. The correspondence between the vertices of a dual arrangement and the slopes of the directions determined by point pairs gives a great deal of structure to these slopes, but does not seem to lead to a sorting of them in $O(n^2)$ time. However, because the graph structure of the arrangement is available in $O(n^2)$ time, we can obtain a "topological sorting" of the intersection points quickly.

Define a directed graph D on the intersection points of the line arrangement as follows: there is a directed arc from vertex v to vertex u iff v is to the right of u, and u and v are connected by an edge of the arrangement. Figure 8.11 shows D for the arrangement in Fig. 8.9. A *topological sort* of a directed graph is an assignment of integers to the nodes such that the number assigned to a node is greater than all the numbers assigned to the nodes that connect to it with a directed arc. One topological sort (usually there are several) is indicated in Fig. 8.11. It is easy to perform a topological sort in time proportional to the size of the graph via a depth-first search (Aho *et al.* 1983); in our case the graph is of size $O(n^2)$. The labels assigned in Fig. 8.11 are also shown in Fig. 8.10, making it evident that a topological sort of the arrangement vertices does not

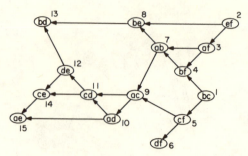

Fig. 8.11. The directed graph associated with the arrangement in Fig. 8.9, and a topological sort.

necessarily correspond to a sorting of the slopes. What Welzl proved, however, is that if the angular sweep algorithm is executed on the slopes organized by any topological sort, it will work just as well as it does with the slopes numerically sorted.

The reason is as follows. Consider all the intersection points on one line of the arrangement. For example, the line T_d dual to point d in Fig. 8.9 is intersected by the lines dual to points $f, a, c, e,$ and b in that order from right to left. The sequence of these intersection points represents a sorting of the directions through d—an angular sweep centered on d. And notice that these intersection points must be sorted properly by the topological sort, since they all lie on a common line of the arrangement: the intersections with T_d are assigned the labels 6, 10, 11, 12, and 13 in Fig. 8.11. As long as all the directions through a common point x are processed in the order of their sorting about x, the angular sweep described previously will produce the correct result, because all of the relevant transitions in the $S_\alpha(x)$ function will be encountered in their correct order. Case (c) in Fig. 8.8 is critical: note that for the update from $S_{\alpha_i}(a)$ to $S_{\alpha_{i+1}}(a)$ to be correct, the value of $S_{\alpha_i}(b)$ must be known. But since the directions through b will be processed in the correct order, $S_{\alpha_i}(b)$ must be correct by the time the direction determined by a and b is considered. Table 8.1 shows the sequence of S_α vectors for our running example when the directions are processed in the topological sort order. Note that all the visibility edges are correctly output in one pass over the directions.

To summarize, Welzl's algorithm consists of the following steps:

(1) Construct the arrangement of lines dual to the endpoints of the line segments.
(2) Perform a topological sort of the vertices of the arrangement.
(3) Perform an angular sweep over the directions in the order given by the topological sort, updating the S_α function at each step, and outputing the edges of the visibility graph.

Each step can be accomplished in $O(n^2)$ time, thus yielding an algorithm for

Table 8.1. Each row shows an endpoint pair determining a direction α, and the S_α vector *after* sweeping past α. S_α elements in italics are the ones modified (or not modified) at direction α. Endpoint pairs shown in italics are output as edges of the visibility graph.

α	a	b	c	d	e	f
	0	2	0	0	0	0
bc	0	0	0	0	0	0
ef	0	0	0	0	0	0
af	3	0	0	0	0	0
bf	3	3	0	0	0	0
cf	3	3	3	0	0	0
df	3	3	3	3	0	0
ab	3	3	3	3	0	0
be	3	0	3	3	0	0
ac	3	0	1	3	0	0
ad	3	0	1	1	0	0
cd	3	0	1	1	0	0
de	3	0	1	1	0	0
bd	3	0	1	0	0	0
ce	3	0	1	0	0	0
ae	0	0	1	0	0	0

constructing the visibility graph in $O(n^2)$ time and space. That this is worst-case optimal follows from the fact that the visibility graph may have $\Omega(n^2)$ edges, for example, when each segment has length zero and no three endpoints are collinear.

It remains an open problem to construct a visibility graph in time proportional to its size, which can be $O(n)$ in special cases. The most recent advance in this direction has been made by Suri, who found an algorithm for constructing the vertex visibility graph of a polygon in time $O(k \log n)$, where k is the number of edges in the graph, using results from Chazelle and Guibas (1985).

8.5. POINT VISIBILITY REGION

In this section we extend the problem of computing a point visibility polygon $V(x)$, considered in Section 8.1, to an environment more general than the interior of a polygon: one consisting of n (perhaps disconnected) line segments. This includes polygons with holes as a special case. Because the resulting object $V(x)$ is not necessarily a polygon (it may be unbounded), we call it the point visibility *region*.

As might be expected, a linear algorithm is no longer possible in this more general case. We first establish that $\Omega(n \log n)$ is a lower bound, and then describe an algorithm that achieves this bound.

8.5.1.   Lower Bound

We prove an $\Omega(n \log n)$ lower bound on the computation of point visibility inside a polygon with holes by reduction from the problem of sorting n integers, $(x_1, x_2, \ldots, x_n)$. Let x_{max} and x_{min} be the largest and the smallest numbers among $x_1, x_2, \ldots, x_n$, and let $\Delta = x_{max} - x_{min}$. Create an instance of the point visibility problem as follows.

The outermost polygon is a rectangle whose vertices are located at $(x_{min} - 1, -\Delta/2)$, $(x_{max} + 1, -\Delta/2)$, $(x_{max} + 1, \Delta/2)$ and $(x_{min} - 1, \Delta/2)$. With each number x_i, $1 \leq i \leq n$, associate a rectangular hole with vertices $(x_i - \varepsilon, -\varepsilon)$, $(x_i + \varepsilon, -\varepsilon)$, $(x_i + \varepsilon, \varepsilon)$, and $(x_i - \varepsilon, \varepsilon)$, where $\varepsilon = 0.1$, for example. Figure 8.12 illustrates the construction for $n = 4$. The point from which the visibility polygon is to be computed is set to be the lower left corner of the outer rectangle: $x = (x_{min} - 1, -\Delta/2)$. It can be easily seen that the lower left corner of each hole occurs at every fifth vertex of the boundary of $V(x)$ in order of increasing values of x_i's. It is therefore easy to extract the sorted order of the x_i's from an algorithm that outputs the boundary of $V(x)$ as a list of vertices. Since sorting n integers is known to require $\Omega(n \log n)$ time in the general algebraic decision tree model, any such algorithm must spend $\Omega(n \log n)$ time in the worst-case.

We now exhibit a simple "angular sweep" algorithm that achieves this lower bound.

8.5.2.   Algorithm

Let S be the set of line segments, assumed to intersect only at their endpoints, and let $P = (p_1, p_2, \ldots, p_n)$ be the set of endpoints of the segments of S. Assume without loss of generality that the given point x is the origin of our coordinate system and the set of points $P \cup \{x\}$ is in general position. Let D be the sequence of n sorted directions determined by x and the endpoints in P. We assume that the ray emanating from x along the X-axis has zero slope and the remaining slopes are measured counterclockwise about x.

The basic idea behind the algorithm is as follows. Let d be any ray. Let $s_1, s_2, \ldots, s_k$ be the sequence of segments of S that intersect d,

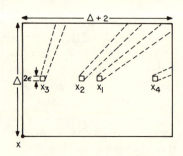

Fig. 8.12.   Construction for the point visibility lower bound.

respectively, at $z_1, z_2, \ldots, z_k$ such that the segments s_1 through s_k are sorted by the rule $(s_i < s_j)$ iff $(|xz_i| < |xz_j|)$, $1 \le i, j \le k$, where $|xz_i|$ denotes the distance from x to z_i. Clearly, s_1 is on the boundary of $V(x)$. The algorithm rotates the ray around x and outputs the sequence of segments that intersect d first. The algorithm is, roughly speaking, an angular plane sweep, and may be described as follows.

Maintain a balanced binary tree T whose leaves are the segments that intersect the ray in the current direction. These segments are sorted by the rule described previously. The current direction is set to slope zero at the start of the algorithm, and then at each step advanced to the head of D, which is organized as a standard queue. The head of D is deleted at each step, and correspondingly a segment is either inserted or deleted from T. An interior node s of T stores the indices of the leftmost and the rightmost segments in the subtree rooted at s. Since the line segments do not cross, information stored with a leaf or an interior node does not change as the ray moves between two consecutive directions in D. For each direction in D, a segment is either inserted or deleted from T. Using the information stored with each node this segment can be inserted or deleted in $O(\log n)$ standard dictionary operations. T, therefore, can be arranged as a standard priority queue that permits the operations *insert, delete,* and *MIN* in logarithmic time per operation.

The correctness of the algorithm is straightforward. The time complexity can be established as follows. The sorted list of slopes, D, can be obtained in $O(n \log n)$ time. Initial construction of T can be accomplished in $O(n \log n)$ time since any ray d intersects $O(n)$ segments. At each step either a segment is added or deleted from T. Since a segment is added and deleted exactly once, and each deletion or insertion can be accomplished in $O(\log n)$ time, the algorithm runs in $O(n \log n)$ time, which is worst-case optimal.

8.6. EDGE VISIBILITY REGION

We generalize in this section the problem of computing the edge visibility polygon $V(e)$ to the general environment of a collection of line segment obstacles. In this environment, $V(e)$ may be unbounded, and it may have holes, so the term "region" is appropriate. Although it is not surprising that this problem has greater time complexity than the polygon case considered in Section 8.3, the magnitude of the complexity is perhaps unexpected: $\Omega(n^4)$. We first establish this lower bound before presenting an algorithm that achieves it.

8.6.1. Lower Bound

The bound is achieved by an example in which $V(e)$ has $\Omega(n^4)$ vertices on its boundary. This yields a lower bound on any algorithm that explicitly

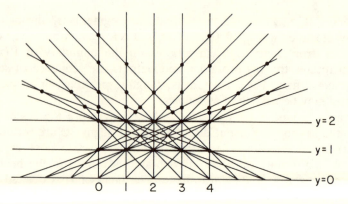

Fig. 8.13. Five gaps on two parallel lines ($y = 1$ and $y = 2$) above e ($y = 0$) produce 29 distinct intersections above the top line; in general, n gaps produce $\Omega(n^4)$ intersections.

constructs the boundary. The main idea of the example is as follows. Let the "luminescent" edge e be horizontal. Place n closely spaced line segments immediately above and parallel to e. The gaps between these segments permit $\Theta(n)$ cones of light to emerge above them. Place a second row of segments above the first, again parallel to e. $\Theta(n^2)$ beams of light escape above this second row. These beams intersect $\Theta(n^4)$ times above the second row, creating a region $V(e)$ with $\Omega(n^4)$ vertices and edges. See Fig. 8.13. A formal specification of this example follows.

Let the segment e have coordinates $\{(-n - 1/2, 0), (2n + 1/2, 0)\}$ for its two endpoints. The first set of segments H lies on the line $y = 1$. Each segment h_i is an open segment from a_i to b_i, where $a_i = (i, 1)$ and $b_i = (i + 1, 1)$ for $0 \le i \le n - 1$. Finally, two more open segments h_{-1} and h_n with the coordinates $\{(-n, -1, 1), (0, 1)\}$ and $\{(n, 1), (2n + 1, 1)\}$, respectively, are included. An identical set of segments H' is constructed on the line $y = 2$. Finally, enclose this set of segments in a rectangular polygon P whose corners have the coordinates

$$\{(-n - 2, -1), (2n + 2, -1), (2n + 2, n + 2), (-n - 2, n + 2)\}.$$

Now let S be the union of H, H', P', and e. Let g_i (respectively, g_i') denote the point gap between two consecutive segments h_{i-1} and h_i (respectively, h_{i-1}' and h_i'). Let G and G' denote the set of gaps for H and H', respectively. It should be clear that every pair of gaps $g_i \in G$ and $g_j' \in G'$, $0 \le i, j \le n$, determines a maximal line segment with one endpoint on e and the other on a side of P, and which does not intersect any other segment. We will call such a maximal line segment a "ray" (in slight abuse of standard terminology). There are $\Omega(n^2)$ rays altogether. Figure 8.13 shows the construction for $n = 4$; the outer polygon P is not shown. Let P' be the intersection of the half space $y \ge 2$ and the region bounded by P. It is clear that the visibility from e within P' is restricted to rays only. Therefore, an intersection point of two rays in P' is a vertex on the boundary of $V(e)$. If we can show that the $\Omega(n^2)$ rays intersect in $\Omega(n^4)$ distinct points in P', the bound will follow immediately. This may seem obvious, but in fact the intersection counting argument is somewhat involved because many rays are parallel, and many intersection points have more than two rays passing through them. One can make an irregular arrangement to avoid parallel beams and multiple intersections, but this also requires considerable care (Suri and O'Rourke 1985). Here we opt for the regular arrangement and proceed with the counting argument.

Let p be a point of intersection above $y = 2$ of at least three rays. Then p is the apex of at least two triangles based on the bottom row, as illustrated in Fig. 8.14. Let b_1 and a_1 be the widths of the left triangle at the bottom and top rows, respectively, and let b_2 and a_2 be the corresponding widths for the triangle that includes the left triangle; again see Fig. 8.14. Then we must have $\dfrac{b_2}{a_2} = \dfrac{b_1}{a_1}$ or $b_2 = \dfrac{b_1 a_2}{a_1}$. Since a_1, a_2, b_1, b_2 are all integers, a_1 must divide $b_1 a_2$. Suppose first that a_1 and b_1 are relatively prime. Then a_1 must divide a_2, and the larger triangle's width is an integer multiple of the smaller's. Suppose second that a_1 and b_1 are not relatively prime. Let $a_1 = ca_1'$ and $b_1 = cb_1'$, with a_1' and b_1' relatively prime. Then $b_2 = \dfrac{b_1' a_2}{a_1'}$, which implies that a_1' divides a_2. Let $a_2 = da_1'$. Substitution yields $b_2 = db_1'$. Thus a_2 and b_2 are not relatively prime. Thus both triangle widths are integer multiples of smaller triangles of widths a_1' and b_1'.

The conclusion of this analysis is that all multiple intersections can be obtained as "scale multiples" of a leftmost, thinnest triangle with relatively prime a and b widths: leftmost because we are treating the scaling as expanding towards the right, and thinnest in that a and b are relatively prime. Thus the number of distinct intersections is equal to the number of leftmost, thinnest triangles. We now proceed to count these triangles.

Let a triangle be determined by a left line through $(b_1, 1)$ and $(a_1, 2)$ on the bottom and top rows, and a right line through $(b_2, 1)$ and $(a_2, 2)$, and let $b = b_2 - b_1$ and $a = a_2 - a_1$ (note the notation here is different from above). Let n be the number of gaps in each row, numbered from 1 to n.

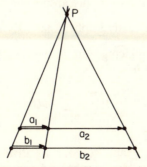

Fig. 8.14. Three lines coincident at one intersection point P determine two triangles, one included in the other.

The number of choices for each of these quantities is as follows:

b: b may take any value from 2 to n. $b = 1$ cannot result in an intersection above $y = 2$.

b_1: b_1 may range from 1 to $n - b$. We will partition this range from 1 to min $(b, n - b)$, and the remainder.

b_2: b_2 is fixed at $b_1 + b$ once b is set.

a: If $a \geq b$, then the triangle does not result in an intersection point above $y = 2$; thus $a < b$. Moreover, a must be relatively prime to b, otherwise the triangle is not thinnest.

a_1: a_1 can range from 1 to $n - 1$ when $b_1 \leq b$, but only from 1 to a when $b_1 > b$, otherwise the triangle would not be leftmost. When $b_1 \leq b$ (and note that min $(b, n - b) \leq b$), the situation is simpler; we will partition this range into two parts, from 1 to $n - b$, and the remainder.

a_2: $a_2 = a_1 + a$ cannot be greater than n, and since $a < b$, it must be less than $a_1 + b$. Within the range $a_1 = 1, \ldots, n - b$, the latter limit applies, and in the remainder the former limit applies.

To simplify the calculations, we will ignore the ranges of b_1 and a_1 that interact with the boundaries of the rows. Thus b_1 will range from 1 to min $(b, n - b)$ and a_1 will range from 1 to $n - b$. Therefore, the quantity we obtain, $S(n)$, is a lower bound on the number of leftmost and thinnest triangles. Concatenating the four choices above yields the following formula:

$$S(n) = \sum_{b=2}^{n} \min (b, n - b)\phi(b)(n - b) \qquad (1)$$

where $\phi(b)$ is the number of numbers less than b and relatively prime to b. We now show that this sum is $\Omega(n^4)$.

It is known that

$$\sum_{b=2}^{n} \phi(b) = \frac{3}{\pi^2} n^2(1 + o(1)) = \Omega(n^2) \qquad (2)$$

See Grosswald (1966). The factors other than $\phi(b)$ in Equation (1) may be moved outside the summation by discarding the first and last quarter of the sum range. Equation (2) easily implies that $\sum_{b=n/4}^{3n/4} \phi(b) = \Omega(n^2)$. Using these summation limits, and replacing min $(b, n - b)$ and $(n - b)$ in Equation (1) by their lower bounds of $n/4$ yields

$$S(n) > \left(\frac{n}{4}\right)\left(\frac{n}{4}\right) \sum_{b=n/4}^{3n/4} \phi(b) = \Omega(n^4).$$

Therefore, $S(n) = \Omega(n^4)$.

Table 8.2 shows the exact number of distinct intersections $I(n)$ for $n = 2, \ldots, 9$, where n is the number of gaps in each row. Figure 8.13 corresponds to the $n = 5$ entry.

Table 8.2

n	2	3	4	5	6	7	8	9
I(n)	0	2	11	29	69	125	224	361

It is necessary to modify the open segments used in the above construction to *closed segments*, to obtain a non-degenerate $V(e)$ with the same lower bound. This requires computing a sufficiently small rational number ε such that modifying the point gaps of our original constructions into ε-gaps, which enlarges the rays to beams, does not merge distinct intersection points. The calculation of epsilon is rather tedious (Suri and O'Rourke 1985); here we simply claim that $\varepsilon < 1/(cn^6)$ suffices, where c is a constant. The important point is that ε need not be exponentially small, which could make the input size larger than n under some models of computation.

8.6.2. Algorithm

We turn now to describing an $O(n^4)$ algorithm for constructing $V(e)$. The algorithm will only be sketched here; details may be found in Suri and O'Rourke (1985, 1986).

First observe that the boundary edges of $V(e)$ are either subsegments of the input segments S, or subsegments of lines through two endpoints in P such that the determined line intersects e.[5] We define a set E of line segments from which the boundary of $V(e)$ will be constructed as follows. First, henceforth consider e, the edge from which visibility is being computed, as a member of S. E consists of all line segments e_i such that:

(1) one endpoint p is in P;
(2) the other endpoint lies on a segment s_i in S, and the interior of e_i intersects no other segments of S;
(3) the line L containing e_i passes through another endpoint p_i in P, which may or may not lie on e_i; and
(4) the line L intersects e, and no other segments of S intersect L between e and p.

It should be clear that E may be constructed in $O(n^2)$ time by slight modification of Welzl's algorithm, described in Section 8.4. Whenever that algorithm outputs a visibility edge between p and p_i, the first segment s_i intersected by the extension of pp_i is available from the data structure. Supplementing the directions swept over with their negations insures that the extension in both directions will be considered. E can be easily constructed from this information.

Let $L(p) = (e_1, e_2, \ldots, e_k)$ be the list of edges of E with an endpoint at p, sorted angularly about p, where e_i terminates on s_i, and the line

---

5. Suri and O'Rourke (1985) for a formal proof of this claim.

containing e_i is determined by p and p_i, as in the definition above. It is somewhat less obvious that $L(p)$ can be obtained in $O(n)$ time for each $p \in P$ from the arrangement of lines used in Welzl's algorithm. Recall that the order of the intersections with the line dual to p in the arrangement corresponds to the directions determined by p sorted by slope. This basic observation can be used to extract $L(p)$ in linear time, as was shown in Asano et al. (1986). We will not prove this assertion here.

The algorithm performs an angular sweep about each $p \in P$ using $L(p)$, and outputs $O(n)$ triangular regions of visibility. The union of the resulting $O(n^2)$ triangles is then found in $O(n^4)$ time, and this constitutes $V(e)$.

Consider the sweep for a particular $p \in P$ from e_i to e_{i+1}. If p remains visible to e throughout the swept angle, then the triangular region between e_i and e_{i+1} is visible to e. There are four distinct cases, depending on the orientation of the segments whose endpoints are p_i and p_{i+1}. These are illustrated in Fig. 8.15, where the visible triangle to be output is shaded. The sweep is made through all of $L(p)$ for each $p \in P$. Note that since e is itself a member of S, triangles whose base is on e will also be output. The following lemma shows that the union of all these triangles is precisely $V(e)$.

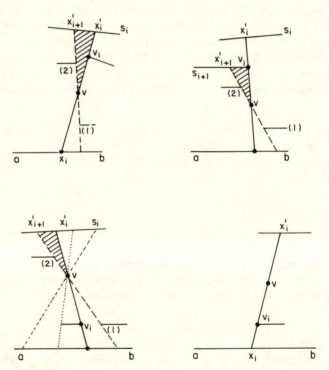

Fig. 8.15. Counterclockwise rotation about v may be blocked by a vertex at position (1) or (2). In (a)–(c), the shaded triangle is output; in (c), triangle $vs_i x_i'$ was output previously; in (d), no rotation is possible.

LEMMA 8.1.   Let $T_i = \bigcup_j \Delta_{i_j}$, where Δ_{i_j} is a triangle rooted at $v_i \in P$ output by the just described algorithm. Then, $\bigcup_i T_i = V(ab)$.

Proof:

$\bigcup_i T_i \subseteq V(ab)$:

Each triangle output by the angular sweep is visible from e by construction.

$\bigcup_i T_i \supseteq V(ab)$:

We prove the claim by contradiction. Let $x \in V(ab)$ be any point such that $x \notin \bigcup_i T_i$. Let $y \in ab$ be any point that is visible from x. Imagine "swinging" the segment xy counterclockwise about x until it hits some vertex $z_1 \in P$. Let $y_1 \in ab$ and $x_1 \in s_x$ be the two points at which segment $z_1 x$ extended in both directions intersects the segments of S, where $s_x \in S$. Now, consider rotating the segment $y_1 x_1$ clockwise about z_1 such that $y_1 x_1$ maintains its contact with ab and s_x. Let z_2 be the first vertex of P contacted by this rotating segment $x_1 y_1$. There are two cases to be considered, depending upon the relative positions of z_1 and z_2 (see Fig. 8.16). Notice

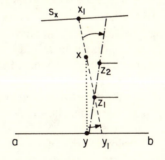

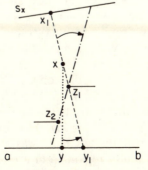

Fig. 8.16. x lies in a triangle rooted at z_1.

that the case $z_1 \in \{a, b\}$ is possible and does not require separate treatment. It is easily seen that in either case x lies in the triangle rooted at z_1 with one side collinear with the segment $z_1 z_2$. But since this triangle belongs to $\bigcup_i T_i$

the assumption that $x \notin \bigcup_i T_i$ is contradicted.   □

All that remains is the actual formation of the union of the $O(n^2)$ triangles. The problem of forming the union of polygons is very similar to a special case of hidden surface elimination: if the polygons are considered parallel to the xy-plane, we want the boundary of the view from $z = +\infty$. McKenna's hidden surface algorithm (McKenna 1987) requires $O(N^2)$ time for a scene with N vertices. Applying this algorithm with slight modification (see Suri and O'Rourke (1985)) to our triangles yields an $O(n^4)$ algorithm for construction of $V(e)$, which is worst-case optimal.

8.7.   RECENT ALGORITHMS

Significant advances in visibility algorithms have been made as this book was being written. Here we mention three of the most important.

It was mentioned in Section 8.3 that the Chazelle–Guibas algorithm for constructing edge visibility polygons creates a data structure that can be used to solve other problems as well. Using this structure (and much else besides), they obtained the following strong result (Chazelle and Guibas 1985). There exists an $O(n)$ data structure for a polygon P that can be computed in time $O(n \log n)$, and which can answer queries of the following form in $O(\log n)$ time: given a point p in P and a direction u, find the first edge of P hit by a ray from p in the direction u. These so-called "bullet shooting" queries are the basis of Suri's output-size sensitive algorithm for construction of the vertex visibility graph of a polygon. In Guibas *et al.* (1986) the preprocessing time for Chazelle-Guibas algorithm is reduced to $O(n \log \log n)$.

Guibas *et al.* recently exploited the new $O(n \log \log n)$ triangulation algorithm to improve the asymptotic worst-case bounds for several visibility problems, most notably the problem of computing the edge visibility polygon (Guibas *et al.* 1986). First they showed how to compute the "shortest-path tree" from a vertex x of a polygon P: the union of all Euclidean shortest paths from x to every other vertex. This step depends heavily on the Tarjan-Van Wyk triangulation algorithm. They then prove that if $e = ab$ can see a portion of $e' = cd$, then the shortest paths from a to c and from b to d are both "outwardly convex," forming an hourglass shape (similar to that shown in Fig. 8.5). With this observation, they can construct $V(e)$ in a single boundary traversal of P using the shortest-path trees from a and from b. The result is an $O(n \log \log n)$ algorithm for computing $V(e)$.

The final result we will discuss here was invoked at the end of the previous section: the visibility region from a point in three dimensions can be computed in $O(n^2)$ time in an environment composed of polygons with a total of n vertices. This is the hidden surface elimination problem. The fastest algorithms developed until recently require $O(n^2 \log n)$ time in the worst-case (Sutherland *et al.* 1974), although they run much faster on the type of inputs encountered in practice. Recently McKenna used the $O(n^2)$ algorithm for constructing line arrangements to obtain an $O(n^2)$ worst-case optimal algorithm (McKenna 1987) for hidden surface removal.[6] This algorithm, however, is likely to be inferior to the standard graphics algorithms in practice. The major open problem in hidden surface algorithms is to find an output-size sensitive algorithm: one that runs in time $O(k \operatorname{polylog} n)$, where k is the number of line segments that are visible in the final scene. Such algorithms have only been achieved in special cases (Güting and Ottmann 1984).

---

6. This problem differs from that of hidden line elimination, which was solved in Devai (1986).

9

MINIMAL GUARD
COVERAGE

9.1. INTRODUCTION

In Chapter 1 it was shown that Fisk's proof of the art gallery theorem can be converted into an algorithm that covers a polygon of n vertices with $\lfloor n/3 \rfloor$ guards in $O(n \log n)$ time. Although $\lfloor n/3 \rfloor$ is necessary in some cases, often this is far more guards than are needed to cover a particular polygon. For example, convex polygons only require one guard, but Avis and Toussaint's algorithm would still place $\lfloor n/3 \rfloor$ guards. It is natural, then, to seek a placement of a *minimal* number of guards that cover a given polygon. We will show, however, that this problem is fundamentally intractable: it is NP-complete.

Finding the minimal number of guards to cover a polygon is a specific instance of a general class of problems on which there is now a considerable literature: polygon decomposition problems. Guards determine star polygons, so minimal guard coverage corresponds to finding a minimal star cover of a polygon. Polygon decomposition problems can be classified along four "dimensions": decomposition type, the shape of the pieces, restrictions on the boundaries of the pieces, and the shape of the polygon being decomposed. We will discuss these dimensions briefly before focusing on our particular case.

(1) Decomposition Type

The term "decomposition" is usually understood to encompass two major types: *partition*, in which the pieces are not allowed to overlap, and *cover*, where overlap is permitted. In both cases, each piece of the decomposition must be a subset of the original polygon, and the union of the pieces must be precisely the polygon. Covers can be significantly more efficient than partitions: Fig. 9.1 shows an example due to Ntafos (1986) that has a star cover of size 2 but the minimum star partition is of size $O(n)$. Since guard lines-of-sight can pass through one another freely, the minimum guard placement problem is a minimal cover problem.

A third type of decomposition, *sum-difference* decomposition, that

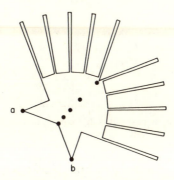

Fig. 9.1. A polygon that may be covered with 2 stars with kernels at *a* and *b*, but that requires 5 stars in a partition, with kernels at the indicated points.

permits both union and difference of pieces, has not been studied yet to the same extent as covers and partitions (Woo 1982).

(2) Shape of Component Pieces

The major shape types that have been studied are convex (Pavlidis 1968, 1977; Chazelle 1980; O'Rourke 1982a, 1982b), star (Maruyama 1972; Avis and Toussaint 1981a), spiral (Feng and Pavlidis 1975; Pavlidis and Feng 1977), monotone (Lee and Preparata 1977), and trapezoidal (Asano, Asano, and Imai 1986). For orthogonal polygons, both rectangle (Pagli *et al.* 1979; Chaiken *et al.* 1981; Franzblau and Kleitman 1984) and square (Albertson and O'Keefe 1981) pieces have been examined; L-shaped partitions were discussed in Sections 2.5 and 2.6. We will only discuss star pieces.

(3) Restrictions on the Boundaries of the Pieces

In addition to the shape restrictions on the pieces, two further restrictions that cut across shape types are important. A *Steiner point* is any point in a polygon that is *not* a vertex.[1] Decompositions are then classified as *with Steiner points* permitted, or *without Steiner points*. The latter are only permitted to use vertex-to-vertex diagonals to compose the boundaries of the pieces. In general, decompositions with Steiner points are more efficient, and harder to find. Figure 9.2 shows a polygon that can be covered with two convex pieces if Steiner points are permitted, but which requires three pieces without Steiner points. A minimum convex partition without Steiner points has no more than four times the number of pieces in a minimal partition with Steiner points, as is established, for example, by the Mehlhorn and Hertel triangulation argument mentioned in Section 1.3.2. (It does not seem to be known if this worst-case bound can be achieved.) The situation for star pieces is less clear. I know of no results comparing the

---

1. Steiner used such points to define what is now known as a *Steiner tree*, a minimal spanning tree employing points in addition to those being spanned.

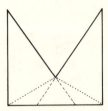

Fig. 9.2. A polygon that may be covered with 2 convex pieces if Steiner points are permitted (dashed), but requires 3 if not permitted (dotted).

efficiency of partitions or covers of star pieces with and without Steiner points.

Other restrictions on the boundaries of the component pieces of decompositions have been considered. The most interesting is to restrict all edges to be subsets of extensions of the polygon edges through the interior of the polygon. This was studied by Pavlidis (1968, 1977) and myself (O'Rourke 1982a,b) for convex partitions, and by Aggarwal *et al.* (1985) for star covers. Figure 9.3 shows an example of the latter authors that requires only two star pieces if diagonals are permitted, but needs three if only edge extensions are used.

(4) Polygon Restrictions

The two most important classes here are polygons with and without holes. In at least one case, convex partitions with Steiner points, the polygon problem can be solved in polynomial time (Section 1.4.2), but permitting holes changes the complexity to NP-hard (Masek 1979) (O'Rourke and Supowit 1983). We will discuss both cases for star covers in this chapter.

Of course, many other polygon restrictions can be considered. We will briefly discuss the restriction to orthogonal polygons.

Our focus in this chapter is minimal star covers with Steiner points. We show in the next section that this problem is NP-hard for polygons with holes, and in Section 9.3 it is shown that the problem remains NP-hard for polygons without holes. Clearly the latter result supersedes the former, but the proofs are quite different, and we present them in the order in which they were discovered. Next we look at two restrictions that permit polynomial-time solutions: guards in "grids," special orthogonal polygons (Section 9.4), and minimal star partitions without Steiner points (Section

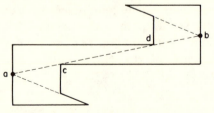

Fig. 9.3. A polygon that can be covered with 2 stars if diagonal *cd* is used, but that requires 3 if only edge extensions are used.

9.5). The former problem can be solved with a graph matching algorithm, and the latter with dynamic programming. Several related algorithms and problems are discussed in the final section.

9.2. NP-HARD FOR POLYGONS WITH HOLES[2]

Although it would take us too far afield to explain the extensive theory of NP-completeness, we will sketch enough of the definitions so that the next two sections can be followed by the uninitiated.

The theory hinges on a division of problems into two complexity classes: P and NP. Problems in P can be solved in deterministic Polynomial time, and problems in NP can be solved in Non-deterministic Polynomial time. The addition of the power of non-determinism seems to widen the class of problems considerably, but although $P \subseteq NP$ follows from the definitions, no one has been able to prove that $P \neq NP$. This is, in fact, the major open problem in computer science today. Despite this uncertainty, the hardest problems in NP, the NP-*complete* problems, seem fundamentally intractable: although over 1000 NP-complete problems have been identified, no polynomial algorithm is known for any of them.

The "hardness" partial order is established by the notion of *polynomial reducibility*. If problem A can be transformed in polynomial time to an instance of problem B such that the solution to B yields a solution to A, then A is said to be polynomial reducible, or just reducible, to B. If A is reducible to B, then B is at least as hard as A, for if B can be solved in polynomial time, so can A. A problem $B \in NP$ to which all problems $A \in NP$ can be reduced is called NP-complete: it is at least as hard as any problem in NP. If an NP-complete problem B is reducible to a problem C, then C is called NP-hard: it is at least as hard as an NP-complete problem. The distinction between NP-complete and NP-hard problems is that the former are members of NP but the latter need not be.

As the classes P and NP are defined for *decision* problems—that is, those that output only "yes" or "no"—we will phrase the minimum guard cover problems as decision questions also. Since it is important to identify clearly the size of the input, we will specify the problems in Garey and Johnson's instance-question format (Garey and Johnson 1979). Our proofs of NP-hardness will start from a known NP-complete problem, Boolean 3-Satisfiability. It may be stated as follows.

Boolean 3-Satisfiability (3SAT)

INSTANCE: A set $U = \{u_1, u_2, \ldots, u_n\}$ of Boolean variables and a collection $C = \{c_1, c_2, \ldots, c_m\}$ of clauses over U such that each $c_i \in C$ is a disjunction of precisely three literals.

---

2. This section is the result of joint work with Ken Supowit; an earlier version appeared in O'Rourke and Supowit (1983), © 1983 IEEE.

QUESTION: Is there a satisfying truth assignment for C, that is, is there a truth assignment to the n variables in U such that the conjunctive normal form $c_1 \cdot c_2 \cdots c_m$ is true?

The minimum guard cover problem is formally stated as follows.

Minimum Star (or Guard) Cover of a Polygon with Holes (StarCH)

INSTANCE: A set of lists of integer-coordinate vertices representing a polygonal region P with holes, and a positive integer bound K.

QUESTION: Is there a cover of P with K or fewer star subsets of P, i.e., do there exist star polygons $S_1, S_2, \ldots, S_k$ with $k \leq K$ such that $S_1 \cup S_2 \cup \cdots \cup S_k = P$?

The goal is now to polynomially transform a given instance of 3SAT into a polygonal region that has a star cover of K or fewer pieces iff the 3SAT instance is satisfiable. The proof proceeds along lines similar to proofs of NP-completeness by Fowler *et al.* on the "box-cover" problem (Fowler *et al.* 1981), and by Supowit on point and disk coverage problems (Supowit 1981).

The usual first step in a proof of NP-completeness is to show that the problem is a member of the class of NP problems, that is, solvable via a non-deterministic algorithm in polynomial time (Garey and Johnson 1979). Often this is easy, merely requiring a demonstration that a solution "guessed" by a non-deterministic program can be checked in polynomial time. With the integer-lattice geometric objects used in our constructions, however, it is unclear how to establish this. In the absence of a proof that StarCH is a member of NP, the argument presented below will establish that StarCH is NP-hard rather than NP-complete.

We will now show that 3SAT is polynomially transformable to StarCH. The goal is to accept an instance of 3SAT as input and construct, in polynomial time, a polygonal region that has a cover with a certain number K or fewer star polygons iff the given set of clauses is satisfiable. As with other 3SAT transformations (Garey and Johnson 1979; Fowler *et al.* 1981; Supowit 1981), the construction forces a truth assignment with n "truth-setting components" that simulate the Boolean variables, and ensures satisfaction with m "clause components" that correspond to the disjunctive clauses.

Truth-Setting Components

The truth-setting components are polygonal regions of a repetitive staircase pattern that have just two distinct minimum star covers; see Fig. 9.4. One of the minimum covers is associated with the truth assignment *true* and the other with *false*. There are certain distinguished points associated with each pattern, labeled with integers in the figures. These points are not part of the construction; they are used in the proof that the polygon constructed has the appropriate cover iff the clause is satisfiable. Note that two of the

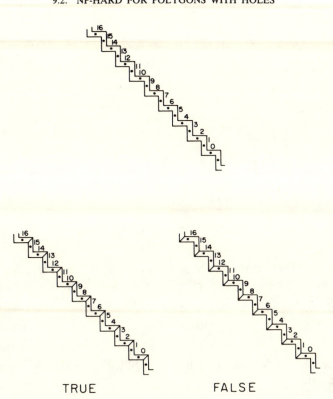

TRUE   FALSE

Fig. 9.4. The truth-setting component has two distinct minimum covers corresponding to assignments *true* and *false*.

distinguished points can be covered by one star polygon iff the two points are consecutive in numerical sequence.

The truth-setting patterns are bent (see Lemma 9.2 below) to form closed loops, called *variable loops*. There will be one such loop per Boolean variable u_k in the final construction.

By the above remarks, each minimum star cover for a variable loop contains exactly $r_k/2$ stars, where r_k is the number of distinguished points in the variable loop corresponding to u_k. We call such a cover *true* if it contains distinguished points i and $i + 1$ for all even i (taken modulo r_k), and we call it *false* if it contains distinguished points j and $j + 1$ for all odd j. Define the bound K used in the definition of the StarCH problem as equal to $\frac{1}{2} \sum_{k=1}^{n} r_k$.

The main properties of variable loops are stated somewhat informally as follows (the proofs, being straightforward, are either omitted or sketched):

LEMMA 9.1. Each minimum star cover is either a *true* cover or a *false* cover.

In constructing the polygonal region P, it will be necessary to cross variable loops over one another, and "bend" them 45°, without these

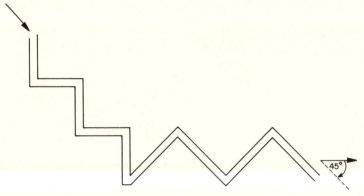

Fig. 9.5. Variable loop 45° bend.

modifications affecting the truth of Lemma 9.1 for any variable loop. The ability to bend a variable loop effectively gives us what is sometimes called an "inverter" in other NP-completeness constructions (Masek 1979).

LEMMA 9.2. The variable loops may bend 45° without affecting their properties.

Proof. See Fig. 9.5. Note that it is not difficult to make all vertices have integer coordinates. ☐

LEMMA 9.3. Two variable loops may cross over one another without affecting their independent coverage properties. More precisely, if two unconnected variable loops require k_1 and k_2 stars in a minimum cover, then one can cross over the other in such a manner that the resulting (connected) polygonal region requires $k_1 + k_2$ star pieces in a minimum cover, and without altering the type of coverage (*true/false*) within either variable loop.

Proof. The construction is shown in Fig. 9.6. It would not be difficult to show that it preserves the desired properties were it not for the possibility that distinguished points i and j may be covered by a single star-shaped polygon Q (shown in shaded in the figure). We can, however, arrange the crossovers to ensure that at each crossover in the complete construction, i and j are both odd. We will argue that this arrangement ensures that each covering that contains no more than K pieces (if there are any) is a *true/false* covering.

Define a *cross star* to be a star polygon containing at least one distinguished point of each of two variable loops—for example, the polygon Q in Fig. 9.6. Since the points i and j are both odd at every crossover, each cross star contains exactly two distinguished points, both of which are odd. Since no star-shaped polygon can contain more than one even distinguished point, and since there are K even distinguished points, every cover must contain K stars to cover the even distinguished points. Therefore, if a cover

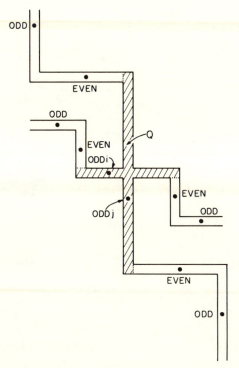

Fig. 9.6. Variable loop crossover. Star Q contains two odd distinguished points.

also includes one or more cross stars, then it must have more than K elements. A similar argument was used in (Supowit 1981).[3] ☐

Clause Junctions

In a minimum cover of a particular variable loop, small triangular areas near the kernels of the star pieces can be added that could be covered "free" (without increasing the number of pieces) if the coverage is of type *true* (say), but that cannot be covered free if the coverage is of type *false* (see Fig. 9.7). This is the key idea in the formation of the clause junctions.

The heart of a clause junction is an isosceles triangle whose equal sides both slope at 45°. (The shape of this triangle is not critical, but it is easier to keep to integer coordinates if its sides slope at 45°.) Arms of three different variable loops are brought to the junction, one for each side of the triangle. Suppose the clause represented by the junction is $c = \overline{u_i} + u_j + \overline{u_k}$. Then variable loop j is arranged so that a setting of *true* will permit the triangle to be covered free, and variable loops i and k are placed so that a setting of *false* will result in free coverage. The result is that the triangle at the clause junction will be covered free iff the clause is satisfied by the truth assignment established by the truth-setting components.

---

3. Use of "planar 3SAT" (Lichtenstein 1982a) apparently obviates the need for this lemma, but it introduces other complications.

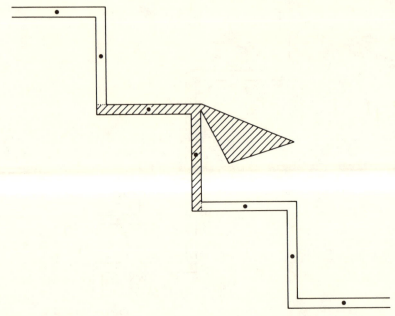

Fig. 9.7. The triangular region is covered free when the truth assignment covers the shaded distinguished points.

The details of clause junction construction are shown in Fig. 9.8. The three important claims concerning the clause junctions are contained in the following proposition.

LEMMA 9.4. The clause junction illustrated in Fig. 9.8 possesses the following properties:

(1) All vertex coordinates are integers.
(2) The central triangle is covered free iff the clause is satisfied.
(3) The junction does not affect the independent coverage properties of the participating variable loops.

Proof. That all vertex coordinates are integers follows from the method of constructing the bends and the use of 45° angles in the clause triangles. Figure 9.7 establishes that the central triangle can be covered free if the clause is satisfied. On the other hand, if the clause is not satisfied, then the construction of the clause junction prevents any piece covering a distinguished point of one of the variable loops to also completely cover the central triangle. Finally, no two distinguished points belonging to different varible loops can be covered by a single piece. Since every piece in a minimum cover must include two distinguished points, there is no interference in their independent coverage properties. □

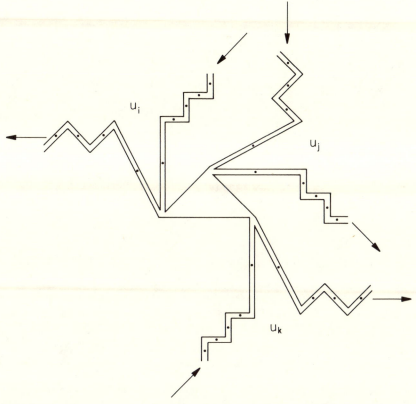

Fig. 9.8. A clause junction. The central triangle is covered free iff the corresponding clause is satisfied.

Complete Construction

The overall structure of the polygonal region constructed for a given instance of 3SAT consists of n variable loops arranged in parallel slanting columns, one for each Boolean variable in U, with m clause junctions placed to the right, one for each clause in C. Arms of the three variable loops corresponding to the three literals that participate in a clause are brought across the other loops to the right, bent in 45° increments until they are oriented properly for the chosen triangle side and according to their complemented/uncomplemented status in the clause, brought to the clause triangle as illustrated previously, and finally returned to their proper slanting columns. A schematic example is shown in Fig. 9.9.

Although the details are complicated, the entire construction can clearly be performed mechanically using the bend, crossover, and clause junction patterns shown previously. The construction requires no more than $O(m)$ bends, $O(mn)$ crossovers, and $O(m)$ clause junctions, so the execution time of the entire procedure is polynomial bounded by $O(mn)$. Note again that

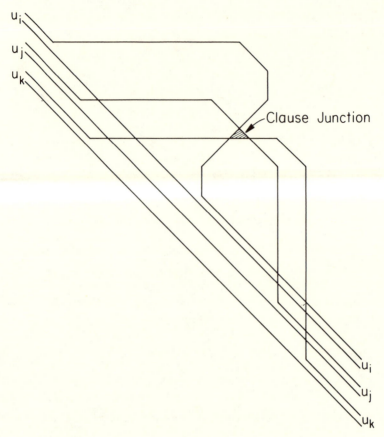

Fig. 9.9. Arrangement of variable loops and a clause junction.

since all of the patterns use integer coordinates, the vertices of the final polygon region will all have integer coordinates. These observations imply the following proposition.

LEMMA 9.5. The construction of the polygonal region requires only polynomial time.

Recall that the bound K was defined to be half the total number of distinguished points. Our argument to this point has shown the following.

LEMMA 9.6. A given set of clauses is satisfiable iff there is a star cover of the constructed polygonal region into K or fewer pieces. (Actually, there can never be fewer than K pieces.)

We may finally state the main result of this section.

THEOREM 9.1 [O'Rourke and Supowit 1982]. The problem StarCH is NP-hard.

Proof. Lemmas 9.5 and 9.6 establish that 3SAT is polynomial transformable to StarCH. Since 3SAT is known to be NP-complete, StarCH is NP-hard. □

COROLLARY. StarCH without Steiner points is NP-hard.

Proof. No Steiner points are needed in any of the constructions. □

9.3. NP-HARD FOR POLYGONS WITHOUT HOLES

The proof in the preceding section constructs a polygonal region with at least n holes, one per variable loop. To prove NP-hardness for polygons with no holes requires, then, a different approach. Recall that for minimum convex covers, the problem is NP-hard with holes but polynomial without, suggesting the same might be true for star covers. But recently Lee and Lin found a clever reduction from 3SAT to a polygon of no holes, proving that finding a minimal star cover (problem StarC) is NP-hard even without holes (Lee and Lin 1986). We present their proof in this section. The proof is simpler if guards are restricted to vertices, that is, if the star kernels always include a vertex; this restriction can be removed later.

The coupling between a variable and its appearance in a clause junction was rather direct in the proof in the previous section: a variable loop is connected to the junction almost as if it were a wire carrying "true" or "false" charge. For a simple polygon construction, the coupling is necessarily more subtle, effected by lines of sight. The truth-setting components of the previous section becomes two distinct components here: a literal pattern, and a variable pattern. The literal patterns appear in clause junctions, and the consistency of the true/false settings of the literals are enforced by the variable pattern.

Literal Pattern

A literal pattern is shown in Fig. 9.10. The distinguished point p shown is visible from vertex t or f. The polygon will be arranged so that no other vertex can see p. As the labels suggest, vertex t will be assigned a guard when the truth value of the literal is *true,* and f when *false.*

Fig. 9.10. A literal pattern. The distinguished point p is visible only to t and f.

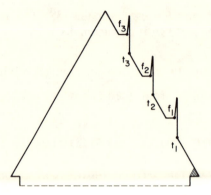

Fig. 9.11. A clause junction. The shaded triangle can be seen only by t_i, $i = 1, 2, 3$.

Clause Junction

A clause junction is shown in Fig. 9.11. Coverage of the three distinguished points in the three literals requires one of $\{t_i, f_i\}$ to be assigned a guard for $i = 1, 2, 3$. At least one of $\{t_1, t_2, t_3\}$ must be assigned a guard in order to cover the shaded triangle. Thus at least one literal must be true for coverage of the junction, which will force each clause to be satisfied.

Variable Pattern

The purpose of a variable pattern is to force all truth assignments of literals of a particular variable to be consistent with one another. This is accomplished with the pattern illustrated in Fig. 9.12. It consists of two "wells," with a vertex at the top of the left well labeled F, and a vertex at the corresponding position on the right well labeled T. In addition each well has s thin spikes, where s is the number of clauses in which the variable u participates, aligned with the F and T vertices and vertices in the clause junctions. One of the two vertices labeled T and F will require a guard in a minimum cover in order to see the distinguished point q illustrated. No other guards will be needed to see the remainder of the variable pattern *if* all the literals for this variable are assigned truth values consistently. This will only become apparent when we examine an example.

Complete Construction

A three variable ($n = 3$), two clause ($m = 2$) example is shown in Fig. 9.13. Here the two clauses are $(u_1 + \overline{u_2} + u_3)$ and $(\overline{u_1} + u_2 + u_3)$. Each variable

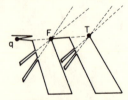

Fig. 9.12. A variable pattern. The distinguished point q can be seen only by T and F.

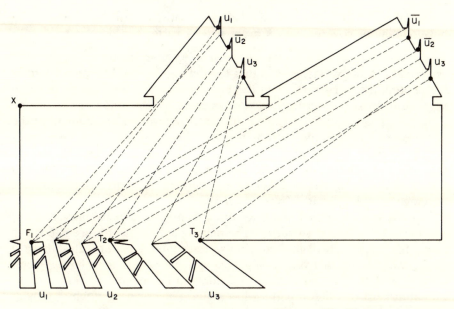

Fig. 9.13. The complete polygon for $(u_1 + \overline{u_2} + u_3) \cdot (\overline{u_1} + \overline{u_2} + u_3)$.

pattern has two spikes, one per well, for each literal in a clause junction that uses that variable. Let u be a variable with distinguished vertices T and F, and let l be a literal in $\{u, \bar{u}\}$ with distinguished vertices t and f. A spike in the left well of the variable pattern for u is collinear with F and t if $l = u$, and with F and f if $l = \bar{u}$. A spike in the right well is collinear with T and f if $l = u$, and with T and t if $l = \bar{u}$. The consequence of these alignments is that a guard placed at F sees down all the spikes of the left well, and a guard placed at T sees down all the spikes of the right well. As mentioned previously, a guard is needed at either T or F to see the distinguished point associated with the variable pattern. Suppose a guard is placed at T, covering all spikes in the right well. Because all spikes in the left well are aligned with F and t_{i_k}, where $t_{i_1}, t_{i_2}, \ldots$ are the t-vertices defined in Fig. 9.11 for all literals using u, and aligned with f_{j_k}, where $f_{j_1}, f_{j_2}, \ldots$ are the f-vertices for all literals $\bar{u}$, all spikes in the left well will be covered if guards are placed at $t_{i_1}, t_{i_2}, \ldots$ and $f_{j_1}, f_{j_2}, \ldots$. This means that if the literals involving u are assigned truth values consistent with $u = true$, then a guard at the F vertex of the u variable pattern is not needed to cover the spikes of the left well, but a guard will be needed at the T vertex. An opposite conclusion is reached for $u = false$. This is the key idea motivating the construction. Thus in Fig. 9.13, u_1 is "set" false by the guard at F_1, and the spikes in the right well of the u_1 variable pattern are covered by a guards at the f-vertex of the u_1 literal in the first clause, and the t-vertex of the $\overline{u_1}$ literal in the second clause.

The total number of distinguished points is $3m + n$: 3 in each of m clause junctions, and 1 in each of n variable patterns.

LEMMA 9.7. A given set of clauses is satisfiable iff the constructed polygon may be covered with $K = 3m + n + 1$ vertex guards.

Proof. If the set of clauses is satisfiable, then there exists a truth assignment to the variables such that each clause is *true*. Placing a guard at the appropraite t or f vertices of the literal patterns in each clause junction necessarily covers the clause junction, because at least one t vertex will be assigned a guard. By the argument presented above, placing a guard at the T vertex of the variable pattern for u if the satisfying truth assignment assigns u *true,* and at F if *false,* covers all the spikes as well as the distinguished point of the pattern for u. Finally, a guard at the vertex x in Fig. 9.13 covers all the wells of all the variable patterns. Thus complete coverage is achieved with K vertex guards.

Suppose there is a cover with K vertex guards. One guard must be at x, otherwise K would not suffice. The remaining $3m + n$ guards are needed to cover the $3m + n$ distinguished points. Each literal pattern must have a guard at either its t or f vertex, and each variable pattern must have a guard at its T or F vertex. Each clause junction will be covered by these guards only if at least one literal pattern has a guard at its t vertex, which implies that each clause will be satisfied. Each variable pattern will be covered by one guard at T or F only if all literals using that variable are assigned consistently, by our previous remarks. But then the guard placement determines a consistent truth assignment that satisfies the given instance of 3SAT.   □

THEOREM 9.2 [Lee and Lin 1984].   The minimum vertex guard problem for polygons (StarC) is NP-complete.

Aggarwal extended the argument to obtain the same result for point guards, guards not restricted to vertices (Aggarwal 1984).

COROLLARY [Aggarwal 1984].   The problem of finding a minimum star cover, with Steiner points permitted, for a polygon without holes, is NP-hard.

9.4. GUARDS IN GRIDS

The negative results in the two preceding sections are not the last word on minimal star covers, as there are many interesting special cases that may be tractable. We present two such positive results in this and the following section.

In this section we study a special restricted class of polygons introduced by Ntafos called "grids" (Ntafos 1986); in fact the restriction is so extreme that they are not even polygons. A *grid* P is a connected union of vertical and horizontal line segments. An example is shown in Fig. 9.14. A grid can be thought of as an orthogonal polygon with holes, consisting of very thin corridors. Visibility retains its usual definition: a guard at x can see point y if

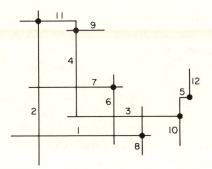

Fig. 9.14. A grid covered by 6 guards (dots).

xy is a subset of P. Of course in a grid all lines of sight are either vertical or horizontal, so star polygons are crosses. Although grids are an extreme specialization of polygonal regions with holes, note that a large portion (but not all) of the constructions used to prove Theorem 9.1 could be accomplished with a grid.

Ntafos offered the following simple algorithm for finding a minimal cover by guards in a grid. A guard must be located in each line segment of a grid. Let G be the intersection graph of the grid: each node of G corresponds to a line segment, and two nodes are connected by an arc iff their corresponding segments cross. Figure 9.15 shows the intersection graph for the grid in Fig. 9.14. A *matching* in a graph is a collection of edges M such that every node is incident to at most one edge of M. A *maximum matching* is a matching of maximum cardinality. Notice that a matching in our intersection graph is a collection of intersections that cover pairs of vertical and horizontal segments of the grid. A maximum matching can be found in $O(V^{2.5})$ time for an arbitrary graph of V vertices (Even 1979). The graph G is, however, not arbitrary: it is bipartite, since only intersections between vertical and horizontal segments can occur; two vertical or two horizontal segments are parallel and cannot intersect. The problem of finding a maximum matching in a bipartite graph is known as the "marriage problem"; one can be found in $O(V^{1/2}E)$ time, where V is the number of vertices and E the number of edges of the bipartite graph (Even 1979). For a grid of n segments, $V = n$

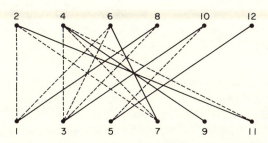

Fig. 9.15. The intersection graph for the grid in Fig. 9.14. The 6 guards are shown as solid lines.

and $E = O(n^2)$, so both the general algorithm and the bipartite algorithm lead to $O(n^{2.5})$ worst-case complexity.

For complete coverage of a grid, each line segment requires a guard, and since only two line segments cross at an intersection, a guard can cover at most two segments. Thus for a grid of n segments, at least $\lceil n/2 \rceil$ guards are necessary. If the intersection graph has a *perfect matching,* a matching of size $\lceil n/2 \rceil$, then $\lceil n/2 \rceil$ guards suffice: place a guard at each intersection of the grid corresponding to an edge of the matching. If a maximum matching has size m, then placing guards at the corresponding intersections covers $2m$ segments. The remaining $n - 2m$ segments can be covered with one guard each, resulting in total coverage by $m + n - 2m = n - m$ guards. Indeed this is a minimal cover: if fewer than $n - m$ guards suffice, more than m guards must cover two segments each that are not covered by any other guards, yielding a matching of size larger than m.

This argument establishes the following theorem.

THEOREM 9.3 [Ntafos 1985].   A minimum cover for a grid of n segments has $n - m$ guards, where m is the size of the maximum matching in the intersection graph of the segments, and may be found in $O(n^{2.5})$ time.

The dividing line between polynomial and NP-hard problems often seems to fall between problem parameters 2 and 3: 3SAT is NP-complete but 2SAT is polynomial, three-dimensional matching is NP-complete but graph matching is polynomial, vertex cover in graphs of degree at most 3 is NP-complete but polynomial if the degrees are at most 2. And Ntafos showed that minimal coverage of three-dimensional grids is NP-complete in contrast to the above theorem for two-dimensional grids. We now turn to this result.

The proof is by reduction from the vertex cover problem in graphs of degree at most three, a known NP-complete problem (Garey and Johnson 1979).

Vertex Cover

INSTANCE.   A graph $G = (V, E)$ with all nodes of degree three or less; a positive integer $K < |V|$.

QUESTION.   Is there a vertex cover for G of size at most K? That is, is there a set of vertices C of size K or less such that each edge of G is incident on at least one vertex of C?

The goal is to construct a three-dimensional grid P such that there is a cover by less than or equal to g guards (the value of g will be specified later) iff there is a vertex cover of G with less than or equal to K vertices. The basic idea is simple. Label the vertices of G 1, 2, . . . , $n = |V|$. The vertices of G are assigned to lattice points along the diagonal line through $(0, 0, 0)$ and $(1, 1, 1)$: each vertex labeled i is assigned the lattice point $v_i = (3i, 3i, 3i)$. Edges of G are represented by grid paths between the lattice points corresponding to the endpoint vertices of the edges. Because each vertex of G is of degree 3 or less, each incident edge can be assigned one of the three orthogonal directions without conflict.

We now describe the construction of the grid P from the given graph G. Suppose all edges incident to vertices $1, \ldots, i-1$ of G have been assigned paths in P, and consider an edge (i, j) of G, with $i < j$. We will use the convention that paths from v_i to v_j with $i < j$ will leave v_i along the positive rays $+x$, $+y$, and $+z$, and approach v_j along the negative rays $-x$, $-y$, and $-z$. Because vertex i has at most degree three, one of the three rays in the directions $+x$, $+y$, or $+z$ emanating from $(3i, 3i, 3i)$ must contain no segments of P. Assume that the $+x$ ray is unoccupied. Then connect $v_i = (3i, 3i, 3i)$ to $v_j = (3j, 3j, 3j)$ with these three grid segments, as long as they do not overlap with any previously constructed segments of P:

$$(3i, 3i, 3i) \rightarrow (3j, 3i, 3i),$$
$$(3j, 3i, 3i) \rightarrow (3j, 3j, 3i),$$
$$(3j, 3j, 3i) \rightarrow (3j, 3j, 3j).$$

The path moves in the $+x$, $+y$, and $+z$ directions in sequence, as illustrated in Fig. 9.16a. If the $+x$ direction is occupied but $+y$ is free at v_i, then the path moves $+y$, $+z$, and $+x$ in sequence. If only the $+z$ ray is unoccupied at v_i, the path follows $+z$, $+x$, and $+y$ to reach v_j. These alternative paths are illustrated in Figs. 9.16b and 9.16c. Note that each of the three alternative paths lies in a distinct plane containing v_i and a distinct plane containing v_j.

Now assume the attempted connection from v_i to v_j overlaps a segment of P containing v_j, due to an earlier connection from v_k to v_j, $k < i < j$. Let the overlap occur on the $-z$ ray from v_j. Then at least one of the rays $-x$ or $-y$ from v_j must be unoccupied. If the $-x$ ray is unoccupied, modify the (v_k, v_j) path as shown in Fig. 9.17a; if the $-y$ ray is unoccupied, modify as shown in Fig. 9.17b. In both cases the overlap on $-z$ is avoided, and the (v_k, v_j) path approaches v_j along the unoccupied ray. Note that the bent path now consists of nine edges. Similar modifications are made if the path overlaps along the $-x$ or $-y$ rays at v_j. Because v_j can have at most three incident paths in P, one of the rays $-z$, $-y$, $-x$ is always unoccupied when a connection is made, so overlap can always be avoided. It may be that a path that is already bent to avoid overlap, will have to bend again to avoid

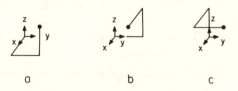

Fig. 9.16. Three paths from v_i (the origin) to v_j.

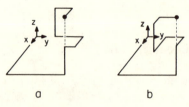

Fig. 9.17. Bending a path to avoid overlap on the $-z$ ray, to enter along the $-x$ ray (a) or the $-y$ ray (b).

overlap with the third incident edge, which would change the 9 segment path into one of 15 segments.[4]

After complete construction, the e edges of G will be embedded as e_3 paths of 3 segments each (when no overlap is encountered), e_9 paths of 9 segments each (when overlap forces bending as in Fig. 9.17), and e_{15} paths of 15 segments each (when overlap occurs twice), where $e = e_3 + e_9 + e_{15}$.

LEMMA 9.8.   There is a vertex cover of size K of G iff there is a cover of the grid P whose construction is described above with $g = K + e_3 + 4e_9 + 7e_{15}$ guards.

Proof.   Suppose there is a vertex cover C of G of size K. Then assign a guard to each intersection in the grid P that corresponds to a vertex in C. Let p_3 be a 3-segment path in P between v_i and v_j. Then because C is a vertex cover, at least one of v_i or v_j is assigned a guard; therefore one additional guard suffices to cover p_3. Let p_9 be a 9-segment path in P between v_i and v_j. Again one of v_i or v_j must be assigned a guard, so that p_9 can be covered with four additional guards, one on every other corner. Similar reasoning show that a 15 segment path requires seven additional guards. The result is complete coverage by $K + e_3 + 4e_9 + 7e_{15}$ guards.

Suppose P may be covered by $K + e_3 + 4e_9 + 7e_{15}$ guards. Each 3-segment path requires one guard on an internal corner—that is, not at a grid point corresponding to some vertex of G. Similarly each 9-segment path requires four guards on internal corners, and each 15-segment path requires seven such guards. This accounts for $e_3 + 4e_9 + 7e_{15}$ guards. Thus at most K guards may be located at grid points corresponding to vertices of G. Suppose the guards assigned to these grid points do *not* correspond to a vertex cover of G. Then some edge (i, j) of G is not incident to a vertex of the cover, which means that its associated path in P does not have a guard at v_i nor at v_j. But then, if the path is a 3-segment path, the one guard at an internal corner does not suffice to cover the path, since this guard can only cover two of the three segments. Similarly, if the path is a 9-segment or 15-segment path, the four or seven guards at internal vertices cover at most 8 or 14 of the 9 or 15 segments, respectively. Thus if the K guards do not correspond to a vertex cover, coverage of the grid P cannot be achieved with $K + e_3 + 4e_9 + 7e_{15}$

---

4. I have modified Ntafos's argument somewhat.

guards. Thus those K guards must correspond to a vertex cover of at most size K. □

THEOREM 9.4 [Ntafos 1985]. Minimal guard coverage of a three-dimensional grid is NP-complete.

Proof. The problem is clearly in NP, as guards need only be located at corners or junctions, and an optimal placement may be guessed and checked in polynomial time. The reduction from Vertex Cover establishes that the problem is NP-complete. □

9.5. PARTITIONS WITHOUT STEINER POINTS

The previous section showed how a version of the minimal guard coverage problem that is solvable in polynomial time can be obtained by severely restricting the class of polygons covered. Another problem solvable in polynomial time can be obtained by restricting the pieces of the decomposition rather than restricting the shape of the polygon being decomposed. Keil showed that the problem of finding a minimal *partition* of an arbitrary simple polygon into star pieces *without* Steiner points can be solved in $O(n^7 \log n)$ time (Keil 1984, 1985b). We showed in Section 9.1 that the number of pieces in a minimal partition into stars can be much larger than the number of guards required for coverage: a partition is quite different from a cover. But it is precisely the restriction to partitions that permits a polynomial algorithm to find the minimum. Consider a diagonal d that lies on the boundary of a star in a minimal star partition of P. P is partitioned into two polygons by d, P_1, and P_2. The crucial observation is that the minimum partition of P is the union of the minimal partitions of P_1 and P_2. Note that this additive property does not hold for covers as d might be overlapped by a piece in a cover. But the fact that the pieces of a partition do not overlap permits a dynamic programming algorithm to build up a minimal partition for P from minimal partitions of subpolygons in P. We now proceed with the details, which are a bit complicated.

Let the vertices of the polygon P to be partitioned be labeled from 1 to n counterclockwise. Let P_{ij} be the subpolygon composed of the boundary of P from i to j, and the diagonal (j, i). P_{ij} is defined only if $i < j - 1$ and i can see j. A minimum partition of P_{ij} will be constructed from minimal partitions of P_{im} and P_{mj} for $i < m < j$. The diagonal (i, j) is called the *base* of P_{ij}, and for any minimal partition M of P_{ij}, $S_{ij}(M)$, the *base star* of M, is the star polygon in M that includes (i, j). Finally, T_{imj} is the triangle whose base is (i, j) and whose apex is m. These definitions are illustrated in Fig. 9.18. The basic idea of the dynamic programming algorithm is to build a minimal partition M of P_{ij} by merging T_{imj} with the minimal partitions A of P_{im} and B of P_{mj}. If $S_{im}(A) \cup T_{imj}$ is a star polygon, then T_{imj} is said to *single merge* with partition A; if $S_{im}(A) \cup T_{imj} \cup S_{mj}(B)$ is a star, then T_{imj} is said to *double merge* with partitions A and B.

Fig. 9.18. The subpolygon P_{ij} and associated regions.

We now concentrate on defining the *states* of the dynamic programming algorithm. First observe that a state cannot be represented by just one minimal partition of a subpolygon. Consider Fig. 9.19. P_{im} is minimally partitioned into two pieces with either diagonal a or b (or others). If diagonal a is used to partition P_{im}, then T_{imj} can single merge with the base star of the partition, while if b is used, the merge produces a non-star polygon. This suggests that each minimal partition of a subpolygon must be a separate state. There are two difficulties with this approach. The first is that there can be an exponential number of distinct minimal partitions: the polygon shown in Fig. 9.20 has 2^{k-1} distinct partitions into k stars, where $k = \Theta(n)$ is the number of steps of the staircase, since there are two independent choices for the diagonal separating adjacent stars. In the figure, $k = 4$. The second difficulty is that sometimes a minimal partition of P_{ij} cannot be constructed from single or double merges. Consider Fig. 9.21. Here P_{ij} is a star, but since the kernel of P_{ij} lies inside every T_{imj} for $i < m < j$, the subpolygons P_{im} and P_{mj} are not both stars. Thus their minimal partitions will contain more than one piece, and simple merges with T_{imj} will never result in the true minimal partition of P_{ij}.

Keil solved these problems by introducing the notion of a pseudo-star. A *pseudo-star polygon* PS_{ij} based on (i, j) is a polygon such that there exists a point x in P but not in PS_{ij} such that x can see all of PS_{ij} *through* (i, j). Thus PS_{ij} is a portion of a star polygon whose kernel lies on the other side of (i, j). For example, P_{im} in Fig. 9.21 is a pseudo-star based on (i, m). Extending minimal partitions to permit a pseudo-star polygon on the base solves the second difficulty mentioned above.

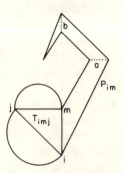

Fig. 9.19. T_{imj} cannot merge with every minimal partition of P_{im}.

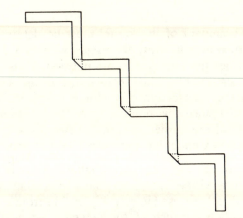

Fig. 9.20. A polygon with 8 distinct partitions into 4 stars.

We now reconsider the first difficulty, the exponentially many partitions of a subpolygon. Although it is not possible to save just one minimal partition for a subpolygon, as Fig. 9.19 showed, only variations in the base star (or pseudo-star) are relevant for merging, as merging only occurs at the base. Thus we need to identify all possible base pseudo-stars. This goal motivates the following definition.

Let L be the set of all maximal line segments internal to P determined by two vertices of P, at least one of which is reflex. Define K to be the vertices of P unioned with the set of all intersection points between the lines of L with each other and with the edges of P. L has size $O(rn)$ for a polygon of n vertices r of which are reflex, and therefore K has size $O(r^2n^2)$. This set K reduces the pseudo-star kernel points to a polynomial-size set of possibilities.

LEMMA 9.9. The kernel of any base star polygon of a minimal partition of a subpolygon P_{ij} contains a point in K.

Proof. Let M be a minimal partition of P_{ij}, and let $S_{ij}(M)$ be its base star. If S_{ij} is convex, then vertex i is in its kernel and in K. If S_{ij} is not convex, then its kernel is a proper subset of S_{ij}. The kernel is the intersection of all

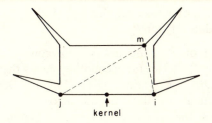

Fig. 9.21. A simple merge of T_{imj} and minimal partitions of the remaining subpolygons will not yield a single star.

the half planes defined by edges of S_{ij}. At least one of the half-planes that form part of the boundary of the kernel must be determined by an edge with a reflex vertex as endpoint; for edges with two convex endpoints extend exterior rather than interior to the polygon. Thus at least one edge of the kernel is determined by a line segment l in L, the set of line segments defined above. If the intersection of l with P lies in the kernel, then the lemma is established since this point is in K. If not, then another line l' containing an edge of the kernel must intersect l. Since l' must be defined by an edge with a reflex endpoint, the intersection of l and l' is in K.   □

Since the kernel of any base star must contain a point in K, we only need consider pseudo-stars visible from the points in K. Let M_x be a minimal partition of P_{ij} with a base pseudo-star PS_{ij} visible from x. Although there may be exponentially many such M_x for a given x, we need only retain one representative. This representative is a state for the dynamic programming algorithm. Although we must store M_x for all $x \in K$, K is of polynomial size. Thus the exponential explosion has been circumvented.

We may finally specify the algorithm.

Preprocessing

(1) Compute the set K. $[O(r^2 n^2)]$
(2) Compute the visibility graph of P. $[O(n^2)]$
(3) Construct the subpolygons and sort by number of vertices. $[O(n^2 \log n)]$
(4) Form a list of all base triangles T_{imj}. $[O(n^3)]$

Dynamic Programming

for each P_{ij} (in order of increasing size) **do**
   for each T_{imj} **do** $[O(n^3)]$
      for each $x \in K$ **do** $[O(r^2 n^2)]$
         double merge:
            if both M_x of P_{im} and M_x of P_{mj} exist
            then T_{imj} can merge with both
         single merge:
            else if M_x of P_{im} exists and j sees x
            then T_{imj} can merge with P_{im}
         no merge:
            else if $x \in T_{imj}$ or x sees T_{imj} through (i, j)
            then candidate M_x for P_{ij}

A smallest partition of P_{1n}, the last subpolygon to be considered, is a minimal partition for P. A careful accounting shows that the algorithm runs in $O(r^2 n^5 \log n) = O(n^7 \log n)$ time (Keil 1985b). Because of this high complexity, it is difficult to illustrate the algorithm by example. We will settle for showing just the final step on a small example.

Let P be the 11 vertex polygon shown in Fig. 9.22, and consider the status of the algorithm when $i = 1$, $j = 11$, and $m = 5$. P_{15} is a star, and so its

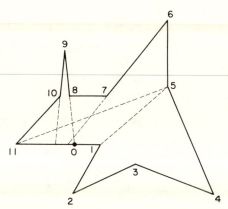

Fig. 9.22. An example of the star partitioning algorithm: the polygon may be partitioned into two stars.

minimal partition is $A = \{(1, 2, 3, 4, 5)\}$. Several pseudo-star partitions would have been computed for P_{15} by the algorithm, including $A_1 = \{(1, 2, 3, 4, 5)\}$, since P_{15} is visible from 1. $P_{5,11}$ is not a star. Its only minimal partition has three pieces: $B = \{(5, 6, 7), \quad (7, 8, 9, 10, 11), \quad (5, 7, 11)\}$. However, it has several more efficient pseudo-star partitions, including $B_0 = \{(5, 6, 7, 8, 9, 10, 11)\}$, where 0 is the intersection of the line containing edge $(8, 9)$ with the boundary of P, since all of $P_{5,11}$ is visible from 0 through $(5, 11)$. Many other pseudo-star partitions exist for $P_{5,11}$, including $B_1 = \{(5, 6, 7, 8, 11), \quad (8, 9, 10, 11)\}$, where all of $(5, 6, 7, 8, 11)$ is visible from 1 through $(5, 11)$. Now consider the attempt to merge $T_{1,5,11}$ with the partitions of $P_{1,5}$ and $P_{5,11}$. First let $x = 1 \in K$. Then since both A_1 and B_1 exist, a double merge is possible. The result is the partition $M_1 = \{(1, 2, 3, 4, 5, 6, 7, 8, 11)(8, 9, 10, 11)\}$. Second, let $x = 0 \in K$. Although B_0 exists, A_0 does not, since no pseudo-star based on $(1, 5)$ is visible from 0. Thus no double merge is possible. However, since B_0 exists and 1 can see 0, a single merge is possible, resulting in $M_0 = \{(1, 5, 6, 7, 8, 9, 10, 11)(1, 2, 3, 4, 5)\}$. Both M_0 and M_1 are minimal partitions of P.

Although we have emphasized that the minimum partition problem is polynomial because it admits a dynamic programming algorithm, whereas the NP-complete minimum cover problem does not, Lingas showed that the proof in Section 9.2 can be modified to establish that minimum partition is NP-complete for polygons with holes (Lingas 1982b). He observed that the stars in the decomposition need only overlap at the crossovers, and that Lichtenstein established that planar 3SAT is NP-complete (Lingas 1982a). Thus Keil's dynamic programming approach cannot work for polygons with holes. Intuitively this is because a diagonal in a multiply-connected polygon P does not necessarily cut it into two pieces, and therefore merging is not confined to one base edge, but must in the worst case be considered along the entire boundary of a subpolygon.

9.6. DISCUSSION

The results discussed in this chapter are summarized, together with two results not yet discussed, in Table 9.1. The results on monotone orthogonal polygons were obtained by Keil (cover) and Liu and Ntafos (partition) (Keil 1985a; Liu and Ntafos 1985). Several interesting open questions remain:

(1) Can a variant of Keil's dynamic programming approach be used to find star partitions permitting Steiner points? Chazelle was able to achieve $O(n^3)$ for minimum *convex* partition with Steiner points via a very complex dynamic programming algorithm (Chazelle 1980), but star partitions seem even more complicated.

(2) What are the complexities of the various problems when restricted to orthogonal polygons? As the table indicates, the first inroads have already been made for monotone orthogonal polygons. It does not seem to be straightforward to extend these results to general orthogonal polygons, however.

(3) Are there other natural restrictions on the pieces that result in polynomially solvable problems? Aggarwal *et al.* investigated star covers where the boundary of the pieces are formed by extensions of the edges of the polygon (Aggarwal *et al.* 1985). They claim that Lee and Lin's algorithm can be modified to establish that this restricted problem is also NP-complete.

(4) Given that most of the interesting problems seem to be intractable, it is natural to seek approximation algorithms that achieve decompositions with, say, no more than a constant times the optimal number of pieces. Such approximation algorithms are just beginning to be explored.

Table 9.1

Decomposition→	Cover		Partition	
	w. Steiner	w/o Steiner	w. Steiner	w/o Steiner
simple polygons	NP-hard	NP-complete	?	$O(n^7 \log n)$
polygons with holes	NP-hard	NP-complete	NP-hard	NP-complete
monotone orthogonal polygons	$O(n^2)$		$O(n)$	
two-dimensional grids	$O(n^{2.5})$		?	
three-dimensional grids	NP-complete		NP-complete	

10

THREE DIMENSIONS AND MISCELLANY

10.1. INTRODUCTION

In this final chapter, four miscellaneous topics are discussed: three dimensions, line segment obstacles, point obstacles, and mirrors.

10.2. THREE DIMENSIONS

Very little is known about art gallery theorems in three dimensions. In this section we present three negative results that collectively show that there is a vast difference between the problem in two and three dimensions, and one positive result concerning convex polyhedra.

10.2.1. Untetrahedralizable Polyhedra

The reason that progress in three dimensions has been difficult is that the main tool used throughout this book for two-dimensional problems—triangulation—does not generalize. Lennes proved in 1911 the surprising theorem that there exist polyhedra (even of genus zero, i.e., without holes) whose interior cannot be partitioned into tetrahedra whose vertices are selected from the polyhedra vertices (Lennes 1911). Schönhardt later gave a simpler example (Schönhardt 1928), which we present here, based on Bagemihl's exposition (Bagemihl 1948).

Let a, b, and c be the vertices (labeled counterclockwise) of an equilateral triangle of unit edge length in the xy-plane. Let a', b', and c' be the vertices of abc when translated up to the plane $z = 1$, as shown in Fig. 10.1a. Define an intermediate polyhedron P' as the hull of the two triangles, including the diagonal edges ab', bc', and ca', as well as the vertical edges aa', bb', and cc', and the edges in the two triangles abc and $a'b'c'$. Now twist the top triangle $a'b'c'$ 30° counterclockwise in the plane $z = 1$, rotating and stretching the attached edges accordingly. The result is shown in Fig. 10.1b; a view from $z = \infty$ is shown in Fig. 10.1c. Call the resulting polyhedron P.

253

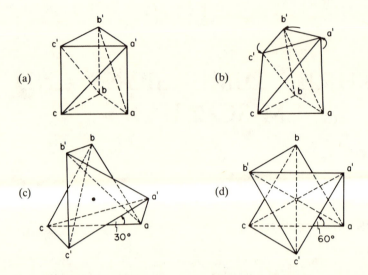

Fig. 10.1. Schönhardt's untetrahedralizable polyhedron, constructed by twisting the top of a triangular prism (a) by 30°, producing (b), shown in top view (c); a twist of 60° would cause face intersections (d).

First note that P is indeed a valid polyhedron: it would take a twist of 60° (shown in an overhead view in Fig. 10.1d) to "pinch off" the interior. Now we show that any tetrahedron whose vertices are selected from those of P includes points exterior to P. This is established with the help of two claims:

(1) Every open segment whose endpoints are vertices of P but which is not an edge of P, is exterior to P.
(2) Every triangle whose sides are edges of P is a face of P.

P has 6 vertices and 12 edges. Since $\binom{6}{2} = 15$, only three segments need be checked to verify claim (1): ac', ba', and cb'. All three are clearly seen to be exterior from Fig. 10.1c. Claim (2) can be checked at a single vertex, say a, as all have the same local connections. And indeed, it is the case that for every pair of edges of P incident to a, either a third edge of P forms a face of P, or there is no third edge of P forming a triangle.

Now, by claim (1), every edge of an interior tetrahedron T must be an edge of P. By claim (2), this means that every face of T is a face of P. But since P is a valid polyhedron, this implies that $T = P$, a contradiction to the fact that P has 6 vertices.

Schöhardt proved that this is the smallest example of an un-tetrahedralizable polyhedron. Bagemihl extended this example to construct a polyhedron of n vertices with the same properties for every $n \geq 6$. As far as I am aware there is no characterization of which polyhedra are tetrahedralizable. It seems likely that there is a nice art gallery theorem for tetrahedralizable polyhedra; this remains an area for future exploration.

10.2.2. $\Omega(n^{3/2})$ Guards Necessary

It seems almost obvious that guards posted at every vertex of a polyhedron cover the entire interior. But this would only be obvious if every polyhedron were tetrahedralizable. For then every tetrahedron would have a guard in a corner (in fact in all four corners), and the tetrahedra would cover the interior. In the absence of tetrahedralization, however, the "obviousness" of complete coverage is less clear. In fact, we describe in this section a polyhedron constructed by Seidel that has these two properties:

(1) Guards placed at every vertex do *not* cover the interior.
(2) $\Omega(n^{3/2})$ guards are necessary, where n is the number of vertices.

The polyhedron that realizes these properties is orthogonal and of genus zero. It may be constructed as follows.

Start with a cube of side length L. On the front face mark squares of side length 1 in a regular $k \times k$ array, with $1 + \varepsilon$ separation between each row and column, where $\varepsilon \ll 1$, as illustrated in Fig. 10.2. Thus L should be chosen to be larger than $(2 + \varepsilon)k$. Attach a $1 \times 1 \times (L - \varepsilon)$ rectangular box behind each square inside the cube, and remove the square on the front face. The result is a deep dent at each square that does not quite reach the back face of the cube. Apply the same procedure for the right face, and for the top face, staggering the $k \times k$ arrays so that none of the box dents intersect. The resulting polyhedron has $n = 8(3k^2 + 1)$ vertices.

Figure 10.3 shows a top-view cross section of the interior. Point x in the figure is confined inside a $(1 + \varepsilon) \times (1 + \varepsilon) \times (1 + \varepsilon)$ cube bound by six box dents, two from each of three directions; x is at the center of this cube. This cube space is not closed, but has $\frac{1}{2}\varepsilon$-cracks along all 12 edges. Nevertheless, it should be clear that x is not visible from any vertex if ε is chosen to be much smaller than 1.

This establishes the first claimed property. The second claim follows by noting that there are $(k - 1)^3$ equivalent points x, no two of which are visible from the same point. Thus at least $g = (k - 1)^3$ guards are necessary, and

$$g = \approx (n/24)^{3/2} \approx n^{3/2}/118 = \Omega(n^{3/2}).$$

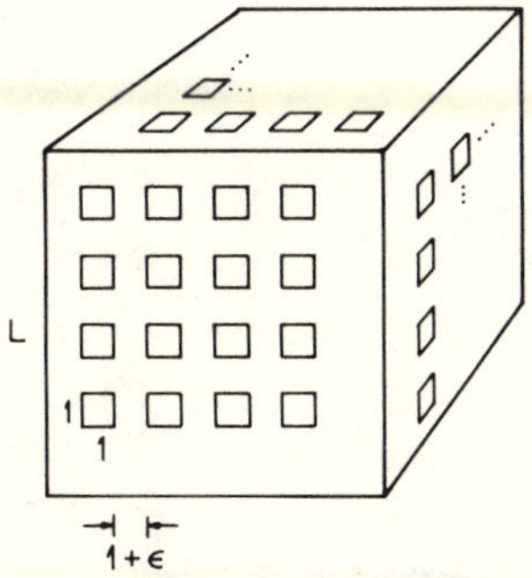

Fig. 10.2. Exterior view of Seidel's polyhedron showing array of dents.

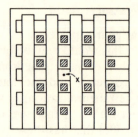

Fig. 10.3. Cross section of Seidel's polyhedron: point x is not visible to any vertex.

Note that the fact that a guard at each vertex does not suffice for coverage implies that Seidel's example is not tetrahedralizable. Finally, the example may be "turned inside-out" to establish the same bound for exterior visibility.

10.2.3. Convex Partitions

In the absence of tetrahedralization, it is natural to attempt to approach three-dimensional art gallery problems through convex partitions, which proved useful in two dimensions (Section 1.4). Our final negative result is that there are polyhedra that require $\Omega(n^2)$ convex pieces in any convex partition of a polyhedron of n vertices. This result was established by Chazelle (1984), who also provided an algorithm that finds a partition into at most $\frac{1}{2}r^2 + \frac{1}{2}r + 1$ convex pieces, where r is the number of reflex edges of the polyhedron, in $O(nr^3)$ time. Chazelle's example may be constructed as follows.

Start with a cube aligned with orthogonal xyz coordinate axes. Cut k thin notches into the bottom face, parallel to the xz-plane. Similarly cut k notches into the top face, parallel to the yz-plane. The result is shown in Fig. 10.4 for $k = 2$. The two sets of notches do not quite meet. The top edges of the notches in the bottom face lie on the hyperbolic paraboloid $z = xy$, and the bottom edges of the notches in the top face lie on $z = xy + \varepsilon$, the same surface shifted up by ε, where $\varepsilon \ll 1$. A hyperbolic paraboloid can be generated by two sets of orthogonal lines (Thomas 1962),

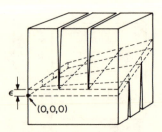

Fig. 10.4. Any convex partition of Chazelle's polyhedron requires a quadratic number of pieces.

so the edges can be chosen to lie on these surfaces. Chazelle proved that the intersection of the warped shape between the two hyperbolic paraboloids with any convex subset of the polyhedron can only have such a small volume that $\Omega(n^2)$ pieces are necessary to make up the volume of the shape. His proof is long and difficult and will not be presented here. His conclusion is that at least $n^2/66 = \Omega(n^2)$ convex pieces are necessary in any convex partition of the polyhedron just described.

10.2.4. Satellite Sentries

The only non-trivial art gallery theorem known for three dimensions is for the very special case of exterior visibility for guards confined to the surface of a convex polyhedron. The equivalent problem in two dimensions is trivial: $\lceil n/2 \rceil$ boundary guards are *always* necessary and sufficient to guard the exterior of a convex polygon. But in three dimensions the situation is not as straightforward. First, there are several quantities that might serve as the basis for a theorem: V, E, and F, the number of vertices, edges, and faces of the polyhedron. It seems that F is the most natural measure, and we will use it in this section.

The theorem is obtained by using matchings in the graph of the dual of the polyhedron. We will need the following theorem of Nishizeki on the size of maximum matchings in planar graphs.

LEMMA 10.1 [Nishizeki 1977]. If G is a connected planar graph of n nodes, with minimum vertex degree $\delta \geq 3$, and with connectivity $\kappa \geq 2$, then for all $n \geq 14$, the number of edges in a maximum matching of G is greater than or equal to $\lceil (n+4)/3 \rceil$, and for $n < 14$, the number of edges is $\lfloor n/2 \rfloor$.

Nishizeki obtained many similar results for different values of δ and κ, all of which are best possible (Nishizeki and Baybars 1977; Nishizeki 1977). We will have occasion to use this powerful theorem in the next section as well.

We may now prove the art gallery theorem.

THEOREM 10.1 [Grünbaum and O'Rourke 1983]. $\lfloor (2F-4)/3 \rfloor$ vertex guards are sometimes necessary and always sufficient to see the exterior of a convex polyhedron of F faces, for $F \geq 10$.

Proof.

Necessity. Let Q be any *simple* polyhedron of f faces, that is, having all vertices of degree 3. From Euler's formula $v - e + f = 2$, and $2e = 3v$, it follows that $v = 2f - 4$. From Q construct a polyhedron P by "truncating" all vertices of Q, that is, replace each vertex of Q by a small triangle so that none of the new triangles share common points. This procedure is illustrated in Fig. 10.5 when Q is a cube. P has $F = f + v = 3f - 4$ faces. Each of the new triangular faces requires its own guard, so the total number required is at least $v = 2f - 4$. But $\lfloor (2F-4)/3 \rfloor = \lfloor (6f-12)/3 \rfloor = 2f - 4$. This establishes necessity when $F \equiv 2 \bmod 3$, since $3f - 4 \equiv 2 \bmod 3$. The

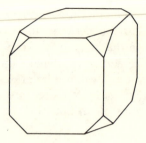

Fig. 10.5.   The result of truncating a cube at every vertex.

other two cases (mod 3) can be shown as follows. If one of Q's vertices is not cut off, then P has $F = 3f - 5$ faces, and needs $2f - 5 = \lfloor[2(3f - 5) - 4]/3\rfloor = \lfloor(2F - 4)/3\rfloor$ guards. If two of Q's vertices are not cut off, then P has $F = 3f - 6$ faces, and needs $2f - 6 = \lfloor[2(3f - 6) - 4]/3\rfloor = \lfloor(2F - 4)/3\rfloor$ guards. Thus for all values of F, polyhedra exist that require $\lfloor(2F - 4)/3\rfloor$ guards.

Sufficiency.   Let G be the dual graph of the surface of the polyhedron P; G has F nodes. G is planar and its minimum vertex degree is three because each face of P must have at least three edges. A *polyhedral graph* is the graph determined by the vertices and edges of a convex polyhedron. G has connectivity of at least three since polyhedral graphs are 3-connected by Balinski's theorem (Grünbaum 1975), and G is polyhedral because it is the dual of a polyhedral graph. Therefore, Lemma 10.1 applies and shows that, for $F \geq 14$, there is a matching M in G of at least $m = \lceil(F + 4)/3\rceil$ edges. Now place a guard on one of the endpoints of the edge of P corresponding to each edge in the matching. This covers $2m$ faces. Assign a separate guard to each of the $F - 2m$ faces of P. The result is complete coverage with $m + F - 2m = F - \lceil(F + 4)/3\rceil$ guards. This quantity is identical to $\lfloor(2F - 4)/3\rfloor$. For $F < 14$, there is a matching of $m = \lfloor F/2\rfloor$ edges, which by the same argument leads to coverage with $\lceil F/2\rceil$ guards. For $F \geq 10$, $\lceil F/2\rceil \leq \lfloor(2F - 4)/3\rfloor$. This establishes the theorem, then, for all $F \geq 10$. $\square$

The necessity holds for all $F \geq 5$, and although I suspect sufficiency also holds in the range $5 \leq F \leq 9$, I have not verified this yet.

10.3.   LINE SEGMENT OBSTACLES

Throughout this book we have concentrated on polygons, but "art gallery-like" questions may be posed for other types of obstacles. In this section we prove an art gallery theorem for n non-intersecting line segments. Visibility is defined as follows: a guard at point x sees point y if the line segment xy does not *cross* the interior of any line segment obstacle; xy may be collinear with a segment, or touch one of its endpoints. Sufficiency follows easily using the same technique just employed for convex polyhedra. Necessity is less obvious, but fortunately a counterexample to a hypothesis on the prison yard problem considered in Chapter 6 may be modified to yield the critical example.

THEOREM 10.2 [O'Rourke 1985]. $\lfloor 2n/3 \rfloor$ point guards are sometimes necessary and always sufficient to cover the plane in the presence of n line segment obstacles, where the guards may be positioned anywhere in the plane, under the following assumptions:

(1) No two segments are parallel (and therefore none are collinear).
(2) No three lines determined by segments intersect in a common point.
(3) $n \geq 5$.

Proof.
   Sufficiency. Partition the plane into $n+1$ regions in a manner similar to that used in Sections 1.4 and 6.5.2 (see Lemma 6.5): extend each segment in both directions until it hits either another segment or a previous segment extension. The induced convex partition is dependent on the order in which the extensions are made, but it always has $n+1$ regions by the non-collinearity assumption (1). Form a graph G from this partition as was done in Section 6.5.2, as follows. Associate a node of G with each convex region of the partition, and connect two nodes by an arc of G if their regions share a common boundary point. An example is shown in Fig. 10.6.
   It is easy to see that assumption (2) ensures that G is a planar graph, and indeed a triangulation, since every face of G (except the exterior face) can be associated with the intersection of two segment lines, and a neighborhood of this intersection point touches three mutually adjacent regions, corresponding to a triangle in G. Without the non-degeneracy assumption, either G would not necessarily be a triangulation, or it would not necessarily

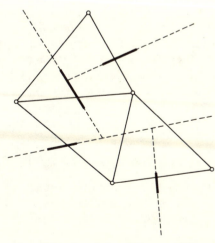

Fig. 10.6. A convex partition of the plane induced by a set of line segments (shown bold) and its dual graph.

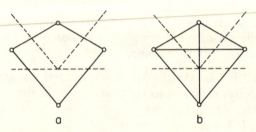

Fig. 10.7. If three segments (dashed) meet at a point, either dual graph is not a triangulation (a) or it is not necessarily planar (b).

be planar, depending on whether adjacency in G required a finite length of common boundary or just a common point, respectively (see Figs. 10.7a and 10.7b). Although these degeneracies are actually "in our favor," the proof is more straightforward if they are assumed not to occur.

We would like to apply Lemma 10.1 to G, which requires a minimum vertex degree δ of 3. However, G may have $\delta = 2$ as illustrated in Fig. 10.6. Since G is a triangulation graph, any nodes of degree 2 must be on the exterior face. Augment G to G' by adding a pseudo-node p adjacent to every node of G on the exterior face. Since G must have at least three nodes on its exterior face, p has degree three or more, and since p is connected to every degree 2 node of G, G' has $\delta \geq 3$.

To show that G' is 2-connected, assume to the contrary that removal of one node disconnects G'. Let x be such an articulation point of G'. Then the convex region R associated with x must divide the plane into two parts that share no boundary points. But this is only achievable if R has parallel edges running to infinity in both directions, which is not possible by the non-parallel assumption (1).

Now apply Lemma 10.1 to the $(n + 2)$-node graph G', for $n \geq 12$, to obtain a matching M of $m = \lceil (n + 6)/3 \rceil = \lceil n/3 \rceil + 2$ edges. Each edge of M not incident on p may be associated with a boundary point shared between two convex regions. Placing a guard at such a point clearly covers the two incident regions since they are convex. At most one edge of M may be incident to p. If there is such an edge, a guard may be used to cover the region associated with the other endpoint. Thus m guards associated with the matching edges cover at least $2m - 1$ regions. Covering the remaining $(n + 1) - (2m - 1)$ regions each with their own guard results in total coverage with

$$m + (n + 1) - (2m - 1) = n - m + 2 = n - \lceil n/3 \rceil = \lfloor 2n/3 \rfloor$$

guards. For $n < 12$, Lemma 10.1 guarantees a matching of size $\lceil (n + 2)/2 \rceil = \lceil n/2 \rceil + 1$ edges, which by the same argument yields coverage with $\lfloor n/2 \rfloor + 1$ guards. Since $\lfloor n/2 \rfloor + 1 \leq \lfloor 2n/3 \rfloor$ for $n \geq 5$, sufficiency is established.

Necessity. Although experimentation with small values of n would lead

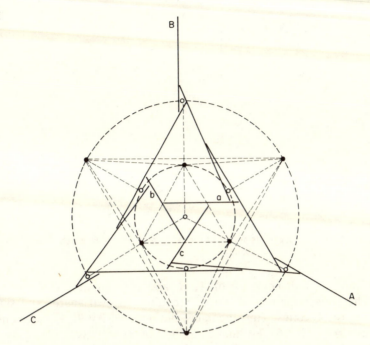

Fig. 10.8. A pattern of 12 line segments that require 7 point guards.

one to expect that at most $\lceil n/2 \rceil$ guards are necessary, the dependence of the sufficiency proof on matching suggests examining graphs with no perfect matching. And indeed, Fig. 6.19, which we used as a counterexample to an approach to the prison yard problem, can be used to establish necessity. Consider the 12 segments and induced convex partition shown in Fig. 10.8. The 13 node dual graph has the property that removal of 6 nodes (solid in the figure) disconnects the graph into seven odd components. Moreover, coverage of three nodes with one guard leaves a graph of 10 nodes that has no perfect matching, because removal of 4 nodes disconnects the remainder into 6 odd components (Section 6.5.2). It is clear that each of the seven triangular regions corresponding to the disconnected nodes (open in the figure) requires their own guard. Since $7 > \lceil 12/2 \rceil$, this example shows that $\lceil n/2 \rceil$ are not sufficient.

In order to show $\lfloor 2n/3 \rfloor$ necessity, we nest the pattern inside of itself as follows. Note that the pattern of segments in Fig. 10.8 has just three edges, A, B, and C, that extend to infinity. Thus the central triangular region formed by edges a, b, and c can be replaced by a copy of the pattern, with A, B, and C replacing the roles of a, b, and c, respectively. If this nesting is repeated k times, $n' = 9k + 3$ segments will be used. Each nesting adds six triangular region that each requires a guard. Since the innermost central triangular region also needs its own guard, $g' = 6k + 1$ guards are necessary.

A final modification yields the critical example. Add three more segments

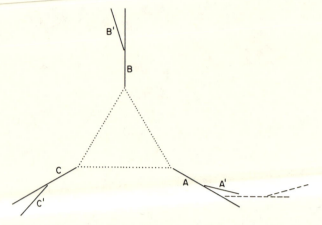

Fig. 10.9. Additional segments added to the pattern of Fig. 10.8, which is nested within the dotted triangle.

A', B', and C' that angle off of A, B, and C to infinity, as shown in Fig. 10.9. The cone bound by A and A' requires its own guard, and similarly for the B and C cones. Thus the figure has $n = n' + 3 = 9k + 6$ segments and requires $g = g' + 3 = 6k + 4$ guards. Since $\lfloor 2n/3 \rfloor = \lfloor (18k + 12)/3 \rfloor = 6k + 4$, the formula has been established when $n \equiv 0 \pmod 3$. This example also establishes the $n \equiv 1 \pmod 3$ case, since incrementing n by 1 does not increase the value of $\lfloor 2n/3 \rfloor$. The $n \equiv 2 \pmod 3$ case can be settled by adding two more segments, shown dashed in Fig. 10.9, forcing the need for another guard. Here $n = 9k + 8$ and $\lfloor 2n/3 \rfloor = 6k + 5$. Thus for every $n \geq 15$, there exists an arrangement that requires $\lfloor 2n/3 \rfloor$ guards. Removing edge A' establishes the same formula for $n = 14$. $\square$

It remains to be explored whether the theorem also holds for the degenerate cases or small values of n ruled out by the theorem's assumptions. Using Lemma 10.1 for $n < 14$ easily establishes that $\lfloor n/2 \rfloor + 1$ guards are sufficient for $n < 14$, which, for $n \geq 5$, is no greater than $\lfloor 2n/3 \rfloor$, but the necessity of $\lfloor 2n/3 \rfloor$ guards for each $n < 14$ has not been established.

If the guards are restricted to vertices the situation changes dramatically.

THEOREM 10.3 [Boenke and Shermer 1986]. *n* vertex guards are sometimes necessary and always sufficient to cover the plane in the presence of *n* line segment obstacles.

Proof. Necessity is established by an arrangement of segments around a circle, as illustrated in Fig. 10.10. Each of the indicated triangular regions is visible only to the two segment endpoints at the base of the triangle. Note the similarity between this example and that used to establish necessity for the prison yard problem (Fig. 6.1).

For sufficiency, partition the plane into $n + 1$ convex regions as in Theorem 10.2. Each region has at least one segment endpoint on its boundary, and each endpoint borders on two regions. Place a guard at any

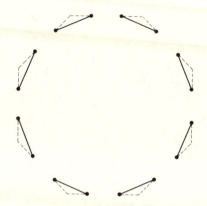

Fig. 10.10. An arrangement of 8 line segments that require 8 vertex guards.

endpoint. This covers two regions. Cover the remaining $n-1$ regions with a guard at an endpoint on their boundaries. □

10.4. POINT OBSTACLES

It may seem that there can be no interesting art gallery questions if the line segment obstacles considered in the previous section are reduced to points, but this is only because we have assumed throughout most of this book that there are no collinear degeneracies. Permitting collinearities and defining visibility to be blocked by points yields two interesting combinatorial-geometric problems, both at least partially unsolved since they were posed in the 1950s and 1960s.

Let P be a set of n points in the plane, not all on a line. Such a point set will be called *non-collinear*. Note that any number $k < n$ of points in P may be collinear. Define points x and y to be visible to one another if the open line segment xy contains no points of P. Let $p^* \in P$ be a point that sees at least as many points of P as any other, and let $M(P)$ be this maximum number. Note that $M(P) = n - 1$ if no three points of P are collinear, with p^* any point of P. Finally define $m(n)$ to be the minimum of $M(P)$ over all point sets of size n. Without the non-collinearity stipulation, $m(n)$ would be 2 for all $n > 2$, since $M(P)$ would be 2 for all sets of collinear points, with p^* any non-extreme point. But if not all points are on a line, it seems a very difficult problem to find $m(n)$. Dirac posed the problem in 1951 (Dirac 1951) and conjectured that $m(n) = \lfloor n/2 \rfloor$.[1]

---

1. His original problem was somewhat different: he sought the minimum over all configurations of the maximum number of lines determined by two points that pass through a third. This is not exactly the same problem, because if the two determining points of a line are on opposite sides of the third, the third sees both, but if they are on the same side, the third only sees the closest.

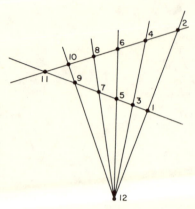

Fig. 10.11. A configuration in which no point can see more than $8 = 12/2 + 2$ other points.

Figure 10.11 shows a configuration that achieves $M(P) = \frac{1}{2}n + 2$ for even n, so $m(n) \le \lfloor n/2 \rfloor + 2$. Dirac offered this simple proof that $m(n) > \sqrt{n}$.

Let p^* be a point that sees a maximum number k of other points. Let L be a line determined by p^* and one of these k points. We claim that L cannot contain more than k points. For suppose it did contain $k' > k$ points. Then because not all points of P are collinear, there is a point $p \in P$ not on L. For each point p_i on L, either p sees p_i, or p sees a point p_i' such that p, p_i', and p_i are collinear in that order. Clearly if p_i and p_j are two distinct points on L, then p_i' and p_j' (if they exist) are distinct also. Thus p sees $k' > k$ points, contradicting the assumption that k is the maximum.

Now count the number of points P in the following way. Each of the k lines through p^* and the k points it sees contains at most $k - 1$ points distinct from p^*. Thus $n \le k(k - 1) + 1$. Therefore, $k > \sqrt{n}$.

Very recently Szemerédi and Trotter proved that $m(n) > cn$ (Moser 1985), but the precise value of c is yet to be determined.

A second art gallery question for point obstacles was posed by Moser in 1966 (Moser 1985). Let P be a set of n non-collinear points. How many guards located at points of P are needed to see the unguarded points of P? Again the problem is trivial if no three points are collinear: one guard suffices. And again the other extreme, all points on one line, is uninteresting: $\lceil (n + 1)/2 \rceil$ are necessary. Moser conjectured that $O(\log n)$ guards suffice for points arranged in an $n \times n$ rectangular lattice. More precisely, let $G(P)$ be the minimum number of points of P that collectively see the other points, and let $g(n)$ be the maximum of $G(P)$ over all sets of n non-collinear points P. We may extend Moser's conjecture to the statement that $g(n) = O(\log n)$.

It seems that progress has only been made in the special case of lattice points. Let L_n be an $n \times n$ square array of integer lattice points. Then, for example, $G(L_5) = 2$, as shown in Fig. 10.12. Abbott (1974) proved that

$$\frac{\ln n}{2 \ln \ln n} < G(L_n) < 4 \ln n.$$

Fig. 10.12. A 5×5 lattice in which two points can see all the other points.

His proofs are number-theoretic; the natural logs in the lower bound come from the prime number theorem. His lower bound establishes that $\eta(n) > (\ln n^2)/(2 \ln \ln n^2)$; that is, this many guards are sometimes necessary, but the sufficiency of $O(\log n)$ guards has only been established for L_n, and even here Abbott's proof is non-constructive, and does not yield an explicit placement of guards.

10.5. MIRRORS

Having opened this book with a problem posed by Klee, it seems appropriate to close with another Klee problem.[2] Let P be a polygon, and imagine that all of its edges are perfect mirrors. Is there always at least one interior point from which P is completely illuminable by a point light bulb? Is P always illuminable from *each* of its points? Assume that the light bulb sends out rays in all directions, and that the standard "angle of reflection = angle of incidence" law of reflection holds. Further assume that a light ray is absorbed if it hits a vertex. Surprisingly, these problems are unsolved for polygons. However, Klee showed the answers to be "no" if curved (differentiable) arcs are permitted. Figure 10.13 shows a region that is not illuminable from the point x, which is the center of both the upper and lower circular arcs. This shows that not every region is illuminable from each of its points. However, the region is easily seen to be illuminable from, for example, point y. Figure 10.14 shows a region that is not illuminable from any of its points. In the figure, a and b, and a' and b', are foci of ellipses forming the upper and lower arcs, respectively. An ellipse with foci

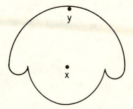

Fig. 10.13. A region not illuminable from x, but illuminable from y.

---

2. The original poser of the problem is unknown; Klee popularized the problem in two articles (Klee 1969, 1979).

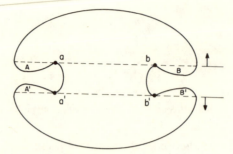

Fig. 10.14. A region not illuminable from any one point.

a and *b* has the following properties:

(1)   A ray through *a* immediately reflects through *b*, and vice versa.
(2)   A ray that intersects the open segment (*a*, *b*) immediately reflects and intersects (*a*, *b*) again.
(3)   A ray that crosses the major axis but does not intersect the closed segment [*a*, *b*] immediately reflects to cross the axis without hitting [*a*, *b*] again.

Thus any light source above the *a'b'* major axis will not illuminate regions *A'* or *B'*, and similarly for below the *ab* axis, by property (2). And a light source in *A* will bounce into *B* and back again by property (3), never illuminating *A'* or *B'*.

Although the problem remains unsolved for polygonal regions, some progress has been made in understanding the behavior of single light rays in a *rational* polygon, one whose angles are all rational multiples of π. (Orthogonal polygons are a very special case of rational polygons.) A single light ray is more usually called a "billiard ball" in the now rather substantial literature on the subject. One of the more accessible results is the following.

THEOREM 10.4 [Boldrighini *et al.* 1978; Kerckhoff *et al.* 1985].   Let *x* be a point in a rational polygon *P*, and θ a direction. Then, except for a countable number of "exceptional" directions θ, the path of a billiard ball issuing from *x* in the direction θ is spatially dense in *P*, that is, passes arbitrarily close to every point of *P*.

One implication of this result is that every rational polygon is illuminable from each of its points in the sense that no finite area region will be left unilluminated; whether an isolated point could remain in the dark is unclear.

For irrational polygons, almost nothing is known. It is not even known if every triangle admits a dense billiard path.

10.6.   TABLE OF THEOREMS

We conclude with a table of the major art gallery theorems discussed in this book.

Table 10.1. Art gallery theorems

Visibility	Polygon Shape	Holes	Guard Type	Lower Bound (necessary)	Upper Bound (sufficient)	Section Discussed
interior	arbitrary	0	vertex	$\lfloor n/3 \rfloor$		1.2.1
				r		1.4.1
		1		$\lfloor (n+1)/3 \rfloor$		5.2
		h		$\lfloor (n+h)/3 \rfloor$	$\lfloor (n+2h)/3 \rfloor$	5.1
		0	diag epts	$\lfloor n/4 \rfloor$		3.2.1
			edge	$\lfloor (n+1)/4 \rfloor$	$\lfloor n/3 \rfloor$	3.2.2
			edge epts	$\lfloor 2n/7 \rfloor$	$\lfloor n/3 \rfloor$	
	star		vertex	$\lfloor n/3 \rfloor$		4.2
				$\lfloor r/2 \rfloor + 1$		
			line	1		
			diagonal	2		
			edge	$\lfloor n/5 \rfloor$	$\lfloor n/3 \rfloor$	
				$\lfloor r/2 \rfloor + 1$		
	orthogonal	0	vertex	$\lfloor n/4 \rfloor = \lfloor r/2 \rfloor + 1$		2.2.2
		1		$\lfloor n/4 \rfloor$		5.3
		2	point	$\lfloor n/4 \rfloor$		
		h	vertex	$\lfloor n/4 \rfloor$	$\lfloor (n+2h)/4 \rfloor$	
		0	diagonal	$\lfloor (3n+4)/16 \rfloor$		3.3
exterior	arbitrary		vertex	$\lceil n/2 \rceil$		6.2.1
			point	$\lceil n/3 \rceil$		6.2.3
	orthogonal		vertex	$\lfloor n/4 \rfloor + 1$		6.2.2
interior+ exterior	arbitrary		vertex	$\lceil n/2 \rceil$	$\lfloor 2n/3 \rfloor$	6.3.1
					$\lceil n/2 \rceil + r$	
	orthogonal			$\lceil n/4 \rceil + 1$	$\lfloor 7n/16 \rfloor + 5$	6.3.2
	segments		point	$\lfloor 2n/3 \rfloor$		10.3
			vertex	n		

267

REFERENCES

H. L. Abbott, Some results in combinatorial geometry, *Discrete Math.* **9** (1974) 199–204.

A. Aggarwal, The art gallery theorem: its variations, applications, and algorithmic aspects, Ph.D. thesis, Johns Hopkins Univ. (1984).

A. Aggarwal, S. K. Ghosh, and R. K. Shyamasundar, Computational complexity of restricted polygon decomposition, unpublished manuscript (1985).

A. V. Aho, J. E. Hopcroft, and J. D. Ullman, *The Design and Analysis of Computer Algorithms,* Addison-Wesley, Reading (1974).

A. V. Aho, J. E. Hopcroft, and J. D. Ullman, *Data Structures and Algorithms,* Addison-Wesley, Reading (1983), 222.

M. O. Albertson and C. J. O'Keefe, Covering regions with squares, *SIAM J. Alg. Disc. Meth.* **2** (1981), 240–243.

K. Appel and W. Haken, Every planar map is 4-colorable, *Ill. J. Math.* **21** (1977), 429–567.

T. Asano, T. Asano, L. J. Guibas, J. Hershberger, and H. Imai, Visibility of disjoint polygons, *Algorithmica* **1** (1986), 49–63.

T. Asano, T. Asano, and H. Imai, Partitioning a polygonal region into trapezoids, *J. ACM* **33** (1986), 290–312.

D. Avis and G. T. Toussaint, An efficient algorithm for decomposing a polygon into star-shaped pieces, *Pattern Recognition* **13** (1981a), 295–298.

D. Avis and G. T. Toussaint, An optimal algorithm for determining the visibility of a polygon from an edge, *IEEE Trans. Comput.* **C-30** (1981b), 910–914.

F. Bagemihl, On indecomposable polyhedra, *Amer. Math. Monthly* **55** (1948), 411–413.

T. Beyer, W. Jones, and S. Mitchell, Linear algorithms for isomorphism of maximal outerplanar graphs, *J. ACM* **26** (1979), 603–610.

C. Boldrighini, M. Keane, and F. Marchetti, Billiards in polygons, *Ann. Prob.* **6** (1978), 532–540.

M. R. Brown and R. E. Tarjan, Design and analysis of a data structure for representing sorted lists, *SIAM J. Comput.* **9** (1980), 594–614.

S. Chaiken, D. J. Kleitman, M. Saks, and J. Shearer, Covering regions by rectangles, *SIAM J. Alg. Disc. Meth.* **2** (1981), 394–410.

B. Chazelle, Computational geometry and convexity, Ph.D. thesis, Yale Univ. (1980).

B. Chazelle, A theorem on polygon cutting with applications, *Proc. 23rd IEEE Symp. Found. Comp. Sci.,* Chicago (1982), 339–349.

B. Chazelle, Convex partitions of polyhedra: a lower bound and worst-case optimal algorithm, *SIAM J. Comput.* **13** (1984), 488–507.

B. Chazelle and D. P. Dobkin, Optimal convex decompositions, *Computational Geometry* (G. T. Toussaint, ed.), Elsevier, North Holland, Amsterdam (1985), 63–133.

B. Chazelle and L. J. Guibas, Visibility and intersection problems in plane geometry, *Proc. 1st ACM Symp. Comp. Geom.,* Baltimore (1985), 135–146.

B. Chazelle, L. J. Guibas, and D. T. Lee, The power of geometric duality, *BIT* **25** (1985), 76–90.

B. Chazelle and J. Incerpi, Triangulating a polygon by divide-and-conquer, *Proc. 21st Allerton Conf.,* Monticello (1983), 447–455.

B. Chazelle and J. Incerpi, Triangulation and shape complexity, *ACM Trans. on Graphics* **3** (1984), 135–152.

N. Chiba, T. Nishizeki, and N. Saito, A linear algorithm for five-coloring a planar graph, *Graph Theory and Algorithms* (N. Saito and T. Nishizeki, eds.), Springer-Verlag, Berlin (1981), 9–19.

V. Chvátal, A combinatorial theorem in plane geometry, *J. Combin. Theory Ser. B* **18** (1975), 39–41.

J. Culberson and G. Rawlins, Turtlegons: generating simple polygons from sequences of angles, *Proc. 1st ACM Symp. Comp. Geom.*, Baltimore (1985), 305–310.

F. Devai, Quadratic bounds for hidden-line elimination, *Proc. 2nd ACM Symp. Comp. Geom.*, Yorktown Heights (1986), 269–275.

G. A. Dirac, Collinearity properties of sets of points, *Quart. J. Math. Oxford* **2** (1951), 221–227.

H. Edelsbrunner, J. O'Rourke, and R. Seidel, Constructing arrangements of lines and hyperplanes with applications, *SIAM J. Comput.* **15** (1986), 341–363.

H. Edelsbrunner, J. O'Rourke, and E. Welzl, Stationing guards in rectilinear art galleries, *Comput. Vision, Graphics, and Image Proc.* **27** (1984), 167–176.

H. ElGindy, Hierarchical decomposition of polygon with applications, Ph.D. thesis, McGill Univ. (1985).

H. ElGindy and D. Avis, A linear algorithm for computing the visibility polygon from a point, *J. Algorithms* **2** (1981), 186–197.

S. Even, *Graph Algorithms*, Computer Science Press, Rockville (1979).

S. Even and R. E. Tarjan, Computing an *st*-numbering, *Th. Comput. Sci.* **2** (1970), 339–344.

H.-Y. F. Feng and T. Pavlidis, Decomposition of polygons into simple components: feature generation for syntactic pattern recognition, *IEEE Trans. Comput.* **C-24** (1975), 636–650.

S. Fisk, A short proof of Chvátal's watchman theorem, *J. Combin. Theory Ser. B* **24** (1978), 374.

A. Fournier and D. Y. Montuno, Triangulating simple polygons and equivalent problems, *ACM Trans. on Graphics* **3** (1984), 153–174.

R. J. Fowler, M. S. Paterson, and S. L. Tanimoto, Optimal packing and covering in the plane are NP-complete, *Info. Proc. Let.* **12** (1981), 133–137.

D. S. Franzblau and D. J. Kleitman, An algorithm for constructing regions with rectangles: independence and minimum generating sets for collections of intervals, *Proc. 16th ACM Symp. Th. Comput.*, Washington (1984), 167–174.

G. N. Frederickson, On linear-time algorithms for 5-coloring planar graphs, *Info. Proc. Let.* **19** (1984), 219–224.

M. R. Garey and D. S. Johnson, *Computers and Intractability: A Guide to the Theory of NP-Completeness*, W. H. Freeman, San Francisco (1979).

M. R. Garey, D. S. Johnson, F. P. Preparata, and R. E. Tarjan, Triangulating a simple polygon, *Info. Proc. Let.* **7** (1978), 175–179.

S. K. Ghosh, On recognizing visibility graphs of simple polygons, Johns Hopkins tech. report JHU/EECS-86/14 (1986).

P. J. Giblin, *Graphs, Surfaces, and Homology,* Chapman and Hall, London (1977), 41–45.

D. H. Greene, The decomposition of polygons into convex parts, *Advances in Computing Research,* Vol. 1 (F. P. Preparata, ed.), JAI Press, Connecticut (1983), 235–259.

E. Grosswald, *Topics from the Theory of Numbers,* Macmillan, New York (1966), 108.

B. Grünbaum, Polytopal graphs, *Studies in Graph Theory* (D. R. Fulkerson, ed.), Mathematical Association of America (1975), 201–224.

L. J. Guibas, J. Hersberger, D. Leven, M. Sharir, and R. E. Tarjan, Linear-time algorithms for visibility and shortest path problems inside simple polygons, *Proc. 2nd ACM Symp. Comp. Geom.*, Yorktown Heights (1986), 1–12.

L. J. Guibas, L. Ramshaw, and J. Stolfi, A kinetic framework for computational geometry, *Proc. 24th IEEE Found. Comput. Sci.*, Tucson (1983), 100–111.

R. H. Güting and T. Ottmann, New algorithms for special cases of the hidden line elimination problem, Univ. Karlsruhe tech. report 184 (1984).

E. Györi, A short proof of the rectilinear art gallery theorem, *SIAM J. Alg. Disc. Meth.* **7** (1986), 452–454.

F. Harary, *Graph Theory,* Addison-Wesley, Reading (1969).

S. Hertel and K. Mehlhorn, Fast triangulation of simple polygons, *Proc. Conf. Found. Comput. Theory,* Springer-Verlag, New York (1983), 207–218.

K. Hoffman, K. Mehlhorn, P. Rosenstiehl, and R. E. Tarjan, Sorting Jordan sequences in linear time, *Proc. 1st ACM Symp. Comp. Geom.,* Baltimore (1985), 196–203.

R. Honsberger, *Mathematical Gems II,* Mathematical Association of America (1976), 104–110.

R. Honsberger, Games, graphs, and galleries, *The Mathematical Gardiner* (D. A. Klarner, ed.), Prindle, Weber & Schmidt, Boston (1981), 274–284.

J. E. Hopcroft and R. E. Tarjan, Efficient planarity testing, *J. ACM* **21** (1974), 549–568.

B. Joe and R. B. Simpson, Visibility of a simple polygon from a point, Univ. Waterloo tech. report (1985).

J. Kahn, M. Klawe, and D. Kleitman, Traditional galleries require fewer watchmen, *SIAM J. Alg. Disc. Meth.* **4** (1983), 194–206.

J. M. Keil, Decomposing a polygon into simpler components, Ph.D. thesis, Univ. Toronto (1983).

J. M. Keil, Decomposing a polygon into simpler components, *SIAM J. Comput.* **14** (1985), 799–817.

J. M. Keil, Minimally covering a horizontally convex orthogonal polygon, *Proc. 2nd ACM Symp. Comp. Geom.,* Yorktown Heights (1986), 43–51.

S. Kerckhoff, H. Masur, and J. Smillie, A rational billard flow is uniquely ergodic in almost every direction, *Bull. AMS* **13** (1985), 141–142.

V. Klee, Is every polygonal region illuminable from some point? *Amer. Math. Monthly* **76** (1969), 180.

V. Klee, Some unsolved problems in plane geometry, *Math. Mag.* **52** (1979), 131–145.

D. E. Knuth, *The Art of Computer Programming*: *Sorting and Searching* (Vol. 3), Addison-Wesley, Reading (1973).

D. T. Lee, Proximity and reachability in the plane, Ph.D. thesis, Univ. Illinois (1978).

D. T. Lee, Visibility of a simple polygon, *Comput. Vision, Graphics, and Image Proc.* **22** (1983), 207–221.

D. T. Lee and A. K. Lin, Computing visibility polygon from an edge, *Comput. Vision, Graphics, and Image Proc.* **34** (1986a), 1–19.

D. T. Lee and A. K. Lin, Computational complexity of art gallery problems, *IEEE Trans. Info. Th* **IT-32** (1986b), 276–282.

D. T. Lee and F. P. Preparata, Location of a point in a planar subdivision and its applications, *SIAM J. Comput.* **6** (1977), 594–606.

D. T. Lee and F. P. Preparata, An optimal algorithm for finding the kernel of a polygon, *J. ACM* **26** (1979), 415–421.

A. Lempel, S. Even, and I. Cederbaum, An algorithm for planarity testing of graphs, *Theory of Graphs*: *International Symposium* (P. Rosenstiehl, ed.), Gordon and Breach, New York (1967), 215–232.

N. J. Lennes, Theorems on the simple finite polygon and polyhedron, *Amer. J. Math.* **33** (1911), 37–62.

D. Lichtenstein, Planar formula and their uses, *SIAM J. Comput.* **11** (1982), 329–343.

A. Lingas, The power of non-rectilinear holes, *Proc. 9th Colloq. on Automata, Languages, and Programming,* Aarhus (1982), 369–383.

R. Liu and S. Ntafos, On partitioning rectilinear polygons into star-shaped components, unpublished manuscript (1985).

T. Lozano–Perez and M. A. Wesley, An algorithm for planning collision-free paths among polyhedral obstacles, *Comm. ACM* **22** (1979), 560–570.

A. Lubiw, Decomposing polygonal regions into convex quadrilaterals, *Proc. 1st ACM Symp. Comp. Geom.,* Baltimore (1985), 97–106.

H. Mannila and D. Wood, A simple proof of the rectilinear art gallery theorem, Univ. Helsinki tech. report C-1984-16 (1984).

K. Maruyama, A study of visual shape perception, Univ. Illinois tech. report UIUCDCS-R-72-533 (1972).

W. J. Masek, Some NP-complete set covering problems, unpublished MIT manuscript (1979).

M. McKenna, Worst-case optimal hidden surface removal, *ACM Trans. on Graphics,* to appear (1987).

G. H. Meisters, Polygons have ears, *Amer. Math. Monthly* **82** (1975), 648–651.

W. O. J. Moser, Problems on extremal properties of a finite set of points, *Discrete Geometry and Convexity* (J. E. Goodman *et al.,* eds.), New York Academy of Sciences, New York (1985), 52–64.

T. Nishizeki, Precise proofs of some lemmas in the paper "Lower bounds on the cardinality of the maximum matchings of planar graphs," Carnegie-Mellon tech. report (1977).

T. Nishizeki and I. Baybars, Lower bounds on the cardinality of the maximum matchings of planar graphs, Carnegie-Mellon tech. report (1977).

J. Nievergelt and F. P. Preparata, Plane-sweeping algorithms for intersecting geometric figures, *Comm. ACM* **25** (1982), 739–747.

S. Ntafos, On gallery watchman in grids, *Info. Proc. Let.* **23** (1986), 99–102.

J. O'Rourke, Polygon decomposition and switching function minimization, *Comput. Graphics and Image Processing* **18** (1982a), 382–391.

J. O'Rourke, The complexity of computing minimum convex covers for polygons, *Proc. 20th Allerton Conf.,* Monticello (1982b), 75–84.

J. O'Rourke, Galleries need fewer mobile guards: a variation on Chvátal's theorem, *Geometriae Dedicata* **14** (1983a), 273–283.

J. O'Rourke, An alternate proof of the rectilinear art gallery theorem, *J. of Geometry* **21** (1983b), 118–130.

J. O'Rourke and K. J. Supowit, Some NP-hard polygon decomposition problems, *IEEE Trans. Info. Th.* **IT-29** (1983), 181–190.

L. Pagli, E. Lodi, F. Luccio, C. Mugnai, and W. Lipski, On two-dimensional data organization 2, *Fundamenta Informaticae* **2** (1979), 211–226.

T. Pavlidis, Analysis of set patterns, *Pattern Recognition* **1** (1968), 165–178.

T. Pavlidis, *Structural Pattern Recognition,* Springer Verlag, Berlin (1977), 236–241.

T. Pavlidis and H.-Y. F. Feng, Shape discrimination, *Syntactic Pattern Recognition: Applications* (K. S. Fu, ed.), Springer-Verlag, New York (1977), 125–145.

F. P. Preparata and K. J. Supowit, Testing a simple polygon for monotonicity, *Info. Proc. Let.* **12** (1981), 161–164.

J.-R. Sack, Rectilinear computational geometry, Carleton Univ. tech. report SCS-TR-54 (1984).

J.-R. Sack and G. T. Toussaint, A linear-time algorithm for decomposing rectilinear star-shaped polygons into convex quadrilaterals, *Proc. 19th Allerton Conf.,* Monticello (1981), 21–30.

E. Schönhardt, Über die Zerlegung von Dreieckspolhedern in Tetraeder, *Math. Ann.* **98** (1928), 309–312.

M. I. Shamos, Computational geometry, Ph.D. thesis, Yale Univ. (1978).

T. Shermer, Triangulation graphs that require extra guards, NYIT Computer Graphics tech. report 3D-13 (1984).

T. Shermer, Polygon guarding II: efficient reduction of triangulation fragments, NYIT Computer Graphics tech. report 3D-16 (1985).

K. J. Supowit, Topics in computational geometry, Ph.D. thesis, Univ. Illinois (1981).

S. Suri and J. O'Rourke, Worst-case optimal algorithms for constructing visibility polygons with holes, Johns Hopkins Univ. tech. report JHU/EECS-85/12 (1985).

S. Suri and J. O'Rourke, Worst-case optimal algorithms for constructing visibility polygons with holes, *Proc. 2nd ACM Symp. Comp. Geom.,* Yorktown Heights (1986), 14–23.

I. E. Sutherland, R. F. Sproull, and R. A. Schumacker, A characterization of ten hidden-surface algorithms, *Comput. Surv.* **6** (1974), 1–55.

R. Tamassia and I. G. Tollis, A unified approach to visibility representations of planar graphs, *Discrete Comput. Geom.* **1** (1986) 321–341.

R. E. Tarjan and C. J. Van Wyk, An $O(n \log \log n)$-time algorithm for triangulating simple polygons, AT & T Bell Laboratories manuscript (1986).

G. B. Thomas Jr., *Calculus and Analytic Geometry,* Addison-Wesley, Reading (1962), 649.

G. T. Toussaint, Pattern recognition and geometrical complexity, *Proc. 5th Int. Conf. Pat. Recog.*, Miami Beach (1980), 1324–1347.

W. T. Tutte, The factorizations of linear graphs, *J. London Math. Soc.* **22** (1947), 107–111.

E. Welzl, Constructing the visibility graph for n line segments in $O(n^2)$ time, *Info. Proc. Let.* **20** (1985), 167–171.

S. K. Wismath, Characterizing bar line-of-sight graphs, *Proc. 1st ACM Symp. Comp. Geom.*, Baltimore (1985), 147–152.

D. Wood and C. K. Yap, Computing the convex skull of an orthogonal polygon, *Proc. 1st ACM Symp. Comp. Geom.*, Baltimore (1985), 311–315.

T. C. Woo, Polygon decomposition and alternating sum, Univ. Michigan tech. report 82-7 (1982).

INDEX

Page numbers in *italics* refer to definitions of the index entry.